CH
R

Facts On File Encyclopedia of

Black Women

IN AMERICA

Business and Professions

Encyclopedia of
Black Women in America

Facts On File Encyclopedia of

IN AMERICA

Business and Professions

Darlene Clark Hine, Editor

Kathleen Thompson, Associate Editor

☑® Facts On File, Inc.

Facts On File Encyclopedia of Black Women in America: Business and Professions

Facts On File
11 Penn Plaza
New York NY 10001

Library of Congress Cataloging-in-Publication Data

Facts on File encyclopedia of Black women in America/Darlene Clark
Hine, editor; Kathleen Thompson, associate editor.
p.   cm.
Includes bibliographical references and index.
Contents: v. 1. The early years, 1619–1899—v. 2. Literature—
v. 3. Dance, sports, and visual arts —v. 4. Business and professions—
v. 5. Music—v. 6. Education—v. 7. Religion and community—
v. 8. Law and government—v. 9. Theater arts and entertainment—
v. 10. Social activism—v. 1I. Science, health, and medicine.
ISBN 0-8160-3424-9 (set: alk. paper)
ISBN 0-8160-3427-3 (Business and Professions)
1. Afro-American women—Biography—Encyclopedias.   I. Hine,
Darlene Clark.   II. Thompson, Kathleen.
E185.96.F2   1996
920.72'08996073—dc20   96-33268

Facts On File books are available at special discounts when purchased in bulk quantities for businesses, associations, institutions or sales promotions. Please call our Special Sales Department in New York at 212/967-8800 or 800/322-8755.

Text design by Cathy Rincon
Cover design by Smart Graphics

Printed in the United States of America

RRD INNO 10 9 8 7 6 5 4 3 2 1

This book is printed on acid-free paper.

CH   7/97

Contents

How to Use This Volume

SCOPE OF THE VOLUME

The *Business and Professions* volume includes entries on individuals in the following subject areas: aviation, arts administration, business, broadcast journalism, journalism, library science, the military, production (film, theater, television, music, and radio), and publishing.

RELATED OCCUPATIONS

Related occupations covered in other volumes of this encyclopedia include the following: architects (*Dance, Sports, and Visual Arts*), clergy (*Religion and Community*), doctors (*Science, Health, and Medicine*), lawyers (*Law and Government*), nurses (*Science, Health, and Medicine*), scientists (*Science, Health, and Medicine*), teachers (*Education*)

HOW TO USE THIS VOLUME

The introduction to this volume presents an overview of the history of black women in business and the professions. Law, medicine, and education are included in this overview, but more extensive coverage of women in these professions can be found in the introductions to other volumes of this encyclopedia. A chronology following the entries lists important events in the history of black women in business and the professions in the United States.

Biographies are presented in alphabetically arranged entries. If the individual or organization you are looking for does not have an entry in this volume, please check the alphabetically arranged list of the entries for all eleven volumes of this encyclopedia that appears at the end of this volume, in addition to tables of contents for each of the other volumes in this series.

Names of individuals and organizations for which there are entries in this or other volumes of the encyclopedia are printed in **boldface**. Check the contents list at the back of this book to find the volume where a particular entry can be found.

Introduction

Ann Fudge sits in an elegant pastel office in White Plains, New York. It looks like a living room from *Better Homes and Gardens* or *Architectural Digest*, with antique furniture, costly carpets and fine paintings. From this room, Fudge, who has an M.B.A. from Harvard, runs the $1.4 billion Maxwell House Coffee Company.

In a Manhattan conference room, **Susan Taylor,** wearing a navy Donna Karan suit, points to a page layout for *Essence* magazine, of which she is editor in chief. The thirty-odd women and one man on her staff listen as Taylor repeats her vision for one of the most influential women's magazines in the country.

Tammy Buford-Herod unlocks the door of Tammy's Hair Gallery in Oxford, Mississippi. She walks past the two chairs in the beauty salon she opened with savings from her minimum-wage McDonald's salary. To reach this goal took more than two years. Last year, she grossed $65,000, but is still some distance from her ultimate goal. "I want to have a huge salon," she says, "with five stylists, a manicurist, and a barber. And I want it to be beautiful."

These are America's new black women, filled with determination, energy, and talent. And each of them has ancestors in the difficult and glorious past.

THE EARLY ENTREPRENEURS

There are records of black businesspeople in this country as early as the 1630s. By that time, at least one black man was a prominent landowner in New Amsterdam. In 1644, the area in New York City that is now Greenwich Village was owned by a group of eleven African Americans. A little later, **Lucy Terry** and Abijah Prince owned two 100-acre farms in Vermont and were prominent citizens of the town of Guilford. These were only a few of the many free black Americans who participated in the business life of early America.

However, as more slaves were freed and became competitors for jobs and trade, there was a white reaction. Beginning in the mid-1600s, laws were enacted restricting the participation of African Americans in business. For example, in 1660, Boston enacted a law forbidding the hiring of black artisans, such as carpenters and masons. In 1670, the Virginia legislature enacted a law forbidding African Americans from having white indentured servants. Over the next several decades, laws were enacted in New York State forbidding African Americans to work as porters, own homes, or sell oysters. And in 1712, the Connecticut Assembly passed a law forbidding blacks to buy land or carry on business in any town without the permission of its white residents.

Still, some African Americans managed to operate businesses and to do so successfully. Among these were a number of women, who fashioned businesses out of the skills they had used as slaves, indentured servants, or paid household workers.

Women who had worked as cooks opened restaurants, catering houses, and bakeries. Often they began as vendors or hucksters, then opened a stall in a town market, later establishing a shop with their profits. Mary Bernoon, for example, opened an oyster and ale house with her husband in Providence, Rhode Island, in 1736. The capital for starting the business was Mary Bernoon's. She had made the money selling illegal whiskey.

A black woman called "Duchess" Quamino became the leading caterer in Newport, Rhode Island, at about the same time. Indeed, according to Stephen Birmingham in his book about the black elite, *Certain People,* "Free blacks virtually invented the catering business in America." He goes on to name four highly successful black caterers in Philadelphia and two in New York City in the first half of the nineteenth century.

For slave women, establishing a business was often the way out of bondage. After paying their owner to allow them to hire out their own time, they saved their profits and bought their freedom. Those who did so were almost always entrepreneurs.

Loren Schweninger has reported on the business activities of a slave called Sally (1790–1849) who was allowed to hire out her own time as a cleaning woman. Using her savings, Sally rented a house in the Nashville, Tennessee, business district and established a laundry and cleaning business while also manufacturing soap for sale.

Jane Minor established a home health care service before she was freed in 1825. Using her skills in nursing, and her knowledge of the pharmacopoeia of folk medicine, Minor used profits from this enterprise to free sixteen women and children from slavery.

In some cases, mistresses deeded property to their former slaves, and this provided the basis for the establishment of rooming houses, inns, restaurants, and cleaning establishments. According to Suzanne Lebsock, Amelia Gallé was proprietor of a bathhouse that she had managed for years before inheriting the business in 1819 from her former slave owner. Other freed slave women with skills as seamstresses, dressmakers, and milliners opened shops on property acquired from their former owners. In this way, they progressed from managers to entrepreneurs.

For a free black woman, survival, rather than freedom, was at stake. Earning a livelihood was very difficult for most black women before the Civil War. Some resorted to illegal activities by establishing taverns or grog shops, often serving "home brew." A few women succeeded as madams, owning houses of prostitution, or as proprietors of luxury boardinghouses. San Francisco's famous **Mary Ellen Pleasant** used investment tips from her prominent clients to build a fortune, which she then used to support abolitionist causes, including John Brown's raid at Harpers Ferry, Virginia, in 1859.

Women who hoped to strengthen their position in the free community worked diligently to buy homes. Home ownership, of course, gave free black women a place to house their families. It also increased their economic and political security. Some free black women centered their work within their households, turning their homes into boardinghouses or devoting domestic space to seamstressing, laundering, or baking goods to sell. Home ownership could also lead to real estate transactions as a way of building on financial successes.

Elleanor Eldridge, a black woman born about 1784, combined real estate with other businesses to make her fortune. Eldridge learned the spinning and weaving of cloth as a teenager, while working as a servant in a white household. When she was in her late twenties, she opened a business with her sister in Warwick, Rhode Island. They wove cloth, made soap, and did some nursing. The business was quite successful, and Eldridge soon bought a lot and built a house on it, which she rented. In 1822, she started a painting and wallpapering business, again bought property, and built a rental house. Soon she owned two more lots and had contracted to purchase a $2,000 house. Because of a legal problem, Eldridge lost her property in 1831, but was able to recover it by coming up with $2,700.

New Orleans merchant Madame Cecee McCarty owned a depot in Plaquemines Parish that provided a base for merchandising her wares outside New Orleans. Madame McCarty sold imported goods, using her thirty-two slaves as a traveling sales force, and by 1848 was worth more than $155,000.

The Remond sisters, Cecilia, Maritcha, and Caroline, operated an exclusive hair salon for black women in Salem, Massachusetts. Their business interests included the largest wig factory in the state. They also manufactured a popular medicated hair tonic, which they sold wholesale and retail, both locally and through the mail-order distribution side of their business.

The Remond family was prominent in abolitionist circles as well as in the Salem business community. Their mother, Nancy, controlled the catering trade in Salem and also ran a small but exclusive restaurant.

The commercial activities of **Elizabeth Keckley**, as the dressmaker of Mary Todd Lincoln, wife of Abraham Lincoln, have been given wide historic recognition. Keckley's business success was due to her expertise as a dress designer. Her Washington, D.C., dress shop employed twenty seamstresses. Keckley's most famous design, Mary Todd Lincoln's inaugural ball gown, is in the Smithsonian Institution, and a re-creation is exhibited at the Black Fashion Museum.

A great many other black women worked as dressmakers, often operating independently. Of course, when all clothing was made by hand, even families of the lower middle class depended on dressmakers the way we now depend on The Gap and J. C. Penney. A small community would support several skilled seamstresses, embroiderers, and designers. A large city needed hundreds. For black women, such work, difficult as it was, represented a major step up from cleaning and laundering, offering a small measure of independence and the possibility of freedom in the future.

THE FIRST PROFESSIONALS

At a time when most of their sisters were still living in slavery, some black women had begun to enter the professions. At a time when it was still illegal to teach African Americans in the South to read, there were black women in the North who were using their own education in the service of their people as teachers and journalists.

The first black professionals were teachers. African-American schools were founded in many cities in the eighteenth century. In 1704, Elie Neau, a white New Yorker, founded the first slave school in North America at his city's Trinity Church. Other schools were established by Puritans in New England and by Quakers in Philadelphia and other towns in Pennsylvania and New Jersey.

The faculties of these early schools were primarily white, often volunteers or poorly paid believers in the cause of abolition. However, from the beginning, black women played important roles as classroom aides. Later, defeating the prejudices of the white reformers, they became teachers. Eleanor Harris was the first teacher of her race in Philadelphia, and Sarah Dorsey and **Margaretta Forten** were among those who followed in her footsteps.

In 1793, an ex-slave named **Katy Ferguson** opened an integrated Sunday school in her home. She took forty-eight black and white children off the streets of her neighborhood and out of the almshouse nearby. She taught them scripture and how to take care of themselves, even helping many find homes and taking several of them into her own home. She supported this venture as a caterer to wealthy white families. Later, she received some support from a neighborhood church.

In the early 1830s, **Sarah Mapps Douglass** returned from New York City, where she had been a teacher, to open a school for black girls in her native Philadelphia. Hers was, at the time, the nation's only high school for black girls. Douglass took the bold step of teaching science to her female students, and later, after taking courses in medicine at the Female Medical College of Pennsylvania and at Pennsylvania Medical University, she traveled widely, lecturing to black women.

Throughout the North in the early decades of the nineteenth century, black women provided and even supervised the education of black girls and, less frequently, black boys. This was far more desirable work than domestic service, but was difficult to find and required education far beyond the reach of most free black women of the period. Teachers were an elite group dedicating themselves to the welfare of an entire people, a tradition that has continued among black professionals to this day.

WRITING FOR FREEDOM

The earliest black journalists, both women and men, did not choose their profession out of personal ambition. They were driven to write by their rage at injustice and their need to speak out for freedom. They usually began writing and speaking publicly as part of the abolition movement.

Free black women before the Civil War used their talents and accomplishments, honed in their literary societies, to protest slavery and racial discrimination on several fronts. **Harriet Wilson, Charlotte** and **Sarah Forten, Harriet Jacobs, Maria Stewart, Ann Plato,** and **Frances E. W. Harper** were foremost among the early black women realists and protest writers.

Mary Prince's *The History of Mary Prince, A West Indian Slave* (1831), a horrifying document of Caribbean slavery, was the first slave narrative written by a black woman in the Americas. The following year, Maria Stewart became the first free African-American woman to publish a book of hymns and meditations. In 1835, Stewart also published a collection of her works, including political speeches, essays, and religious meditations.

Ten years later, Ann Plato became the first African American to publish a book of essays, and Harriet Wilson was the first black person in the United States to publish a novel. Her 1859 text, *Our Nig: or, Sketches from the Life of a Free Black*, details some of the excruciating problems of free families of color, and the abuse of African-American servant women and children.

Two years later, Harriet Jacobs' *Incidents in the Life of a Slave Girl* personalized the plight of the Southern female slave by detailing episodes of psychological torture, sexual abuse, physical intimidation, and loss of family in her own life. Jacobs' testimony expresses her determination to resist abuse and claim her humanity and femininity as much as it describes her life as a slave. It was an invaluable defense of abolition and the character of black women.

Some women also published in various anti-slavery journals and literary magazines. The writings of Charlotte Forten [Grimké], for example, appeared in the *Liberator*, the *Christian Recorder*, the *Anglo-African Magazine*, the *National Anti-Slavery Standard*, the *Atlantic Monthly*, and the *New England Magazine*. An avid scholar and educator, Forten also had impressive linguistic abilities, translating for publication the French novel *Madame Thérèse: or, The Volunteers of '92* by Emile Erckmann and Alexandre Chatrian.

One of the first black women to make a living from writing was Frances E. W. Harper, a free woman from Baltimore who had worked as a domestic, seamstress, and teacher before turning to writing and lecturing full-time for the Maine Anti-Slavery Society. Harper's poems were published in three volumes: *Poems on Miscellaneous Subjects* (1854), *Poems* (1871), and *Sketches of Southern Life* (1872). Harper used much of the income from her first book of poems to support William Still and his efforts on behalf of the Underground Railroad.

Mary Ann Shadd [Cary] not only was an influential abolitionist writer and activist but also was the first African-American woman editor. Determined not to have her political views or social critiques censored, Shadd Cary created her own newspaper, the *Provincial Freeman*, in 1853. For six years Shadd Cary juggled key positions on the fledgling anti-slavery and emigrationist journal, serving as its editor, writer, promoter, and fund-raiser. She was a pioneer in an all-male profession, however, and few were willing to provide her with long-term support.

Black women would find themselves facing double discrimination again and again over the years, especially with regard to this crucial question of entering business and professional life. In many areas of life—housing, public accommodations, social equality, to name just a few—racism is clearly a more significant factor than discrimination because of gender. However, women were so thoroughly shut out of professional life for so long, in all parts of the world, that sexism in this area is enormously powerful. And black women have had to contend with both sexism and racism.

AS THE WAR APPROACHES

Black pioneers in business and the professions faced obstacles that are difficult for us to imagine today. Laws were against them. Custom stood in their way. Jacques

Brissot de Warville, a French traveler of the time, wrote, "Those Negroes who keep shops live moderately, and never augment their business beyond a certain point. The reason is obvious; the whites . . . like not to give them credit to undertake any extensive commerce nor even to give them the means of a common education by receiving them into their counting houses."

Even when African Americans managed to prosper, they had to be careful. In 1834, whites rioted against black businesses and workers in both New York City and Philadelphia. Such riots occurred again in Philadelphia in 1838 and 1843, and in Pittsburgh in 1839. Black businesspeople knew that success brought with it an element of danger.

Still, they strove for success. Stephen Birmingham quotes statistics saying that, in New York State in 1853, African Americans owned property worth more than $1 million and had invested $839,000 in businesses in the New York City area. Statistics from 1856 show that, in Philadelphia, African Americans owned real estate worth $800,000. And just before the Civil War, African Americans in Washington, D.C., owned property worth about $630,000.

There was even considerable black wealth in the South. Indeed, among all American cities, black prosperity reached its height in New Orleans. There, in 1860, African Americans owned $15 million worth of taxable property.

According to Birmingham, "The total personal and real wealth of free blacks in America in that year [1860] has been placed at $50 million, and this is considered an estimate on the conservative side. Blacks owned nine thousand homes, fifteen thousand farms, and two thousand businesses."

It's important to remember, though, that the majority of those homes, farms, and businesses belonged to black *men*. Black women faced, in addition to racism, the discrimination that confronted all women of the time. If they married, they could not own property. As a result, most women who had business and professional ambitions gave up family life. If they didn't, they risked having their husbands take over all their financial assets.

Also, the demands of married life were far greater on a woman than on a man, just as they are today. Black women were somewhat freer to participate in business and public causes than white women, but they were still expected to fulfill their roles as wives and mothers as faithfully as if they had no other interests. And so, the lists of publicly active black women at that time contain few names of married women.

Jarena Lee, for example, believed that she had a vocation to preach the gospel. As early as 1809, she asked to be allowed to preach at the Bethel African Methodist Church of Philadelphia. Her request was denied, but years later, after the death of her minister husband, she became a traveling minister. **Elizabeth Clovis Lange** founded an order of Roman Catholic nuns called the **Oblate Sisters of Providence** in Baltimore, Maryland, in 1829. **Elizabeth Taylor Greenfield** went on the concert stage and, in 1854, performed for Queen Victoria at Buckingham Palace in London.

All of these women, in addition to dress designer Elizabeth Keckley, real estate investor Elleanor Eldridge, lecturer Sojourner Truth, financial wizard Mary Ellen Pleasant, were either unmarried or widowed. In any list of successful black businesspeople, there are far more married men than married women.

However, in 1860, the world of both women and men was about to change dramatically. The long-awaited day of freedom was in sight. The Civil War would bring emancipation to all African Americans. To the small black business and professional class, it would bring changes no one foresaw.

THE IMPACT OF THE CIVIL WAR

Wars create millionaires. That has been true throughout history, and it was certainly true of the American Civil War. Before the years of war contracts and government loans and the vast expansion of railroads, there had been some very wealthy people in this country. But the wealth that came in the wake of the war was immense. The Civil War was the basis of the financial empires of men such as Cornelius Vanderbilt, Jay Gould, and J. P. Morgan.

For African Americans in business, these people were the competition. Where black capital had once been a small but significant factor in American business, it was now virtually irrelevant. The gap had widened enormously between the rich and powerful on one side and everyone else on the other. It had never been clearer on which side of the gap African Americans lived.

This widened gap was one of the results of the war. Another was a repetition of what had happened in the middle of the eighteenth century, when the number of free blacks had increased. White Americans, particularly Southerners, became angry, afraid, and hostile. In the first few years after the war, and again when federal troops were pulled out of the South in 1877,

Southern states began enacting laws limiting the rights of African Americans. The Ku Klux Klan began its night-riding. White laws and white terrorism combined to keep black Americans from taking their rightful place in society.

There were many people, both black and white, who tried to make exceptions for the educated, property-owning class that had arisen before the war. It was clearly not fair, they claimed, that these worthy members of society should be treated the same as "ignorant ex-slaves." But no such distinction could be upheld. The black middle class suffered an immediate and severe setback to its financial and social aspirations.

Still, there were business and professional successes. At first, according to Arnold Taylor in *Travail and Triumph*, "they generally came from the class of pre–Civil War free blacks or were the mixed-blood descendants of favored house slaves. Robert Church, Sr., of Memphis, for example, who by the time of his death in 1912 had amassed a fortune in excess of $1 million through dealings in white real estate, was the mulatto son of a wealthy white man."

Black women, too, built on the successes of the past. In 1860, 15 percent of free black women were dressmakers and hairdressers, including women who owned their own businesses. Five percent operated boardinghouses or small shops. In the second half of the nineteenth century, black businesswomen continued to work in the areas marked out by the women who had come before them, especially fashion and beauty. Speaking of dressmaking, Jacqueline Jones, in *Labor of Love, Labor of Sorrow*, wrote, "In at least some late nineteenth-century cities (among them

Charleston, Louisville, and New Orleans), this general category of working women constituted the largest group of 'artisans,' or skilled tradespeople, of either sex within the black population."

At first, they continued to offer their services primarily to white customers. Fanny Criss, for example, designed clothes for wealthy white women in Richmond, Virginia. That city's Valentine Museum has in its collection several of Criss' designs, including a white wool Second-Day (wedding reception) dress from 1896. Criss continued her career in New York City after moving there about 1918. There were many Fanny Crisses who are now unknown to us by name but who were hard at work designing and creating the fashion images of the white elite.

After a time, these businesswomen began to turn to their own communities to market their goods and services. Some black women set up small but successful shops where they adapted illustrations from *Vogue* and *Harper's Bazaar* for the women in their communities. Others operated more informally but nonetheless developed a regular clientele for their dressmaking. Church and community socials were their advertising venues. Mamie Garvin, a twenty-five-year-old South Carolina schoolteacher, spent the summer of 1913 in Boston with two other young women. Together they opened

a sewing room at home. . . . Very few if any of the neighborhood ladies could afford to buy the dresses *Vogue* magazine advertised, but they did have the taste for them, and some of them had enough money to buy nice material and the various trimmings. I knew how to make patterns and get the most up-to-date lines.

Ellestine and Myrtle knew how to do everything else, so we got busy copying the expensive dresses we found in *Vogue*.

Our "factory" was Ellestine's bedroom, which overlooked Wallpole Street, a well-traveled street in Roxbury. We made a display out of magazines and made a big sign for the window: "Parisian Vogue." A lady passing by would come up to see what we were working on; the next thing you know, here she comes back with an order. Or Miss so-and-so would appear in church wearing a suit we made; Wednesday or Thursday, Miss such-and-such wants one like it (but not *just* like it, of course). The word got out quickly that we were stylish girls who knew all about clothes . . . and soon we had more business than we knew what to do with. . . . Each of us got to the point where we specialized in a certain part of the job.

The other favorite business enterprise was hairdressing. Black women who had been trained as servants to dress their employer's hair and attend to other grooming and beauty tasks built on those skills to start businesses in the area of beauty culture.

Beauty culture has been a source of opportunity, self-expression, and, at the same time, controversy for black women. Work in hairdressing, beauty salons, and door-to-door sales promised economic advancement to black women, whose job opportunities were extremely limited. At the same time, the new emphasis on appearance and grooming fostered by beauty culture promoted a larger debate about African-American identity, social participation, and cultural modernity. If, on the one hand, beauty culture encouraged a notion of the "New Negro Woman," it simultaneously raised troubling questions about whether African Americans should copy and try to become a part of white culture.

Even before the Civil War, hairdressing and skin care had been concerns of black women. Women in slavery used herbs, berries, and other natural substances to heal, soften, and color the skin. Moreover, a number of enslaved and free women of color worked as hairdressers for white women, and probably compounded simple pomades and lotions to use on their patrons. By the 1870s, some urban black women owned hairdressing parlors, manufactured beauty products for sale, and profited in the "hair trade."

It was not until the late nineteenth century, however, that commercial beauty culture took off as part of the more general development of an African-American consumer market. Limited by poverty and racial discrimination, most African Americans had little spending money for anything beyond what was essential for survival. Still, the black middle class was expanding. Urban workers had more disposable income than farm laborers of the past. And, for African Americans after the Civil War, grooming, stylishness, and adornment were ideals that signified freedom and respectability. Both black-owned and white-owned companies responded to those desires with a range of commercial beauty products and services. Not until the beginning of the twentieth century, however, would beauty culture truly become big business for African Americans.

Indeed, all of the businesses black women formed or participated in prior to the twentieth century were small and of strictly local importance. They were making something out of nothing in the tradition of American entrepreneurs of all ages, but they had much more going against them than the average European immigrant man with a pushcart.

On the other hand, the end of the nineteenth century saw a significant expansion of the professional class among black women. The growing middle class greatly emphasized education for young women, and many of those women used their education to embark on careers.

TEACHERS AND WRITERS OF THE NINETEENTH CENTURY

It is difficult to estimate how many black women were teaching in the United States in the second half of the nineteenth century. Many were only part-time teachers and would probably have named other occupations to a census taker. However, the 1910 census listed 17,266 African-American women teachers in the Southern states. There were three times as many black women teaching as black men. They represented 1 percent of all black working women in the South.

Many of these women, in another day, might have become doctors or lawyers or ministers. At that time, however, those professions were either completely or virtually closed to them. And so they taught.

Jacqueline Jones points out that teaching black children at that moment in history "implicitly involved a commitment to social and political activism." Education had been a radical act before the Civil War, when it was illegal to teach slaves. It remained a radical act after the war. As a result, many of the time's most important black political leaders came from the ranks of women teachers. They included **Fannie Jackson Coppin, Lucy Laney, Charlotte Hawkins Brown, Hallie Quinn Brown,** and **Nannie Helen Burroughs.**

Journalism also remained both a profession and a political act. Black American women writers showcased their intellectual and creative talents in journals and magazines, including the *Repository of Religion and Literature and of Science and the Arts*, a journal, begun in 1858, of the African Methodist Episcopal Church, and the *Anglo-African Magazine* founded in 1859. Scores of other women followed the print tradition; among them were professor Mary V. Cook, editor of the education section of *Our Women and Children*, Meta E. Pelham, reporter for the *Detroit Plain Dealer*, **Gertrude Mossell**, correspondent for the *Indianapolis Freeman*, and Lillian A. Lewis, who wrote a column called "They Say" for the *Boston Advocate* under the pen name Bert Islew.

The one woman who dominated journalism at the end of the nineteenth century was **Ida B. Wells-Barnett.** Wells-Barnett was the fiery editor of *Free Speech and Headlight*, a small weekly in her hometown of Memphis, Tennessee. She used scathing language in her crusading efforts against lynching, introducing the idea that white women were culpable in these crimes. She redefined lynching, its causes and consequences. At considerable cost, with the burning of the *Free Speech* office and her subsequent exile from Tennessee (induced by letters to editors all over the South that warned she would be torched next if she returned), Wells-Barnett became only the second black female journalist (Mary Ann Shadd [Cary] preceded her) to step outside the content boundaries reserved for women, and to successfully mobilize both black and white readers through print.

The post-Reconstruction period also introduced the first periodicals targeting a female audience and featuring the work of black women. In 1887, A. E. Johnson, a woman poet from Baltimore, Maryland, founded a monthly literary journal, *The Joy*, perhaps the earliest of these efforts. The magazine was published until 1889–90 and received complimentary reviews from both black and white contemporaries, a striking testament to the journalistic skills of black women.

By the close of the nineteenth century, an increasing number of black women were firmly entrenched in the black press. Yet writer and activist Gertrude Mossell admonished her female colleagues for remaining "willing captives, chained to the chariot wheels of the sterner element." She also criticized black men for not fully including their female colleagues.

Feminism had come of age during this time, and black women were exploring their own version of it. They were seeking liberation in a totally new way. Nowhere was this more evident than in the field of medicine.

THE FIRST DOCTORS

Black women entered both the medical and legal professions during the second half of the nineteenth century, in spite of tremendous obstacles. At that time most colleges and universities were closed to women, black and white, and the doors to medical schools were shut tight.

In 1849, a white woman named Elizabeth Blackwell battled her way into and through a small, rural medical school in west central New York State to become the first woman doctor in the United States or Britain. In 1864, fifteen years after Blackwell became the first American woman medical graduate, the first black woman graduate, Rebecca Lee, received a doctor of medicine degree from the New England Female Medical College in Boston.

Three years later, the second black American woman physician, **Rebecca J. Cole**, graduated from the Woman's Medical College of Pennsylvania. In 1870, **Susan Smith McKinney Steward** completed her studies at New York Medical College for Women. Lee, Cole, and Steward signaled the emergence of black women in the medical profession.

Black women physicians such as Rebecca J. Cole skillfully combined private medical practice with community service among white and black women. Cole worked for a time with Elizabeth and Emily Blackwell at the New York Infirmary for Women and Children as a "sanitary visitor." The infirmary's Tenement House Service, begun in 1866, was the earliest practical program of medical social service in the country. As a sanitary visitor or tenement physician, Cole made house calls in slum neighborhoods, teaching indigent mothers the basics of hygiene and "the preservation of the health of their families." Elizabeth Blackwell described Cole as "an intelligent young coloured physician" who conducted her work "with tact and care" and thus demonstrated that the establishment of a social service department "would be a valuable addition to every hospital."

The majority of early black women physicians were the daughters of socially privileged black families or others who, perhaps to protect them from menial labor or domestic servitude, encouraged their daughters to educate themselves. **Caroline Anderson** was the daughter of William Still, a founder of the Underground Railroad, chairman of the General Vigilance Committee in ante-bellum Philadelphia, and author of *The Underground Railroad* (1872). **Halle Johnson** was the daughter of Bishop B. T. Tanner of the African Methodist Episcopal Church in Philadelphia. **Susan Steward** was the daughter of a prosperous Brooklyn, New York, merchant. Sarah Logan Fraser's father was Bishop Logan of the Zion Methodist Episcopal Church in Syracuse, New York. Sarah G. Boyd Jones' father, George W. Boyd, was reputed to be the wealthiest black man in Richmond, Virginia.

To be sure, not all of the first generation of black women physicians belonged to illustrious families. Some, such as **Eliza Grier**, were former slaves who worked their way through college and medical school, occasionally receiving limited financial assistance from parents or siblings. Grier apparently completed the medical program by working every other year, since she was admitted in 1890 and graduated seven years later, in 1897.

The late nineteenth century witnessed a dramatic increase of women doctors in America. In 1860, there were about 200. Twenty years later, in 1880, there were 2,423, more than ten times as many. When another twenty years had passed, that number had tripled, to more than 7,000. During this forty years, nineteen medical schools for women were founded. By 1895, eleven of them had disbanded, but by that time a tiny number of all-male medical schools were admitting a few women.

Black women at first seemed to benefit from these new opportunities for women in medicine. In the twenty-five years after the ending of slavery, and during the height of racial segregation and discrimination, there were 115 black women physicians in the United States. However, by the 1920s, the U.S. Census listed only sixty-five black women as practicing physicians.

Black nurses had once been tolerated in white hospitals because of the servant-like status of nurses in general. As nursing grew in prestige, however, they were shut out of both hospitals and training schools. The only alternative was to found their own network of nursing schools and hospitals.

In 1886, John D. Rockefeller contributed funds for the establishment of a nursing school at the Atlanta Baptist Seminary (now Spelman College), a school for black women. This was the nation's first nursing school to be part of an academic institution. The earliest nursing schools within black hospitals began to appear in the 1890s. They were formed mostly by black physicians and the members of black women's clubs, who played a vitally important role in black health care.

By 1920 there were thirty-six training schools for black nurses. Unfortunately, training in the hospital nursing schools was poor, and opportunities for their graduates to find fulfilling work were limited because discrimination against black nurses was rampant in the profession. And black nurses were denied admission to the American Nurses' Association.

In medicine, the end of the nineteenth century was a time only of bare beginnings, of first tentative steps for black women. This was also true in the legal profession.

THE FIRST LAWYERS

In 1872, black women entered the legal profession. At that time, women did not have the vote. Opposition to educating women was at its height as some universities began to become timidly coeducational. The idea of a woman lawyer was, to most people, laughable. And yet, in that year, **Charlotte E. Ray**, an African-American woman, graduated from Howard University Law School and was admitted to the bar in the District of Columbia.

A few white women had been admitted to the bar of this state or that—none in the District of Columbia—but hardly any of them had attended law school. Usually, they were wives of attorneys who had studied with their husbands, in their husbands' offices, then took the bar examination. Also, few of them practiced. The most prominent white woman lawyer of the time was Myra Bradwell, who edited the *Chicago Legal News* instead of practicing law.

Charlotte Ray opened a law office in Washington, D.C., and proved herself an able attorney. But discrimination against both African Americans and women was so strong that she was unable to make a living. However, Ray was a strong feminist and became active in the suffrage movement, attending the annual convention of the National Woman Suffrage Association in New York City in 1876.

In 1883, Mary Ann Shadd Cary became the second black woman to earn a law degree, also graduating from Howard University Law School. She could have been the first, having attended Howard's law school in 1869, but she was "refused graduation on account of her sex," according to a letter she wrote in 1890.

Both of these women, though legally eligible to argue in the nation's courts, were unable to vote in the nation's elections. And neither of them lived to see the day that women in this country would be allowed to enter voting booths.

THE BUSINESS OF BEAUTY

In the first half of the twentieth century, black women began to carve out a significant place for themselves in business and the professions. They made progress primarily by expanding their scope in the areas they had already staked out. In business, that meant beauty and fashion.

Some white-owned firms cultivated the African-American market for cosmetics as early as the 1890s. Patent medicine manufacturers and toiletry goods companies promoted hair tonics to black Americans through almanacs, trade cards, and newspaper advertisements. Promising to straighten "kinky" hair and lighten dark skin, these ads blatantly appealed to racial prejudice and the desire among some African Americans for social acceptance. By the 1920s, white-owned firms like Plough and Nadinola had so expanded their marketing that they were the leading advertisers in many African-American newspapers. Highly controversial within the black community, these companies were at times targeted for protest over their competitive tactics, failure to employ black workers, and alleged disregard for product safety.

In this same period, a hair and beauty industry emerged that was developed and controlled by African Americans. Anthony Overton, **Annie Turnbo Malone, Madam C.**

J. Walker, and **Sarah Spencer Washington** were among the most successful African-American entrepreneurs to sell hair tonics, pressing oils, face creams, and other products. Some firms developed out of the drugstore supplies trade or began as small cosmetics companies.

Anthony Overton, who by 1916 owned one of the largest African-American businesses in the United States, began his career as a peddler and baking powder manufacturer in 1898. He shifted into cosmetics when his daughter's formula for a face powder proved popular in their local community. Overton sold his High-Brown Face Powder through an army of sales agents who aggressively pushed it into mainstream routes of distribution, making Overton the first African American to place his products in Woolworth's.

Another cosmetics firm, Kashmir Chemical Company, was founded in 1918 by Claude Barnett, head of the Associated Negro Press. Although the company was short-lived, Barnett's advertising for the Nile Queen cosmetics line was particularly ingenious because it targeted the popular interest among black Americans in Cleopatra and the African origins of Egyptian culture.

Black women entrepreneurs were even more significant to the development of African-American beauty culture. Beginning around 1900, such pioneers as Annie Turnbo Malone and Madam C. J. Walker created new techniques and products to assure black women of smooth, manageable hair. These women, who started out with little capital but boundless energy, sold their goods by traveling door to door and teaching women the art of hairdressing.

By the early 1900s, Malone's Poro products and the Walker System had spread throughout the country, not only in urban areas, but in the rural South and Midwest. Both companies also exported their goods to Africa, Cuba, the West Indies, and Central America. Initially emphasizing hair care products, Malone and Walker began to manufacture skin preparations, including face powders, rouges, creams, and skin lighteners, after World War I.

Beauty culture offered new employment opportunities in a labor market that relegated most black women to domestic service, laundering, and farm labor. The trade required little capital, was easy to

Madam C. J. Walker was the first woman self-made millionaire in the United States. Her Walker Manufacturing Company created a complete line of beauty care products. Hundreds of agents sold the products aggressively throughout the country. (A'LELIA BUNDLES)

learn, and was in demand. Beauty parlors could be operated cheaply in homes, apartments, and small shops, and hair and skin care products could be purchased cheaply or mixed in the kitchen for use on clients.

Because most drugstores, chain stores, and department stores refused to locate in black communities, door-to-door agents and salon beauticians largely controlled the distribution and sale of the products. From about 1910 through the 1920s, thousands of women were trained in different, competing systems of hair and beauty culture. Advertising was generally limited to black-owned newspapers, although large companies like Poro purchased space in various newspapers throughout the country.

Beauty culture in the early twentieth century was seen as a path toward individual mobility and also as a means of collective economic and social advancement. Both Walker and Malone were known not only for their business acumen but also for their generous support of African-American educational, charitable, and civic institutions. Local beauty salons and clubs of cosmetologists similarly emphasized service to the black community.

In the absence of many commercial outlets, female entrepreneurs sought relationships and clientele in black women's organizations, colleges, and churches. They offered promotions, beauty shows, and product sales to raise needed funds. Moreover, the sales methods they employed—salon operatives and door-to-door agents selling to friends and neighbors—probably enhanced the web of mutual support and assistance integral to black women's culture. This integration of the industry with aspects of black commu-

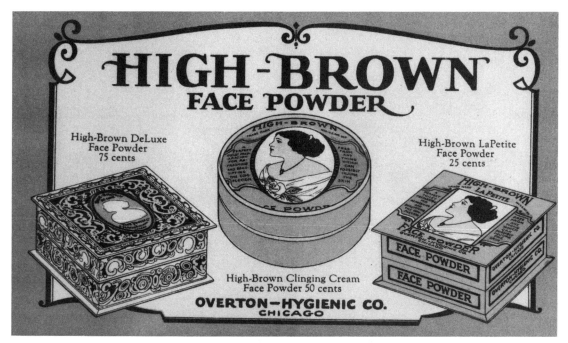

The advertising of the highly successful Overton-Hygienic Company featured light-skinned, refined-looking women and appealed to respectability and gentility. (LAKE COUNTY ILL.] MUSEUM/CURT TEICH POSTCARD ARCHIVES)

nity life and politics sets it apart from the white beauty industry.

Aspects of beauty culture, especially hair straightening and skin bleaching, were highly controversial in the black community. Products with names like Black-No-More and No-Kink (many of which were manufactured by white-owned as well as black-owned companies) adhered to racist European aesthetic standards. Journalists, politicians, novelists, and others debated the legitimacy and meaning of such practices, relating the question of beauty not only to the definition of female respectability but also to "race consciousness" and black resistance to white domination.

In the eyes of many critics, hair straighteners and skin bleaches were a way of copying white beauty standards that could only reinforce a degrading sense of physical and psychological inferiority in black people. Skin bleaching, in particular, represented an admission of loathing for blackness and denial of African heritage.

Others astutely observed a more complicated dynamic at work in African-American appraisals of "good" and "bad" hair and hierarchies of skin colors. Black women with lighter skin and straighter hair, critics like Nannie Burroughs maintained, gained higher-paying jobs in the labor market and fared better socially, especially in marriages to wealthier black men, who tended to choose women with these characteristics. Overlooked in this debate was the degree to which whites—working-class and middle-

The significance of Madam C. J. Walker's life and career lies both in her innovative, and sometimes controversial, hair-care system and in her advocacy of black women's independence and her creation of business opportunities for black women. In 1919, the year Walker died, Mary McLeod Bethune called her "the greatest demonstration . . . of Negro woman's ability recorded in history." (A'LELIA BUNDLES)

class, native-born and immigrant—used skin bleaches, hair pullers, and hairpieces to attain the same beauty standards.

African-American beauty culturists replied to this criticism by emphasizing the economic opportunities they produced. They also declared that their products were cultural weapons in the hands of women who used them. White racism had symbolically linked the supposedly natural inferiority and backwardness of black Americans to an appearance marked by unruly or "kinky" hair, poor grooming, and slovenly dress. The beauty products did not challenge this stereotype, but they allowed black women to escape it.

In particular, a "refined" appearance helped black women to avoid the charge of sexual immorality that was often leveled against them. Thus, hair care and grooming visually signified personal success, cultural modernity, and racial progress. The beauty industry asserted and exploited this view in its advertising. The Madam C. J. Walker Company, for example, ran a full-page newspaper ad in 1928 whose headline announced: "Amazing Progress of Colored Race—Improved Appearance Responsible" (*Oklahoma Eagle*, March 3, 1928).

Madam Walker herself had certainly made amazing progress. When she died in 1919, she was generally considered to be the wealthiest black woman in America and the first black American woman millionaire. She was the first self-made American woman millionaire. Hetty Green, an eccentric white financier who had amassed a huge fortune during approximately the same time, started with an inheritance of more than a million dollars. Walker started with nothing.

The African-American beauty industry was hard hit by the Great Depression of the 1930s. Many beauty salons closed, sales declined, and women's dominance in the trade eroded. The modern development of the industry, starting in the 1950s with Johnson Products, was controlled largely by men. In the early decades of the twentieth century, however, African-American beauty culture appealed to women as workers and consumers to take control of their destinies and challenge the stereotypes that limited them. The extraordinary growth of this industry suggests that beauty culture had great meaning for black women, as they generated new self-definitions and collective responses to decades of abuse, poverty, and discrimination.

SUCCESS BY DESIGN

Dressmaking and design also continued to be important business fields for black women. They were instruments of self-sufficiency for the businesswoman and for her customers.

In the 1920s, black women were denied the opportunity to shop in fashionable white department stores. They saw the latest fashions in magazines and shop windows, but they couldn't buy them. So, black women of the middle and upper classes throughout the South sought ways to obtain the current fashions without traveling to stores in the North and Midwest. Thousands of black women dressmakers throughout the South provided that opportunity. They also frequently branched out to design for customers outside the black community.

Ann Lowe was one such woman. The granddaughter, daughter, and niece of experienced seamstresses, Lowe began her career when, as a teenager, she completed the inaugural ball gown for the wife of an Alabama governor (a work begun by her mother). Soon many wealthy Alabama society and political women were requesting Lowe's services.

This was at the time of the great northern migration, and at the age of sixteen Lowe moved to New York. There she enrolled in a design school that admitted her but requested she place her sewing table in the hall outside the classroom, away from the white students. Within a year, Lowe had opened her own dressmaking shop on Madison Avenue, eventually numbering among her clients the Astors and Rockefellers.

Although Lowe's designs were featured nationally on the covers of fashion magazines and women's magazines, her name was not well known outside of debutante circles until the 1953 wedding of Jacqueline Bouvier and John Fitzgerald Kennedy. Ann Lowe designed the mother-of-the-bride and bridesmaids' dresses, as well as the bridal gown. At last she was acknowledged as a designer as well as a dressmaker/seamstress, an artist as well as a craftsperson.

Similarly, milliner Mildred Blount's talents went without public recognition, despite her designing for Joan Crawford,

When the St. Luke Penny Savings Bank opened in 1903, Maggie Lena Walker became the first woman bank president in the United States. When St. Luke's merged with two other banks to become the Consolidated Bank and Trust Company, Walker became chairman of the board of the only black bank in Richmond. (SCHOMBURG CENTER)

Gloria Vanderbilt, and other society and Hollywood women. Her creations adorned the casts of *Gone With the Wind*, *Easter Parade*, and *Back Street*, and her hats were featured on the cover of *Ladies' Home Journal*. Blount and other black women designed for Hollywood for more than half a century before, in 1972, Hollywood acknowledged the fact. That year, Elizabeth Courtney became the first black woman to be nominated for an Academy Award in Costume Design (*Lady Sings the Blues*).

Outside the areas of business traditionally associated with women, black women also made their mark. The most prominent of them was **Maggie Lena Walker**, of Richmond, Virginia.

THE OTHER WALKER

The free black community in America had, from its earliest days, formed societies for mutual aid and support. After the Civil War, these societies became even more popular, and many of them were founded by women. One of these societies was the vehicle for Maggie Lena Walker's remarkable success.

By the close of Reconstruction, black women in Richmond had formed twenty-five "female benevolent orders." Doubtless, the most important among these was the Independent Order of St. Luke, which had expanded to Richmond from Baltimore, where it had been founded in 1867 by an ex-slave, Mary Prout. By 1899, the order had fallen on hard times.

Maggie Walker was active in the Order of St. Luke from the age of fourteen, while also teaching in Richmond's public schools. She worked in the office and, for a time, collected the small dues that the order used to provide funeral benefits. She was also an active participant in meetings, conventions, and planning for the organization. In 1899, she was elected secretary.

Walker headed a reorganization of St. Luke that expanded the order into twenty-two states and converted the provision of funeral benefits into a full-fledged insurance enterprise. She traveled widely, speaking of the necessity for black business and for community cooperation in building black businesses.

In 1902, the order began publishing the *St. Luke Herald,* a newspaper that carried on a major anti-lynching campaign. In 1903, the St. Luke Penny Savings Bank opened. It was the fourth black bank in Richmond, and Maggie Walker became its president. Most historians agree that she was the first woman bank president in the United States.

In 1905, Walker and her organization opened the Emporium, a department store that served the black community. It was not as successful as the other St. Luke ventures, and was closed in 1911.

The insurance arm of the organization gradually grew to be its major activity. Indeed, the bank had to be separated from the order in order to comply with new federal banking and insurance regulations. Eventually, it combined with other black banks to become the Consolidated Bank and Trust Company, headed by Emmett Burke, the original St. Luke cashier, with Maggie Walker as chairman of the board. It became the only black bank in Richmond and is still prospering today.

At this point, Maggie Lena Walker was clearly one of the most successful women, of any color, in American business. She was also one of the most active in community service. She believed that black business should support the community just as strongly as she believed that the community should support its entrepreneurs and businesspeople. Besides, the black women's club movement was a critically important networking tool then, just as it is today.

In the professions, as in business, significant progress was made in the first half of the twentieth century. Final victories were not won, but black women triumphed in many important battles.

GAINING A FOOTHOLD

If teaching was the black women's profession of the late 1800s, journalism was their profession of the early 1900s. There were now close to fifty newspapers and forty magazines and periodicals published by African Americans, and women played a central role in their publication. These women journalists represented the cultural, political, and economic diversity of the larger black community.

In 1900, for example, the Boston-based *Colored American Magazine* hired the young novelist and writer **Pauline Hopkins** to edit its women's section. Three years later Hopkins was literary editor of the magazine, and today she is best known for her four novels serialized in its pages.

Margaret Murray Washington began as editor of *National Notes.* She was the wife of Booker T. Washington as well as the dean of women at Tuskegee Institute. Washington figured prominently in the women's club movement and black self-help activities, and she continued as editor until 1922.

West of the Mississippi, the first decade of the twentieth century witnessed the publication of two black women's periodicals.

Alice Dunbar-Nelson, not often identified as a journalist, published widely and even tried unsuccessfully to launch her own syndicated newspaper column. (SCHOMBURG CENTER)

Women's World was founded in Fort Worth, Texas. *Colored Women's Magazine* began in Topeka, Kansas, in 1907 and was edited by two women, C. M. Hughes and Minnie Thomas, as a monthly family magazine. It was published until at least 1920, and women maintained editorial control throughout its history.

Black women also figured prominently in periodicals targeted toward a more general audience. **Josephine Silone Yates**, a teacher at Lincoln Institute in Missouri and a two-term president of the National Association of Colored Women, served as associate editor of the *Negro Educational Review,*

founded in Vincennes, Indiana, in 1904. Agnes Carroll, a music teacher in Washington, D.C., helped edit the *Negro Music Journal,* published in that city during the same period. **Amanda Berry Smith**, an evangelist, itinerant preacher, and perhaps the most colorful woman journalist of the period, published the *Helper* (1900–1907), a magazine that focused on the issues of child care, temperance, and religion.

The turn of the century brought an era of development and growth for such influential African-American newspapers as the *Baltimore Afro-American*, the *Chicago Defender*, and the *New York Age*. The polemical, romantic writing of nineteenth-century American journalism gradually was replaced with a quest for objective reporting of the news, and powerful black newspapers were part of this developing professionalism. Black women were reporters, columnists, and editors for these papers but little is known about their efforts beyond the heroic story of Ida Wells-Barnett.

Some black women writers of the early 1900s included journalism among the other literary forms they practiced. **Alice Dunbar-Nelson**, wife of poet Paul Laurence Dunbar, is not often identified as a journalist, but she wrote for both black and white newspapers at the beginning of the century, including the *Pittsburgh Courier*, the *Washington Eagle*, the *Chicago Daily News*, the *Chicago Record-Herald*, and the *New York Sun*. She published poetry and short stories in numerous periodicals, and she wrote reviews of other black writers' works as well as news stories. She also edited the *Wilmington Advocate*, served as an associate editor for the *AME Church Review*, and later tried unsuccessfully to launch her own syndicated newspaper column.

Others among Dunbar-Nelson's contemporaries devoted their energies more exclusively to journalism, including **Delilah Beasley**, who began her career writing for a black newspaper, the *Cleveland Gazette*, and went on to contribute to white-owned papers such as the *Cincinnati Enquirer*. After moving to California, Beasley wrote a regular column for the *Oakland Tribune*—the state's largest circulation daily at the time—from 1915 to 1925.

California was home base for another journalist, **Charlotta Bass**, who is thought to be the first black woman to own and publish a newspaper in the United States. Bass started her career in 1910 as a writer for the *California Eagle*, a black-owned weekly in Los Angeles, and she purchased the paper two years later. She supported Marcus Garvey's **Universal Negro Improvement Association** and numerous civil rights organizations on the West Coast. Bass published the *Eagle* for nearly forty years, but she is perhaps best known as the first black woman to run for vice president when she joined the Progressive Party ticket in 1952.

Political activism frequently became a partner to black women's journalistic work. Marvel Jackson Cooke began her career as an editorial assistant to W. E. B. DuBois at the *Crisis* in 1926. Two years later DuBois helped Cooke obtain a position at the *New York Amsterdam News*, where she struggled to improve the newspaper's quality and expand coverage of the black community. Her efforts to organize a union local and lead a strike against the paper in 1935 prompted a move to the *People's Voice*, founded by Adam Clayton Powell, where she served as assistant managing editor. In 1950, Cooke became the first full-time African-American woman reporter for a mainstream newspaper when she joined the staff of the *Daily Compass*, where she worked with the renowned journalist I. F. Stone.

By the 1940s, black women had seized new challenges within the black press. Hazel Garland broke into the newspaper business as a stringer for the *Pittsburgh Courier*. In 1946, she was hired as a full-time reporter, and she traveled the country to cover crucial issues such as lynching and African

The ultimate success of black women in journalism and publishing is Essence *magazine. The first issue, whose cover is reproduced above, was published in May 1970. As of 1996, it had a circulation of over 800,000. Among the executives and former executives included in this encyclopedia are Susan Taylor, Marcia Ann Gillespie, and Linda Villarosa. (ESSENCE)*

Americans' responses to World War II. In an interview she recalled writing an award-winning series titled "The Three I's: Ignorance, Illiteracy, Illegitimacy," based on her travels through poor black communities in the South. During her years at the *Courier*, Garland served as entertainment editor, radio-television editor, women's editor, and finally editor in chief. Garland's daughter, Phyllis, also became a journalist, beginning her career at *Ebony* magazine in 1966, later teaching at Columbia University's Graduate School of Journalism.

Elizabeth Murphy Moss was connected with one of the black newspaper giants at mid-century, her family's paper, the *Baltimore Afro-American*. She began her career with the paper at age eleven and was a correspondent in England during World War II. She eventually rose to the position of vice president and treasurer for the *Afro-American* newspaper chain.

To one degree or another, in the first half of this century most professions became open to black women, with the clergy among the exceptions. But medicine, law, and even the military admitted them, and gained by their participation.

OFFICERS OF THE COURT

The first wave of black women attorneys appeared shortly after the Nineteenth Amendment gave women that most important right of citizenship, the right to vote. In 1920, **Violette N. Anderson** became the first black woman to practice law in Illinois. She later became the first black woman to argue a case before the United States Supreme Court. She was also Chicago's first woman prosecutor.

In 1925, **L. Marian Fleming Poe** was admitted to the Virginia bar. She is believed to be the first black woman to practice law in a Southern state. Her distinguished career in private practice continued into the 1960s, when she was twice the Virginia delegate to the National Associaton of Woman Lawyers, a biracial organization.

In 1927, **Sadie Tanner Mossell Alexander** became the first black woman to be admitted to the bar and to practice law in Pennsylvania. She was in partnership with her husband, Raymond Pace Alexander, until 1959, when he became a judge. The Alexanders were among the founders of the National Bar Association, which is the professional organization of African-American lawyers.

In 1939, **Jane Bolin** became the nation's first black woman judge when Mayor Fiorello La Guardia appointed her Justice of the Domestic Relations Court in New York City. The first black woman to be elected to a judgeship would be **Juanita Kidd Stout**. Two full decades later, in 1959, she was elected to a judgeship of the Philadelphia Municipal Court.

Black women lawyers frequently found government agencies offered greater opportunities than private practice. **Eunice Hunton Carter**, became New York State's first black woman district attorney upon joining the New York County District Attorney's office shortly after graduation from Fordham Law School in 1934. She eventually became chief of the Special Sessions Bureau, which handled more than 14,000 criminal cases each year.

Edith Sampson, the first woman to graduate from Loyola University Law School in Chicago, practiced law in that city, coming to public attention through the **National**

Council of Negro Women. In 1949, that organization chose her to be their representative in a program called America's Town Meeting of the Air which traveled worldwide debating issues of interest.

Sampson's work with Town Meeting led President Harry S Truman, in 1950, to appoint her an alternate delegate to the United Nations General Assembly. Later, she became a member-at-large of the North Atlantic Treaty Organization (NATO) and of the United Nations Educational, Scientific, and Cultural Organization (UNESCO). Back in Chicago, she was assistant corporation counsel, associate judge of the Municipal Court, and judge of the Cook County Circuit Court.

These women were not isolated examples. There were black women lawyers in cities around the country. Still, their numbers were small. Most law schools in the South refused to admit black students. Other law schools around the country discriminated against women, either by policy or custom. The same was true of medical schools. And the situation was even more dire for would-be women medical students. Those women who succeeded in creating careers for themselves in medicine were truly pioneers.

THE NEED TO HEAL

Even today, only a small number of black women have become physicians. In 1920, sixty-five black women practiced medicine. Fifty years later, the number had increased to 1,051. By 1989, the number had grown to 3,250, but this represented less than 1 percent of practicing physicians in the United States. Until the advent of affirmative action programs in the 1970s, most black women graduated from the two predominantly black medical schools, Howard University and Meharry Medical College. Indeed, the doors of most medical schools in the United States were closed to *all women* until the early 1960s.

In the twentieth century, black women physicians faced a new obstacle. They had to gain access to hospitals, which had become essential for medical education, medical practice, and medical specialization. Several states had even passed laws requiring the completion of an internship as a prerequisite for a medical license. But African Americans could not get internships in white hospitals. And women could not get internships in black hospitals. For the most part, black women were welcome only in the handful of women's hospitals that existed, and not in all of those.

The opportunities, therefore, for black women to obtain hospital appointments and specialty training were severely limited. A few black women were able to gain admission to programs at government hospitals. **Dorothy Ferebee**, after several rejections from white hospitals, secured an internship at Freedmen's Hospital in Washington, D.C. In 1926, **May Chinn** became the first black woman intern at New York City's Harlem Hospital.

Still, examining the work of twentieth-century black women physicians demonstrates the significant contributions that they have made to medicine and their communities. These women founded hospitals, established civic organizations, practiced medicine among the underserved, and challenged barriers in a profession that has been, and continues to be, white and male dominated.

Nurses continued their fight for respect during this time. In 1908, they founded the **National Association of Colored Graduate Nurses** (NACGN). In 1912, the NACGN members numbered 125, and by 1920 it boasted a membership of 500. In the mid-1930s, grants from the General Education Board of the Rockefeller Foundation and the Julius Rosenwald Fund made it possible for the organization to employ **Mabel K. Staupers** as executive secretary and to move into permanent headquarters at Rockefeller Center in New York City, where all the major national nursing organizations had offices. Following a long and relentless struggle, Staupers and NACGN president **Estelle Massey Osborne** succeeded in winning recognition and acceptance for black nurses. In 1948, the American Nurses' Association (ANA) extended membership to black nurses.

With the removal of the overtly discriminatory barriers to membership in the ANA, members of the NACGN recognized that their needs would now be served by the ANA, which agreed to take over the functions of the NACGN. Thus, during the NACGN's 1949 convention, its members voted the organization out of existence, and the following year, Staupers, then president, presided over its formal dissolution.

A major battle had been won but, as it turned out, the war was far from over. Discrimination continued against black nurses, as it did against black women in every area of business and professional life. But this first half of the twentieth century did see black women enter an entirely new area of professional life, an area where war really was war—the military.

THE FIGHT TO SERVE

Much of the Spanish-American War took place in Cuba and in the Philippines. As Teddy Roosevelt made his famous charge up San Juan Hill, the Twenty-fourth Infantry, an all-black unit, provided cover. Additionally, the Ninth and Tenth Cavalry and the Twenty-fifth Infantry were all-black units that participated in combat during the ten-week war. Though the United States won the war, thousands of black and white soldiers contracted various tropical diseases.

In July 1898, the Surgeon General asked that a corps of black women be organized as nurses for black soldiers. Thirty-two black nurses were sent to tend black troops located at Camp Thomas, Georgia. These trailblazers were so well received that Congress created a permanent Army Nurse Corps in 1901. The Navy Nurse Corps was established in 1908. Thus, women had finally become an official part of the military.

Ironically, black women did not serve in either of these corps for another four decades. The groups they had inspired were closed to them.

However, black nurses were accepted into the Red Cross. The opportunities created for black nurses to serve the military directly and through the Red Cross were important during the era of Jim Crow, when there were very few black hospitals and health care facilities, and when black nurses were barred from working in white hospitals.

During World War I, 650,000 black men served in the U.S. military, with approximately a third of them serving in France. Hundreds of black nurses registered with the American Red Cross. In June 1918, the Secretary of War issued a call for black nurses who were affiliated with the Red Cross to volunteer for overseas duty as well as for service at home. Among those who responded was **Adah B. Thoms**, the president of the National Association of Colored Graduate Nurses. Many others served the more than 38,000 black troops confined to base hospitals in Kansas, Illinois, Iowa, Kentucky, Ohio, and New Jersey.

In December 1941, the United States entered World War II. During World War II and throughout the 1940s, a number of developments improved opportunities for black women who wanted to serve in the military. Pressure from civil rights activists such as A. Philip Randolph, from the **National Association for the Advancement of Colored People** and the black press, and the efforts of **Mary McLeod Bethune** and other members of Franklin D. Roosevelt's "Black Cabinet," combined with the military's changing needs to open new doors.

Perhaps the most important development for black women during World War II was the creation of the Women's Army Auxiliary Corps (WAAC) in May 1942. The WAAC was incorporated into the U.S. Army in 1943 when it became the Women's Army Corps (WAC). Black and white women were accepted into both of those organizations, but segregation and discrimination often occurred. By the end of World War II more than 4,000 black women had enlisted in the WAC.

The first black woman in U.S. history to be commissioned as a military officer was a WAC, **Charity Adams Earley**. She was also the highest-ranking black woman

Charity Adams Earley was the highest-ranking black woman in the military during World War II. (CHARITY ADAMS)

during World War II. Adams described her military experience in the book *One Woman's Army: A Black Officer Remembers the WAC* (1989). The 6888th Central Postal Battalion, comprised of 800 women, was the first all-black female unit to deploy overseas. They served in England.

The WAC trained in Des Moines, Iowa. The first graduating class consisted of thirty-nine black women representing every region of the country. The WACs also had a renowned black band known as the 404th Army Service Band. The band sang and performed at black and white military, civilian, and church functions across the country.

Company 8 of the Women's Auxiliary Corps is shown here in formation at Fort Des Moines, Iowa. One of its officers was Charity Adams Earley, the first black woman commissioned in the army. (CHARITY ADAMS)

The navy opened its doors to black women during World War II with a plan to raise black recruitment to 10 percent of the navy's total personnel and to form the Women's Reserve of the United States Navy, most commonly known as the WAVES (an acronym for Women Accepted for Volunteer Emergency Service). In 1944, Bessie Garret became the first black woman accepted. The first WAVES officer graduates from Smith College included two black women, Frances Wills and Harriet Pickens. The Coast Guard admitted five black women during World War II. Among them were Olivia J. Hooker, currently a practicing clinical psychologist. The first black WAVES to enter the Hospital Corps were Ruth C. Isaacs, Katherine Horton, and Inez Patterson.

While the navy announced big plans, it fell short of its goals. The 10 percent black quota was never achieved during World War II, and as of 1945 there were only fifty-six black WAVES. However, the navy became the first armed service to accept women in its regular forces when, in 1948, the WAVES were incorporated into the regular navy. The WACs, in contrast, did not become part of the regular army until 1978. With the elimination of these separate auxiliaries, the navy and the army decreased some problems with sexism and made more soldiers (regardless of sex) part of the core organization.

The army and the navy, despite these changes, continued to maintain separate nurse corps. While both branches formed their nurse corps at the beginning of the twentieth century, black nurses were not admitted until the start of World War II. Susan Elizabeth Freeman became one of the first black women to join the Army Nurse Corps (1941), while Phyllis Mae Daley was the first African American inducted into the Navy Nurse Corps (March 8, 1945).

There were considerably more black women, however, in the army's nurse corps than in the navy's. Black nurses served in all-black military hospitals as well as in four general hospitals, the regional hospitals, and at least nine station hospitals. Additionally, black women nurses served in Africa and Europe during World War II.

The U.S. military assisted the United Nations and its mission in Korea during the early 1950s, and the women who went to Korea were nurses with the Red Cross, the Army Nurse Corps, or the Navy Nurse Corps. A few others served during the Korean War in Tokyo, Japan, and other places in the Far East Command that were not in the battle zone.

When the Korean War began, there was a total of about 29,000 women in all branches of the military services. The number increased to nearly 100,000 by 1956. It is not known how many of these were black, but it is clear that most were white. (One black soldier, I. C. Rochell, was on duty in Korea for more than seventeen months and reported seeing only one black woman, a nurse with the Red Cross.)

According to the description of this photo in the National Archives, these women are the "first group of Army Corp and Air Corp enlistees from the New York area sworn in—3 black, 2 white." The armed services were becoming an equal opportunity employer. —(NATIONAL ARCHIVES)

One of the lasting achievements for women during the Korean War was the formation of the Defense Advisory Committee on Women in the Armed Services (DACOWITS), a group that still functions today in the interest of women in the military. One of the black women who later served on this powerful committee was **Clara Adams-Ender**, a general in the Army Nurse Corps.

President Truman's executive orders in the late 1940s and the 1954 *Brown* v. *Board of Education* Supreme Court ruling began the long desegregation process. The Civil Rights Act of 1964 then pushed the U.S. military into the modern age.

By 1973, toward the end of the Vietnam War, almost 10 percent of the American troops who had served in Vietnam were black, including thousands of black women. From this point on, a series of new firsts signaled the gains made by black women.

The Reverend Alice Henderson became the first woman military chaplain in the country in 1974. During that same year, Jill Brown became the first black woman in U.S. military history to qualify as a pilot. In 1975, the Naval Medical Corps appointed its first black female physician, Donna P. Davis. Black women were being admitted to all of the military academies by 1976, where the entrance requirements were the same for both sexes, except for weight and height.

In March 1980, **Hazel W. Johnson** (later Hazel Johnson-Brown) became the first black woman in U.S. history to hold the rank of general. Johnson, who also had a Ph.D., was the Chief of the U.S. Army Nurse Corps. Two other black women were promoted to the rank of general during the 1980s as well, General **Sherian Cadoria** in the army, and General Clara Adams-Ender in the Army Nurse Corps. The fourth black female general, **Marcelite J. Harris**, in the air force, received her rank in 1990.

Today, black women are allowed to join all areas of the U.S. armed services, except combat arms units (infantry, armor, artillery, and combat engineers). Women are attached to the combat arms units in support capacities. During operations Desert Shield and Desert Storm, Captain Cynthia Mosley commanded Alpha Company of the Twenty-fourth Forward Support Battalion, Twenty-fourth Infantry Division. Mosley's company was responsible for refueling vehicles and resupplying troops located in the combat zone. Moreover, the first Scud missile was shot down in the Gulf War by a black woman, Lieutenant Phoebe Jeter. As many as forty percent of the 3,500 female soldiers involved in the Gulf War were black, and three black women lost their lives.

THE PROFESSIONS IN THE MODERN AGE

Historically, the black middle class has been more likely to be involved in the professions—education, law, medicine, journalism, and so forth—than in business. In part this is because of the tremendous value placed on education in the African-American community. In part it is because success in business requires the cooperation of the white community even more than success in the professions.

However, obstacles placed in the way of black women in the professions have been much more formidable than those faced by black men. And they have remained so, despite progress. A black woman is far more likely today to be president of a business enterprise than to be a neurosurgeon or dean of a law school.

Throughout most of the twentieth century, most black women physicians had general practices because of their limited opportunities to obtain specialist training. Since World War II, many have entered the more prestigious and financially rewarding medical specialties. But black women in medicine are still racking up surprising and unnerving firsts.

In 1946, **Helen O. Dickens**, the daughter of a former slave, received her certification from the American Board of Obstetrics and Gynecology. Four years later, she became the first black woman admitted to the American College of Surgeons. The American Board of Surgery certified its first black woman, Hughenna L. Gauntlett, in 1968, and the American Board of Neurological Surgery certified its first, **Alexa Canady**, in 1984. As of 1995, Canady was still one of only four black women neurosurgeons in the country.

Black women have begun to assume some leadership roles within the profession. In 1958, Edith Irby Jones broke the racial barriers of Southern medical schools when she became the first black person, male or female, admitted to the University of Arkansas School of Medicine. In 1985, Jones became the first woman president of the National Medical Association, a predominantly black medical society. By 1991, two other black women, Vivian Pinn-Wiggins and Alma R. George, had headed the organization.

In 1991, Pinn-Wiggins was appointed the first permanent director of the National Institutes of Health Office of Women's Health Research. **Roselyn Payne Epps**, in 1990, became the first black physician to be president of the American Medical Women's Association. In 1992, **Joycelyn Elders** became Surgeon General of the United States. Despite these achievements, only a few black women have assumed prominent roles in the medical hierarchy. Few have been named department chairs, and none has been named a medical school dean.

Black women have long been a force in African-American journalism. Today, they are becoming increasingly visible in mainstream journalism, both in print and on the air.

During the 1940s, **Alice Allison Dunnigan** became the first African-American woman to cover the White House when she was the Washington correspondent for the *Chicago Defender*. In the mid-1960s, **Ethel L. Payne** spent ten weeks in Vietnam covering the war. She traveled extensively throughout Asia and Africa during her career and became one of the first black women in broadcasting when she provided commentary for CBS News.

The death of **Philippa Duke Schuyler** in Vietnam in May 1967 at the age of thirty-four, as she tried to evacuate Vietnamese children trapped in an orphanage, is a tragic episode among the stories of black women journalists. Schuyler was best known as a child prodigy who performed as a classical pianist when barely in her teens. She began her second career, as a journalist, in the 1960s, first covering the war in the Congo, and later Vietnam, for the *Manchester Union Leader*.

These diverse and courageous women served as role models for a new generation of journalists who emerged in the 1960s and 1970s. Individuals like Dorothy Gilliam, the first black woman columnist for the *Washington Post*, and Pamela M. Johnson, the first black woman publisher of a white-owned daily newspaper, the *Ithaca Journal*, have continued this pioneering legacy. Black women have also become increasingly visible in broadcast news, following the lead of **Charlayne Hunter-Gault** in public broadcasting, and **Carol Jenkins**, Renee Poussaint, and others associated with the networks. In 1993, **Pearl Stewart** became the first black woman to serve as editor of a major U.S. daily newspaper, the *Oakland Tribune*.

Today's black women journalists face the challenge of increasing their numbers and visibility in every facet of the news media. Their predecessors demonstrated that black women are a vital link in the nation's quest for free expression and social justice.

However, in spite of the accomplishments of black women in law, teaching, journalism, medicine, and the military, the most impressive change for black women today has occurred in business.

THE NEW ERA IN BUSINESS

The Civil Rights Act of 1964 was the single most important piece of legislation, short of constitutional amendments, in African-American history. And one section of it had a major impact on black women in business. That section was Title VII, which was designed to prevent discrimination in employment.

There was a remarkable parallel between this law and the Fifteenth Amendment, which, in the nineteenth century, gave black men the vote. Black men were the proposed beneficiaries of Title VII, just as they were beneficiaries of the Fifteenth Amendment. Though the law would theoretically have protected black women as well, there is little doubt they would have continued to be deprived of employment and advancement, with gender used as an excuse, if nothing else.

Again paralleling the nineteenth-century situation, there were women who felt that Title VII should apply to them as well as to men. However, before those women got a chance to add the word "sex" to the bill, somebody else did.

That somebody else was Representative Howard Smith of Virginia, who was against the bill. It was his belief that adding women to those covered by the bill would make it appear so ridiculous that no one would vote for it. However, as **Paula Giddings** relates it in *When and Where I Enter*, "There *was* much ribaldry in the Congress; the day Smith made his proposal was called 'Ladies Day' in the House. But evidently the good ol' boys were laughing so hard they missed a step. Some of their colleagues, particularly Representative Martha Griffiths of Michigan, were able to marshal forces sufficient to pass the bill—with the sex provision."

Title VII, and its enforcement arm, the Equal Employment Opportunities Commission, changed the face of American business. With the force of the government behind them, black women were more frequently able to find jobs that fit their talent and their education, as were black men, and women of other races.

Title VII was particularly effective when it was supplemented by what came to be known as "affirmative action." The phrase, which is now loaded down with political and emotional baggage, had a very simple meaning in the beginning. Title VII was all about negative action. It was about *not* doing discriminatory things. Then a series of presidential directives added the concept of positive, or affirmative, action. These were about actively correcting discrimination.

In many ways, affirmative action has worked. Between the 1970s and 1990s, the percentage of African Americans in the work force has risen by 50 percent. Many black workers were hired by the government itself. Between 1966 and 1976, according to *Business Week*, 850,000 African Americans found work in the social-welfare arms of federal, state, and local government.

As a result of these changes, the black middle class has expanded enormously. But what about the upper reaches of business and professional life in America? Have the changes of the last few decades extended to the executive suite and the boardroom? Just how far have black women come?

To begin to answer that question, it's important to understand that we are now talking about black women inside the corporate structure. There are still many entrepreneurs, and their accomplishments are sometimes remarkable. But black women have for the first time in history entered mainstream businesses in large enough numbers to be a significant presence.

In 1966, two years after the passage of the Civil Rights Act, 1 percent of all managers in U.S. business were black. In 1989, the number had risen to 5 percent. In a country where just over 12 percent of the population is black, that number certainly leaves room for improvement, but it also

represents outstanding determination, commitment, and achievement on the part of African Americans.

However, black women have not risen equally with black men. When *Black Enterprise* magazine published its "25 Hottest Black Managers" in corporate America in 1988, for example, there was not a single woman on the list. In explaining this, the magazine pointed out that, of the 125 final candidates, women represented less than 1 percent. In other words, there was only one. The article went on to say that "only one or two" (of the one woman among the finalists) "held top management positions in which they headed major divisions or departments directly impacting the fiscal health and overall direction of the companies in which they worked." (In other words, had any clout.) And finally, "none of the female candidates had compensation packages (including salary, bonuses, stock options, and pension plans) of at least $250,000."

To simplify, the magazine put together a roster of 125 finalists for their "Hottest Black Managers," and among those finalists was one woman. She had clout in her company, but she didn't make much money, comparatively speaking, so she didn't make the list.

Less than four years later, in 1991, the same magazine published another list— "21 [Black] Women of Power and Influence in Corporate America." There were seven women on this new list who would have met the qualifications of clout and compensation set for the "Hottest Black Managers" list.

In 1993, *Black Enterprise* published a list of forty of "America's Most Powerful

Black Executives." There were four women on that list.

Four years after that, a black woman became president of a major American corporation. At the age of forty-four, Ann M. Fudge was named president of Maxwell House Coffee, a $1.4 billion business.

How did things change so quickly? The answer is simple. They didn't. They had been changing slowly all along. To reach the top of the corporate ladder, you need talent, determination, luck—and time. Black women are relatively new entrants into the corporate world, but there is finally a substantial number who have been around long enough to be considered for upper-level positions. They've been in the "pipeline" for a decade or two and are now ready to emerge.

To keep things in perspective, it's important to remember that corporate power is still very much in male hands. *Fortune* magazine published a study in 1990 that showed that of the 4,000 highest-paid officers and directors employed by 799 of the largest public corporations, 19 were women. For the number of women to be in proportion to women in the general population, that number would be more than 2,000. For it to be in proportion to women in the work force, it would be more than 1,500. Instead, it was 19. And not one of those women was black.

Or, to look at it another way, there are now more black women than black men in corporate America, according to statistics released by the U.S. Equal Employment Opportunity Commission in 1993. There was a 125 percent increase of black professional women between 1982 and 1992. And yet, among officers and managers, black men still significantly outnumber

black women, and the salaries of black women in the work force still trail those of black men by fourteen percentage points.

Still, there are more and more women like Ann Fudge. They are highly educated, highly motivated, and finally coming into their own. **Sylvia Rhone** has climbed the ladder at Atlantic Records to become president of their Elektra/EastWest Records division. She was the first black woman to head a major record label. Paula A. Sneed is president of General Foods USA's Foodservice Division. Carolyn H. Baldwin is president of Coca-Cola Financial Corporation. Dorothy Terrell is president of SunExpress, Inc., the direct marketing unit of Sun Microsystems, Inc., which is the leading supplier of workstation computers in the world. Michele J. Hooper is president of the International Business Group of Caremark International, Inc., which is the nation's leading provider of alternate site health care.

In 1994, there were a dozen black women who sat on the boards of directors of at least three Fortune 500 companies. And in 1995, there was one black woman, **Oprah Winfrey**, among the 400 richest people in America. She represents a different group of black businesswomen, the entrepreneurs.

OPRAH AND OTHERS

Oprah Winfrey could have ended up just another show business personality. Certainly the salary she received, and still receives, for standing in front of an audience and talking about the problems of daily life would be enough to satisfy most people. But Winfrey was a born entrepreneur.

She built her business on her success as a talk-show host. What's important to remember is that there have been many successful television personalities—though not many as successful as Winfrey—but few of them have been able to capitalize on their entertainment achievements as she has. Early in her career, she formed her own production company.

Winfrey is the highest-paid performer in show business. She also owns and produces her show. She has also produced a number of other television shows, including *The Women of Brewster Place*. In 1988, she founded Harpo Studios, becoming the first African American to own her own television studio.

Winfrey is one of many black women entrepreneurs. Black women own or control more than one-third of all black-owned businesses. And there are more than 400,000 such businesses in the U.S. Most black women entrepreneurs face obstacles that the remarkable entertainment mogul was able to circumvent. These include difficulty finding financial backing and difficulty being accepted by the business world in which they function. But contemporary black women have shown the same sort of ingenuity and vision that made Madam C. J. Walker a millionaire almost a century ago.

Ernesta G. Procope founded E. G. Bowman Co., Inc., in the 1950s. It was the first, and is still, the largest minority-owned insurance brokerage firm on Wall Street. More than 2,000 large corporations and government entities make up the company's blue-chip roster of clients.

Barbara Gardner Proctor left her position at a white advertising agency in 1970 to form her own company, Proctor & Gardner Advertising. She offered expertise in targeting the African-American market to such clients as Sears of Chicago, Jewel Food Stores, and Kraft Foods. Within a few years, Proctor & Gardner was the largest black advertising company in the world, with annual billings of more than $4 million. Today, it remains an important force in advertising.

Claudette F. Hayle is an example of the new wave of black women entrepreneurs who have been able to use the resources currently available to women and minorities. She co-founded Goodman & Hayle Information Systems, Inc., in 1985. Although she received help from the Small Business Administration (SBA), she was at first unable to get credit from a bank. However, with the help of the National Association of Women Business Owners (NAWBO), she finally established a relationship with Chemical Bank. In 1986, the company landed a $700,000 contract with McDonnell Douglas Corporation's software development division. The next year, Goodman & Hayle grossed $3 million.

Dolores Robinson's firm, Dolores Robinson Entertainment, has managed the careers of such Hollywood stars as Martin Sheen, Rosie Perez, Montel Williams, and Wesley Snipes. She is very clear about the advantages of working for yourself. "Because it's my own business," she told *Essence* magazine in 1995, "I don't run into as much racism and sexism as I would if I worked for someone else. I find that white clients are not reluctant to work with me. They take a look at my track record. That speaks for itself."

There are thousands of black women entrepreneurs in entertainment, public relations, insurance, and most other service industries. In manufacturing, they have historically been involved primarily in the beauty industry. Although the field was largely taken over by men in the 1930s, women have now made a comeback.

In the 1970s and 1980s, black women again began to enter the beauty industry as entrepreneurs. The first and most prominent of these was former model **Naomi Sims**. The fashion model who made history as the first black woman to appear on the covers of *Ladies' Home Journal* (1968) and *Life* (1969), then quit the business in 1973, at the age of twenty-three.

Frustrated with the wigs and makeup given her for photo shoots, Sims eventually created a line of wigs and hairpieces for black women. She reached the market for her products by writing four books: *How to Be a Top Model* (1979), *All about Success for the Black Woman* (1982), *All about Hair Care for the Black Woman* (1982), and *All about Health and Beauty for the Black Woman* (1986). Then, in 1987, she created the Naomi Sims Skin Care Collection, a thirteen-product line that took ten years to develop. Her success, as well as that of a handful of other start-up cosmetics companies founded by black women (e.g., Juin Rachele Cosmetics, directly distributed, founded in Houston in 1986; Gazelle International, based in Paris, founded in 1983 by Georgia native Patricia A. French), continues to inspire black women entrepreneurs.

Many black women start their own businesses because they are tired of battling discrimination in mainstream corporate America. And many simply enjoy being in control of their own destinies. It will be a clear sign of success for black women when one of these businesses becomes a major American corporation, when the Fortune 500 list finally includes a company that not only employs but was founded by a black woman.

INTO THE FUTURE

It is difficult to predict what the future holds for black women in business and the professions. There are many factors involved.

What will happen in this country with regard to affirmative action? If ever there was a debate with more than two sides, this one is it. Some say that affirmative action is a form of reverse discrimination, that African Americans are being handed jobs on a platter. Others say that affirmative action scarcely exists anymore, that Reagan took the teeth out of it.

Some black Americans believe that, without affirmative action, business will retreat into the Dark Ages, or rather the White Ages. Others say that affirmative action stigmatizes black workers as incompetent and unworthy of hiring and promotion on their own merits.

Affirmative action is now a hot political issue, and how that issue is resolved will almost certainly have a tremendous impact on the position of black women. On the other hand, there are now a large number of black women in place in business and the professions. They are on the way to greater responsibility and power. They are, or will soon be, in a position to hire and to serve as mentors to other black women. There may be a step back in the future, but it will certainly not be all the way back, or even close.

In addition, many large corporations are realizing that a purely white male management team is unfeasible in today's world.

To manage a diverse work force, they are going to need a diverse group of managers and executives. Also, women and minorities are often more effective at dealing with customers and colleagues from other cultures than are traditionally socialized white American men.

The number of black women in law, medicine, and the other professions will certainly increase as the black middle class continues to expand. Women entering those fields will continue to face the subtle forms of discrimination that can be so destructive and so difficult to confront. But here, too, the world has changed and will not ever go back.

There will never again be a time when black women are banned from medical schools. Never again will they be denied entrance to bar associations. And never again will all the faces on the evening news be white ones that have to be shaved before they go on the air. It is indeed a new era for black women.

A

Andrews, Rosalyn (1953–)

A gifted businesswoman who turned her experience in education and marketing into leadership of multimillion-dollar ventures, Rosalyn McPherson Andrews is a modern executive who oversees the creation of world-changing products. As vice president of marketing for Time Life Inc.'s Education Division, she develops and markets culturally diverse products to schools and libraries across the nation. Her first product for Time Life, *African Americans: Voices of Triumph,* has been a feat of marketing skill and cultural integrity.

Born in New Orleans on March 27, 1953, Andrews is the daughter of Major James G. McPherson and Lillie Webb McPherson. Her father was an army officer who later became a nursing home administrator. Her mother was an elementary school teacher.

In 1973 she earned a bachelor's degree in secondary education from Southern University & A & M College, in Baton Rouge. From 1975 to 1976 she taught mathematics and social studies in the public schools of Roosevelt, New York. Then, in 1976, Andrews became an editor for CBS, Inc., in New York City, developing social studies textbooks and related products.

Andrews stayed with CBS until 1979, when she left to join McGraw-Hill, where she was again an editor in a social studies textbook program. She stayed until 1980, when she was recruited to Scholastic, Inc., to be a product manager for children's paperbacks. Andrews was primarily in charge of marketing products, producing catalogs and promotional materials for a line that generated in excess of $6 million in revenue.

In 1982, Andrews received her M.B.A. from Fairleigh Dickinson University in Teaneck, New Jersey. The following year she left Scholastic to become circulation manager of college agent sales at Time, Inc., which publishes not only *Time* but *Sports Illustrated* and *Discover,* among other magazines. Andrews was in charge of marketing these and other magazines to college students and faculty. She was responsible for more than $12 million in profits.

By 1985, Andrews had decided to strike out on her own, opening McPherson Andrews Marketing, Inc. She began as a lone free-lancer with only three clients. She ended up with more than twenty specialists working for her, and more than twenty corporate clients. Her specialty was research, development, and distribution of multicultural products to schools, libraries, and individual consumers. During this period Andrews also found time to teach marketing at Rider College and at Rutgers, The State University of New Jersey.

In 1992, Time Life, Inc., asked Andrews back to become director of multicultural markets. Her primary project was the development of the three-volume set *African Americans: Voices of Triumph.* The first volume, *Perseverance,* chronicled individual struggles from slavery through the civil rights movement. The second, *Leadership,* covers accomplishments in business, education, religion, science, and politics. The third, *Creative Fire,* deals with achievement in the arts, music, literature, theater, and film.

Andrews is head of the project, which includes distinguished board members such as writer Maya Angelou and Harvard historian Henry Louis Gates, Jr. In a project managed and staffed by black professionals, Andrews was careful to keep the books culturally accurate and appropriate. In order to introduce the series, one set of books was donated to every public school, secondary school, and library in the country, a total of some 50,000 books.

In September of 1993, Andrews was promoted to vice president of marketing for Time Life's Educational Division. Major corporations have recognized the potential of ethnically targeted educational products, and they need businesswomen like Andrews to deliver.

ANDRA MEDEA

Avant, Angela L. (1959–)

One of an extraordinary new breed of corporate executives, Angela L. Avant has reached a level of achievement that would be envied even by those who have not had to face the obstacles of race and gender. She was born on August 16, 1959, in Portsmouth Virginia, to E. Loretta Avant Miller and George S. Allen. Her mother is an administrator and her father a quality control specialist at the United States Naval Air Station. Avant earned a bachelor's degree in accounting at Virginia State University and then went to work for Arthur Andersen & Com-

Angela Avant was responsible for staggering amounts of money as manager of mergers and acquisitions for the Opto-Electronics Business Group of Corning Incorporated. Earlier in her career, she was the first black woman in the position of manager in Arthur Andersen company's audit practice. (CORNING, INC.)

pany, one of the nation's largest accounting firms.

While she was with Arthur Andersen, she progressed steadily up the ladder, becoming the first black woman to hold the position of manager in their audit practice. Her experience there and at Ryder Systems served her well when in 1992 she moved to Corning Incorporated, a $6 billion company.

At Corning, Avant was first manager of the mergers and acquisitions accounting department, a remarkable achievement for a woman her age—she was thirty-three at the time—and only the beginning. After about six months in that position, she rose to director of internal audit for Corning. A year and a half later, she was named manager of mergers and acquisitions for the Opto-Electronics Business Group of Corning.

While many black women find themselves stalled in the human resources departments of large corporations, Avant is dealing with staggering sums of money as she takes responsibility for the coordination of the acquisition, joint venture, and divestiture process as well as management of the deal valuation and transaction structuring process. She also coordinates the due diligence process and third-party negotiations.

At the same time, Avant is in her second term as president of the National Association of Black Accountants (NABA). In 1994, she was chosen to be part of a select group of executives participating in *Black Enterprise* magazine's Corporate Executive Women's Roundtable. Still in her thirties, she is a woman to watch in the future.

KATHLEEN THOMPSON

B

Baker, Augusta (1911–)

Augusta Baker, the distinguished children's librarian, storyteller, teacher, administrator, and anthologist, spent her thirty-seven-year career at the New York Public Library. She began as a children's librarian in 1937 at the 135th Street Branch (now the Countee Cullen Regional Branch) and retired as coordinator of children's services in 1974.

Augusta Baker was born on April 1, 1911, in Baltimore, Maryland, the daughter of teachers Winfort J. and Mabel Gough Braxston. She was educated in the public schools of Baltimore and graduated with honors from high school. Her father encouraged her to attend an integrated college

When Augusta Baker was appointed assistant coordinator of children's services in 1953, she became the first black woman to hold an administrative position with the New York Public Library, one of the world's largest public library systems. Later promoted to coordinator of children's services, she used her experience as a storyteller to bring children and books together. (SCHOMBURG CENTER)

where, he thought, contact with people from other cultures would broaden her outlook. She studied for two years at the University of Pittsburgh and then transferred to New York State Teachers College in Albany, where she received a bachelor of arts degree in 1933 and a bachelor of science degree in library science the following year. Having grown up in a family that valued scholarship, good books, and a career in teaching, Baker taught school briefly before finding her true calling in public library work. When she became an assistant children's librarian at the 135th Street Branch of the New York Public Library in 1937, the Harlem facility already housed a sizable collection of books on black history and culture. Under the leadership of Ernestine Rose, branch librarian, and Arthur Schomburg, curator of the Negro Collection, the library had established programs on popular culture and education and had developed services directed especially at the black community.

Baker plunged into children's work, telling stories and organizing clubs, trips, and concerts. As part of a dedicated staff, she worked with parents, teachers, and community groups to enrich the cultural lives of children, noting that the children who used the library did not know very much about their heritage. Moreover, she found few books that would instill pride in, or encourage children to read about, black culture. With the assistance of a group of women from the community, Baker tried to correct this problem by collecting worthwhile books that were available. This landmark collection of children's literature, called the James Weldon Johnson Memorial Collection, was selected according to language, theme, and illustration. A bibliography of this pioneering collection was published in 1957 as *Books about Negro Life for Children;* the list has gone through successively larger revisions and eventually was retitled *The Black Experience in Children's Books.*

In 1953, Baker became the first black librarian to be appointed to an administrative position in the New York Public Library, one of the largest public library systems in the world. As assistant coordinator of children's services for the New York Public Library, she was well regarded for her hard work and effectiveness as a children's librarian at the now renamed Countee Cullen Branch. In her new position, she used her skills as a creative manager and experienced storyteller to bring children and books together and to help parents understand the importance of reading.

Baker was a persistent and convincing spokesperson for the improvement of children's literature about black people, promoting sensitivity to pictorial, cultural, and intellectual standards. She talked to editors, authors, and publishers about the need for better books about black life, enlisting the help of interracial organizations in the cause. In so doing, Baker helped to advance the idea that books can help children of different cultures and traditions understand and respect one another while instilling pride in their own cultural traditions. Her commitment to locating materials that would meet this end led Baker to study African folklore and to publish folk tales in anthologies for children. She believed that "folklore makes one aware of the brotherhood of man."

During the 1950s, Baker received nationwide recognition for her efforts. She was the recipient of the first E. P. Dutton–John Macrae Award of the American Library Association (ALA). Her project was to assess the role of books in intercultural education and survey libraries around the country. As a consultant, she organized children's services of the Trinidad Public Library in Port-of-Spain, Trinidad. She taught children's literature, storytelling, and library work with children at Columbia University and the New School for Social Research and was invited by other universities here and abroad to lecture and conduct workshops.

In 1961, Baker was appointed to the highest position in the New York Public Library's Office of Work with Children. As coordinator of children's services, she was responsible for the development and coordination of policies and programs for children throughout the system's eighty-two branches and six bookmobiles. She expanded the children's collections by adding audiovisual and other special materials.

Following in the tradition of her predecessors and mentors, Frances Lander Spain, Frances Clarke Sayers, and Anne Carroll Moore, Baker encouraged flexibility, relating library services to the various needs of children from the culturally and economically diverse communities of New York City. Working with a varied staff of more than one hundred, Baker forged relationships and maintained a dialogue with schools and community groups, including those involved in the war on poverty. As an adviser to publishers and authors of children's books, a consultant for the television program *Sesame Street,* and a moderator of TV and radio programs, Baker was a visible and vocal advocate for children's services. Following her retirement from the New York Public Library in 1974, she was appointed storyteller-in-residence at the University of South Carolina in Columbia.

Throughout her career Baker was an active participant in professional, literary, and civil rights organizations. She held important offices at the ALA, including chair, Newbery-Caldecott Awards Committee, 1966–67; president, Children's Services Division, 1967–68; and member, executive board, 1968–73. Among her many awards for life-long contributions to library work with children, children's literature, and to books and American culture are the Parents Magazine Medal Award (1966), the ALA Grolier Award (1968), the Women's National Book Association, Constance Lindsay Skinner Award (1971), the Distinguished Alumni Award from the State University of New York at Albany (1975), honorary membership, American Library Association (1976), an honorary doctorate from St. John's University (1980), and the Catholic Library Association's Regina Medal (1981).

Baker is the widow of James Baker and has a son, James. She is now married to Gordon Alexander.

BETTY L. JENKINS

Beasley, Delilah   (1872–1934)

Delilah Leontium Beasley stood supreme in challenging education that portrayed the idealism, misconceptions, and contradictions inherent in white America's attitudes toward black Americans and their proper place in the nation's history. Beasley was a thorough writer and journalist, an intense black woman with an uncompromising commitment to refute misunderstandings and prove that black people had made great contributions to the history of California. Her book, *The Negro Trail-Blazers of California*, published in 1919, was nominated for inclusion in the *Guide to the Best Books* because of its great value to students of sociology, and scholars at the University of California at Berkeley found the book to be comprehensive, with a measure of wisdom for all Americans. This acclamation was well earned.

Delilah Beasley was born on September 9, 1872, in Cincinnati, Ohio. The first child born to Margaret Beasley and her husband, Daniel, Delilah began her writing career at age twelve when she became a "correspondent" for the Cleveland *Gazette*. At age fifteen, she published her first column in the Sunday Cincinnati, Ohio, *Enquirer* under the headline "Mosaics."

After moving to California in 1910, Beasley attended lectures on history at Berkeley, but never registered as a student. Instead, she spent her time writing short essays for presentation at churches.

The experience of researching California history and writing articles as a news contributor for the *Oakland Tribune* affected her whole career. The best known of her works came in 1919, when she was forty-seven, with the completion of her one book, *The Negro Trail-Blazers of California,* which was based on more than eight years of careful research.

Her journalistic career began at the *Oakland Tribune* with a weekly Sunday column entitled "Activities among Negroes." As a featured columnist for nearly two decades, she had an impact far beyond the publication of her column. Through her efforts, the local white press stopped using the terms "darkie" and "nigger" and began to capitalize the "N" in Negro. She became widely known as an outspoken activist in the struggle for equality for and between the races. She once said that the value of the book lay in

Newspaper columnist Delilah Leontium Beasley chronicled California's early black settlers in her 1919 book The Negro Trail-Blazers of California. *(SCHOMBURG CENTER)*

its ability to promote understanding between the races. Beasley also used her column as a vehicle for social progress to educate and celebrate Negro History Week and black art in Oakland.

Beasley died August 18, 1934, at Fairmont Hospital in San Leandro, California. Death was caused by arteriosclerotic heart disease. Her funeral was held at Saint Francis de Sales Catholic Church in Oakland.

Beasley sensed the value of education in developing moral understanding between different peoples. She also has the distinction of being the first person to have presented written proof of the existence of black Californians.

LORRAINE J. CROUCHETT

Bowen, Ruth (1924–)

Ruth Bowen is president of Queen Booking Corporation, once the largest black-owned talent clearinghouse in the world. Born in Danville, Virginia, on September 13, 1924, the product of an interracial marriage between her black/French mother and her Irish father. Ruth never was made to feel inferior growing up with three older white half-sisters.

She attended New York University for two years prior to her 1944 marriage to Billy Bowen, one of the original Ink Spots, a vocal group renowned as one of the first black acts to break the racial barrier in entertainment of the 1950s. They remained married until his death in 1982.

Managing her husband's business affairs provided Bowen with much of the background and practical business experience that led to her long and successful career in the entertainment business. Bowen spent a great deal of time traveling with the Ink Spots in the 1940s and 1950s, during which time she learned firsthand about racism and the treatment of African Americans as second-class citizens. Although the Ink Spots were a major act, after World War II there were still hotels that would not rent rooms to them. In an interview Bowen stated that on one such occasion, "Arrangements had been made for us to stay in a guest house in Salt Lake City. When we pulled up I said, 'I'm not staying here.' Billy asked where were we going to stay. I said, 'Take me to the best hotel in the city.' . . . I left Billy and Harold Francis, the piano player, in the car, and scared to death I marched into the hotel and asked for two rooms," Bowen continued. "When the bellboy went to the car to get the luggage and Billy and Harold, I knew it was over. But there were no problems, and we spent the night in the best hotel in Salt Lake City."

Major Robinson, a nationally syndicated columnist, introduced Bowen to **Dinah Washington** in 1945, and Bowen became Washington's press secretary in 1946. Soon, Washington began urging Bowen to assume personal management responsibilities for her because of the rampant exploitation that she faced as a performer.

In 1959, Bowen set up her business, Queen Artists, with an initial investment of $500. The office was so small that her staff of four "had to back in and out," according to Bowen. Before long, Queen Artists began handling the press and bookings for Earl Bostic, Johnny Lytle, Kenny Burrell, and the Basin Street East nightclub. The number of clients grew, and the staff increased to thirty. By 1969, Queen Booking Corporation had become the largest black-owned entertainment agency in the world. The more than 100 acts handled by Queen Booking ran the gamut from individual singers to soul-rock groups to gospel choirs to comedians. The most famous single performers included Sammy Davis, Jr., **Aretha Franklin**, and Ray Charles.

Among the other popular acts handled by Queen Booking were the Drifters, Harold Melvin and the Bluenotes, **Patti LaBelle** and the Blue Belles, Curtis Mayfield and the Impressions, **Gladys Knight** and the Pips, the Isley Brothers, Kool and the Gang, the Dells, the ChiLites, the O'Jays, Teddy Pendergrass, Smokey Robinson, Bobby Womack, Marvin Gaye, Ike and **Tina Turner**, the Four Tops, the **Marvelettes**, Dee Dee Warwick, the Delfonics, the Staple

Singers, the Stylistics, Barbara Mason, Ben E. King, Al Green, Tavares, the Reverend James Cleveland, Shirley Caesar, the Mighty Clouds of Joy, Andrae Crouch, **Clara Ward**, Richard Pryor, Slappy White, Willie Tyler, and Stu Gilliam.

REGINA JONES

Bowser, Yvette Lee (1965–)

A successful television producer, Yvette Lee Bowser is the creator of the hit series, "Living Single." Acting as writer and executive producer, Bowser designed a series about young black woman that could speak to the young black women of today.

Born on June 9, 1965 in Philadelphia, Bowser was the only child of an interracial marriage. She attended Stanford University, where she majored in political science and psychology. After graduating from Stanford she went to Hollywood.

Bowser started the bottom of the ladder, making coffee as an apprentice for "A Different World" in 1987. By 1988 she was writing scripts for the show. By 1992 she had worked her way up to producer.

Bowser's skills at comedy writing and production won her positions with a series pilot, "Sweet Home Chicago," and then with an existing series, "Hangin' With Mr. Cooper."

After working on "Hangin' With Mr. Cooper" for a season, Bowser wanted a job that was more in line with her talents. She was in luck. Warner Brothers approached her to develop a comedy series with a black female ensemble. Instead of the tired old stereotypes, Bowser created fresh characters that were a little like her, and a little like her friends. The show was to be about four young professional women making their way in the world—in short, about real people the audience could relate to. The result was "Living Single."

"Living Single" premiered on the Fox television network, a competitor of the Big Three networks. While the show got off to a slow start in its 1993 pilot season, Fox executives continued to have faith in Bowser. Two seasons later, their faith paid off. The series caught on and became a hit.

Bowser is a hands-on producer in every sense of the word. She chose the writing staff of eleven scriptwriters, assembling one of the most diverse teams in television today. As a part of the writing team, Bowser selects the script ideas or comes up with them herself. She oversees the taping of the actual show and edits it herself. She often works twelve to sixteen hours a day, but she gets the product she wants.

Bowser founded her own production company, SisterLee Productions, which is involved in developing additional entertainment products. She is a creative consultant to *The Waylan Brothers*, a series on another Big Three challenger, the Warner Bros. TV network. Bowser is also planning a venture with her husband, Kyle Bowser, who is a director of creative affairs for HBO Independent Productions.

As Bowser describes her work, "My vision is to depict African Americans in television in a realistic, humorous way. I think the key to the show is that it is honest. . . . Maybe not all people interact the same way, but (the show) is about my life. It's about my friends. It's about people I know."

ANDRA MEDEA

Bradford, Martina Lewis (1952–)

As the highest-ranked black female executive at communications giant AT&T,

Martina L. Bradford is among the most successful figures in corporate America. A corporate vice president at the age of only thirty-five, Bradford combined savvy career planning with the right university degrees to make her way to the top.

Born in Washington, D.C., on September 14, 1952, Bradford is the daughter of Martin Lewis and Alma Ashton. She attended American University in Washington, D.C., graduating in 1973 with a bachelor's degree in economics. She went on to law school at Duke University in North Carolina, receiving her J.D. in corporate law in 1975. Before graduating, she completed a corporate legal internship with Southern Railways, Incorporated, in 1974.

Bradford developed a career plan early and held to it. She knew she had to position her skills where they would be most useful. The road to corporate glory is not always found by people who produce or sell a product. In this complicated age, sometimes corporate superstars are the lawyers who can manage complex legal problems or manipulate the web of regulations that govern corporate life. Bradford took her first jobs with the federal government to learn to work within the maze.

Her first job out of law school was as a lawyer in the Interstate Commerce Commission (ICC), Financial Division, a post she held from 1976 to 1978. From 1978 to 1981, she was a counsel for the House of Representatives' Committee on Appropriations. From 1981 to 1983, she was chief of staff to the vice chairman of the ICC. In 1982, she taught as an adjunct professor at the law school of her alma mater, American University.

After years of learning how things work within the federal government, Bradford decided to make the shift to private industry. AT&T looked promising. It was a high-growth company with a good track record in promoting women and minorities. And they would need the skills that she possessed. As she states, "(When) I selected AT&T, I sat down and analyzed where my skills would fit in best and targeted my efforts toward the company. I studied the industry and I felt it would be dealing with regulatory issues for a long time."

Communications companies such as AT&T are strongly affected by government regulations and so they need astute individuals who can keep track of regulations and lobby to affect bills going through Congress. Some legislation can improve the company's bottom line. Other laws can jeopardize its very existence.

Bradford started with AT&T as an attorney in their legal department in New York City in 1983. She worked primarily on divestiture issues, as the giant AT&T divided itself into "Baby Bells" and other off-shoot companies. She next worked as an attorney in AT&T Corporate Public Affairs Division in Washington, D.C., staying from 1985 to 1988.

Bradford took on high-profile assignments and did superlatively well. One project involved monitoring the progress of certain bills going through Congress and preparing witnesses to testify on the legislation. Another was dealing with legislation that allowed local "Baby Bell" companies to provide long distance services and manufacture their own telephone equipment, two of the most important profit areas for the telecommunications industry.

After such a successful performance, AT&T sent Bradford to the highly acclaimed Executive Program in Telecommunications, an intensive month-long session held at Duke University. This prestigious program focuses on issues important to the industry, such as deregulation, market globalization, and financial and management techniques.

In 1988, Bradford was made vice president of external affairs for the New York/New England region. She was based in an office in New York City but regularly commuted to Washington. By then she had acquired all the trappings of power, including the cherrywood desk and the office with a view of Manhattan.

In 1991, Bradford was promoted to vice president of government affairs, headquartered in her hometown of Washington, D.C. The stakes were still high. She was tracking and attempting to influence legislative changes that could affect billions of dollars in corporate profits.

Like many businesswomen, Bradford saw the value of networking. She was founding vice president of the Women's Transportation Seminar in 1978, minority counsel for the House of Representatives from 1978 to 1979, and minority counsel for the U.S. Senate from 1979 to 1980.

ANDRA MEDEA

Bragg, Janet Harmon   (1907–1993)

I'm not afraid of tomorrow because I've seen yesterday, and today is beautiful.

Janet Harmon Bragg, 1991

Janet Harmon Bragg simultaneously and successfully pursued two careers, one in the more traditional field of nursing and one in a field reticent to accept either African-Americans or women, aviation. Janet

After passing her flight exam, Janet Bragg was turned down for her pilot's license because the Alabama examiner had "never given a colored girl a commercial license and don't intend to." Bragg went to Illinois, got her license, and became a leading proponent of black aviation. (ELIZABETH FREYDBERG)

Harmon was born on March 24, 1907, to Cordia (Batts) and Samuel Harmon in Griffin, Georgia, about thirty miles south of Atlanta. She was the youngest of seven children. Her maternal grandmother was a full-blooded Cherokee, and her maternal grandfather, Oss Batts, was a freed slave of Spanish descent.

Janet Harmon completed her primary education in Griffin and her secondary education in Fort Valley, Georgia. Always independent, she broke with family tradition and attended **Spelman College** in Atlanta rather than Tuskegee Institute. She graduated from Spelman with an R.N.

degree, intending to fulfill her childhood ambition of becoming a nurse. Soon after graduation she moved to Rockford, Illinois, to live with an older sister. She worked as a supervising nurse at Wilson Hospital and attended night school at Loyola University, receiving a graduate certificate in public health administration.

Janet Harmon married Evans Waterford, but the two divorced after five years, citing incompatibility. After the divorce, she worked for a dentist, a general practitioner, and an eye, ear, nose, and throat specialist while doing graduate work in pediatric nursing at the Cook County Hospital School of Nursing. By 1933, she was a health inspector for the Metropolitan Burial Insurance Company, which became the Chicago Metropolitan Insurance Company. In 1951, she married Sumner Bragg, a supervisor whom she had met earlier at Metropolitan. Sumner, a graduate of Fisk University and an accomplished athlete, had majored in sociology and later studied hospital administration at Northwestern University. The couple later established two nursing homes in the Hyde Park area for elderly black people.

Janet Harmon Bragg's pursuit of aviation was inspired by a roadside billboard that read: "Birds learn to fly. Why can't you?"

Although Chicago was the center of aviation in the 1930s, Bragg could not gain admission to an aviation school there because black Americans were considered mentally and physically incapable of piloting airplanes. Eventually she registered in the inaugural class of the Aeronautical University, founded by Cornelius R. Coffey and John C. Robinson, two black men who had graduated from Chicago's Curtiss Wright School of Aeronautics in 1928.

Both men had been initially denied admission because of their race, but the school relented after the men, who were automobile mechanics, threatened the school with a lawsuit endorsed by their employer, Emil Mack, president of Elmwood Park Motors.

In spite of relentless harassment, Coffey and Robinson graduated with distinction in 1928, after which the school enlisted them as instructors with a mandate that they recruit African-Americans. Bragg was the only woman during the first semester in this segregated class of twenty-seven students. The class increased to thirty-two during the second semester, including four more women. The students were taught airplane construction, the function and operation of the airplane engine, and airplane safety inspection.

Although the classes were coeducational, the men initially harassed Bragg during her first semester by refusing to lend her tools to complete her assignments and by preventing her from working on the airplanes. Since she had remained financially independent by continuing to work as a nurse, she was able to buy her own tools, which her fellow students soon wanted to borrow. The antagonism was also lessened through Janet's demonstrated mechanical competence and by the presence of four more women during the second semester. In 1933, after this group built an airport and hangar together in Robins, Illinois, Bragg bought their first airplane and shared it in return for maintenance of the aircraft.

The Coffey School of Aeronautics at Harlem Airport in Chicago was the site of the first Civilian Pilot Training Program (CPTP) for black aviators. Pilots who completed basic training at Harlem were sent to

Tuskegee for advanced training. Charles Johnson and Bragg established an additional coeducational, interracial flight school at Harlem Airport for prospective pilots who were ineligible for Coffey's CPTP school.

Bragg continued to meet opposition in her pursuit of a career in commercial and military aviation. During World War II, she applied to work with the Women's Auxiliary Service Pilots (WASPs), transporting military aircraft to England. Her application was accepted, but during an interview, Ethel Sheehy, vice president of the Ninety-Nines and a Women's Flying Training Detachment executive officer, told her that she did not know what to do with a black woman and that she would refer the case to her superior, Jacqueline Cochran. Bragg, undaunted, forwarded a letter of interest to Cochran, the Army Air Corps' director of women pilots in Washington, D.C., and received a reply validating Sheehy's statement. Although she was well educated, a registered nurse, and a licensed pilot with her own airplane, Bragg was rejected because of her race.

Only emboldened by this dismissal, Bragg went to Tuskegee, where black male pilots were enrolled in the CPTP, to earn her commercial and instrument certificates. She held a private pilot's license, had already completed theory courses, and had passed the written exam for a commercial license, but Chicago's inclement weather had delayed her flight test. In Alabama, however, Bragg was denied certification by a white examiner, the only person with the authority to license pilots in that region. Although she had unequivocally passed her flight exam, she was denied her license because no black woman had ever been

given a commercial license, and the examiner refused to pass her. Imbued with an even stronger conviction to be certified as a commercial pilot, Bragg returned to Chicago, took the flight test at Palwaukee Airport, and picked up her license at Chicago Municipal Airport (now Midway Airport) within a week.

Bragg once again attempted to serve her country after reading an article in the *Chicago Tribune* summoning 60,000 or more nurses for the military nurse corps. Upon application, however, she was told that the quota for black nurses was filled.

Bragg continued to fly as a hobby and encouraged others to pursue careers in aviation. During the 1920s and 1930s, she wrote a weekly column, "Negro in Aviation," in the *Chicago Defender* and reported the exploits of Colonel John C. Robinson, a black American aviator in charge of the Imperial Ethiopian Air Forces in Addis Ababa under Emperor Haile Selassie. She also reminded her readers that the late **Bessie Coleman** had inspired African Americans to engage in aviation, and she rallied them to continue where Coleman had left off.

Janet Harmon Bragg was a founding and charter member of the Challenger Air Pilots Association (1931), a national organization of black American aviators, inspired by the legacy of Bessie Coleman, which constructed its first airstrip in the black township of Robins, Illinois, in 1933—the Chicago airports were off limits to African Americans at that time. She was a founding member of the National Airmen's Association of America, an organization that has sent representatives across the United States to visit black colleges and universities and to inspire interest in, and inform students about, aviation. Bragg, along with Willa Brown, Cornelius Coffey, and Dale White, was among a group of black pilots who flew the first memorial flight over Coleman's grave in 1935, a commemoration that continues today.

Janet Harmon Bragg has only recently begun to receive acknowledgments, awards, and honors for her tireless efforts in promoting aviation careers among youth. In June 1991, she was inducted into the International Forest of Friendship. Most notably, in 1984, she received an award from the Civil Rights Division of the Federal Aviation Administration (FAA) acknowledging her as a pioneer black female aviator and aircraft owner, as a charter member of the National Airmen's Association of America, and honoring her for her role in establishing a place for black people in American aviation. In 1985, Bragg received the Bishop Wright Air Industry Award (created by Wilton Wright, the father of Orville and Wilbur Wright) for outstanding contributions to aviation. Bragg has also received awards from the Tuskegee Airmen and from the Chicago Graduate Nurses Association.

Janet Harmon Bragg lived the last years of her life in Tucson, Arizona, where she frequently spoke at churches, libraries, and schools to encourage youngsters to consider aviation as a career. She died on April 11, 1993 in Blue Island, Illinois.

ELIZABETH HADLEY FREYDBERG

Bricktop (Ada Smith)   (1894–1984)

Ada Beatrice Queen Victoria Louise Virginia Smith ("Bricktop"), vaudevillian, saloon entertainer, international host, and

In the Paris of the 1920s and 1930s, Bricktop's was the place to find royalty, from the Prince of Wales to the great Duke Ellington. Ada "Bricktop" Smith performed and presented such entertainers as Mabel Mercer.   (LIBRARY OF CONGRESS)

nightclub owner, was born August 14, 1894 in Alderson, West Virginia. Ada Smith was the youngest of four children born to Thomas and Hattie Thompson Smith. After her father's death (c. 1898), Ada's mother moved the family to Chicago, where she ran rooming houses and worked as a maid. Ada Smith attended Keith School.

Smith's stage debut, at four or five years old, was as Harry in Uncle Tom's Cabin at Chicago's Haymarket Theatre. At age fourteen, after persistent appearances at the stage door of the Pekin Theatre, she acquired a job in the chorus. A diligent truant officer, however, ended the job ten days later.

At age sixteen, Smith toured the Theater Owners' Booking Association (TOBA) and Pantages vaudeville circuits with entertainers such as Miller and Lyles, McCabe's Georgia Troubadours, Ten Georgia Campers, the Kinky-Doo Trio, and the Oma Crosby Trio. Barron Wilkins, the owner of Barron's Exclusive Club in New York City, gave her the name "Bricktop." The name referred to her flaming red hair and freckles.

By the time Smith was twenty, she was entrenched in a life style that included traveling, performing, and living in a wide variety of locations throughout the United States and foreign countries. Smith's work and adventures took her from Chicago to San Francisco, from Vancouver to New York. At Barron's Exclusive Club in Harlem, she convinced the owner to hire Elmer Snowden's Washingtonians, a band that included Duke Ellington.

Her first performance in Paris, France, was in 1924 when she replaced Florence Jones at the nightclub Le Grand Duc. It was during this period that Smith's ability as an entertainer combined with her skills as a host. She caught the attention of the rich and famous, notably F. Scott Fitzgerald and Cole Porter, with whom she became friends. Porter wrote the song "Miss Otis Regrets She's Unable to Lunch Today" for her. She

With the approach of World War II, "Bricktop" returned to New York, where her attempts with nightclub enterprises were not as successful as before. Between 1943 and 1951 she opened and closed clubs in Mexico City, Paris, and Rome.   (LIBRARY OF CONGRESS)

soon began hosting and entertaining at private parties for the wealthy, and at benefits for various charities.

In 1926, Smith's involvement with Paris nightclubs became more vigorous. She opened and closed The Music Box and Le Grand Duc. She later opened a club she called Bricktop's that featured American music and a society clientele. Among her distinguished guests, who often performed unannounced, were Jasha Heifetz, Duke Ellington, Noel Coward, the Prince of Wales, and Paul Robeson. She and **Josephine Baker** became friends during this time.

Smith married musician Peter Duconge in 1929. Two years later, she moved

One of the most prolific journalists among black women of the nineteenth century, Mary E. Britton was also a physician and an early proponent of alternative medicine. (SCHOMBURG CENTER)

Bricktop's to 66 rue Pigalle, with Mabel Mercer as the main attraction. Business thrived until the mid-1930s, when an economic depression hit Paris. Smith separated from her husband in 1932, though they never divorced. From 1938 to 1939 she did radio broadcasts for the French government, but as World War II approached, she returned to the United States, urged to do so by the Duchess of Windsor and Lady Mendl.

She settled in New York City, where her nightclub enterprises were not as successful as some of her previous undertakings. Between 1943 and 1951 she opened and closed nightclubs in Mexico City, Paris, and Rome. Continuing to name many of the clubs Bricktop's, she was usually successful in attracting international celebrities.

"So Long Baby," her only recording, was made in 1972 with Cy Coleman. Afterwards, she performed occasionally in nightclubs and at charity events. She had a heart attack in 1975, but continued to perform into the early 1980s. Ada "Bricktop" Smith's autobiography, *Bricktop,* written with James Haskins and published in 1983, appeared in print just months before her death. She died on January 31, 1984, in New York City.

ARTHUR C. DAWKINS

Britton, Mary E. (18??–?)

M.D., elocutionist, teacher, journalist, and metaphysician, Mary E. Britton was prominent among nineteenth-century black women leaders in the South whose work and writings advanced the causes of both racial and sexual liberation. She was born in Lexington, Kentucky, to Henry and Laura

Britton. Her birthday is unknown. An exceptionally bright child who loved reading, she excelled in the primary and secondary schools she attended in Lexington, which were run, for the most part, by the American Missionary Association. In order to give their children the best college education available in the state, the Brittons moved to Berea, where Mary attended Berea College from 1869 to 1874. Before her graduation, in March of 1874, her father died, and four months later, in July, her mother died.

To support herself, Mary became a schoolteacher, working for a short time in Chilesburg, Kentucky, before accepting a position, in 1876, with the Lexington public schools, where she gained recognition for her brilliance as a teacher and her talents as an elocutionist, often ranked with Hallie Q. Brown.

But Britton Britton earned her place in the annals of black women's history as a journalist. She was considered one of the leading women journalists of the nineteenth century, writing for a number of newspapers, among them the *Courant*, the *Cleveland Gazette*, the *Lexington Herald*, the *Indianapolis World*, the *Cincinnati Commercial*, and the *Ivy*. Using the pen name "Meb" or "Aunt Peggy" (the latter for a column devoted to the interests of children), Britton wrote passionately about racial discrimination, woman's suffrage, temperance, abstinence from tobacco, the influence of teachers and preachers on the morals of youth, and health.

Britton continued her education at the American Missionary Medical College in Chicago, from which she graduated in 1903, and at Battle Creek Sanitarium, which was famous at the time. She was a specialist in hydrotherapy, electrotherapy, and massage. She believed in metaphysics and in phrenology and, as a devout Seventh-Day Adventist, in vegetarianism. During her life, she was one of the most loved, respected, and honored black women in Kentucky and a very visible and prominent black woman leader in the nation.

GLORIA WADE-GAYLES

Brooks, Hallie   (1907–1985)

"Nobody's going to rain on my parade, including me." That was Hallie Beachem Brooks' response when asked if her retirement from Atlanta University after forty-seven years of service would be tearful. Brooks retired on May 13, 1977, having served the university, the library science profession, and the community with distinction.

Hallie Beachem Brooks was born in West Baden, Indiana, on October 9, 1907, the daughter of Hal and Mary Lucy Beachem. After graduating from Shortridge High School in Indianapolis, she earned an A.B. at Butler University, a B.L.S. degree at the Columbia University School of Library Service, and a master's degree at the University of Chicago. She studied an additional year at the University of Chicago, where she completed course work toward a doctorate in library science, aided by grants from the Carnegie Corporation and the General Education Board. In 1936, she married Frederic Victor Brooks.

Brooks' entire professional career was spent in the field of librarianship. In 1930, President John Hope of Atlanta University recruited her—she was then a public librarian in Indianapolis—to organize library services for the university's new Laboratory

High School. The high school was closed in 1941, and after serving as director of Field Services to Schools and Libraries in thirteen Southern states financed by a grant from the Carnegie Corporation of New York, Brooks was appointed to the faculty of the Atlanta University School of Library Science, which had been established the previous year. During her long association with Atlanta University, she also served as acting dean of the library school and as chairperson of every committee in the school. She was a member of Beta Phi Mu, the international honorary fraternity for library and information science, and, in 1983, was awarded the status of professor-emerita of Atlanta University.

Brooks held offices or committee memberships in the American Library Association, the Association for Library and Information Science Education, the Southern Library Association, the Georgia Library Association, and the Metropolitan Atlanta Association.

Brooks' knowledge of the art of bookmaking was extensive. In 1948, she published a *Panoramic Chart of the Manuscript Period in Bookmaking,* which is still used in graduate library schools throughout the United States and Canada. In addition, she authored numerous articles on reading and communications. She died October 10, 1985.

ARTHUR C. GUNN

Brown, Willa Beatrice (1906–1992)

Willa Beatrice Brown, pioneer aviator, was born on January 22, 1906, to Reverend and Mrs. Eric B. Brown in Glasgow, Kentucky. She was reared and educated in Indiana.

Brown, an exceptional student, attended elementary schools in Indianapolis and Terre Haute, Indiana. She graduated from Sarah Scott Junior High School in 1920 and from Wiley High School in 1923, after which she attended Indiana State Teachers College where she received her B.A. in 1927. She earned an M.B.A. in 1937 from Northwestern University in Evanston, Illinois.

After Brown had completed her traditional education, she pursued her interest in aviation. Following **Bessie Coleman**'s example, Brown also enlisted the assistance of *Chicago Defender* editor Robert Abbott when she embarked upon her career in aviation. During the early 1930s Abbott financed tours by African-American aviators to African-American colleges and universities for the purpose of encouraging young people to get involved in aviation. He also lobbied Congress to include African-Americans in federally sponsored aviation programs.

Brown enrolled in the Aeronautical University in Chicago, earning a Master Mechanic certificate in 1935. She studied with Cornelius Coffey, certified flight instructor and an expert aviation and engine mechanic, and earned her private pilot's license on June 22, 1938, passing her exam with a near-perfect score of 96 percent. Brown received her Civil Aeronautics Administration (CAA) ground school instructor's rating in 1940.

After a short-lived marriage to Wilbur Hardaway, an alderman in Gary, Indiana, Brown later married Coffey, and together they established the Coffey School of Aeronautics, where they trained black pilots throughout the Depression at the Harlem Airport in Chicago. Brown handled administrative and promotional responsibilities as well as teaching. An activist for racial equality, Brown used her position as president of the Chicago branch of the National Airmen's Association of America to petition the United States government to integrate African Americans into the U.S. Army Air Corps and to include African Americans in the Civilian Pilot Training Program (CPTP), a government-funded aviation training program designed to prepare a reserve of civilian pilots who could serve in the event of a national emergency. The United States military forces were segregated, African Americans were not permitted to enlist in the Air Corps, and there was no indication that the government would award contracts for the training of African-American pilots.

Brown also promoted the efforts of Chauncey Spencer (son of Anne Spencer, poet and Virginia's literary salon queen of the Harlem Renaissance) and Dale White, two licensed pilots and members of the association who flew from Chicago to Washington in an antiquated airplane to lobby for African-American inclusion in the CPTP.

Their efforts met fruition when, in 1939, legislation based on the separate-but-equal policy was adopted by Congress, authorizing African Americans to be admitted to the civilian flight-training programs. Although the majority of the government contracts were awarded to ten black colleges, Brown was awarded contracts to train African-American pilots at the Coffey School of Aeronautics in a noncollege unit. She became the coordinator for the CPTP in Chicago.

In addition to training some of the most celebrated African-American pilots of World War II under the CPTP (several went on to become members of the celebrated Tuskegee Airmen), together Brown and Coffey paved the way for integration of the aviation industry as they trained both black and white American pilots. Brown was promoted to the rank of lieutenant, becoming the first African-American officer in the Civil Air Patrol. She was a member of the Federal Aviation Administration's (FAA) Women's Advisory Board, and by 1943 she was the only woman in the United States concurrently holding a mechanic's license, a commercial pilot's license, and the presidency of a large aviation corporation.

Willa Beatrice Brown's achievements are numerous. She founded the National Airmen's Association of America (1939), along with Cornelius R. Coffey and Enoch P. Waters, Jr., and served as national secretary. She taught aviation subjects for the Works Progress Administration (WPA) Adult Education Program during 1939–40, was

A pioneer aviator, Willa Brown and her husband trained black pilots throughout the Depression at the Harlem Airport in Chicago. In 1939, she was a cofounder of the National Airmen's Association of America. (ELIZABETH FREYDBERG)

selected by the U.S. Army Air Corps and the CAA to conduct experiments for the admission of black aviators into the U.S. Army Air Corps in 1940, and served as ground school instructor for the CAA during 1940. She was director of the Coffey School of Aeronautics, aviation mechanic's instructor for the Chicago Board of Education during 1940–41, president of the Pioneer (Chicago) branch of the National Airmen's Association of America for 1940–41, and vice president of the Aeronautical Association of Negro Schools in 1941.

Brown also had a strong interest in politics. She was the Republican candidate for the House of Representatives from the First Congressional District in Illinois in 1946 (surely one of the first black women candidates for the House from a major party). She lost that race and was also unsuccessful in subsequent tries in 1958 and 1960. She also ran for Chicago alderman in 1947. She taught aeronautics at Westinghouse High School until the 1970s. She died on July 18, 1992.

ELIZABETH HADLEY FREYDBERG

Brunson, Dorothy Edwards (1938–)

Dorothy Edwards Brunson was America's first and, for some time, its only black woman to own a radio station. She was also the first to own a television station. In the 1970s, she revolutionized radio programming by airing pop music that appealed to youths both black and white. Her formula, called "urban-contemporary" or "adult-contemporary," created many new listeners and was adopted by stations nationwide.

Dorothy Edwards was the older of two daughters. Six months after her birth in Georgia on March 13, 1938, her family moved to New York City's Harlem. Her father died during her childhood, and her mother remarried and supported the family by doing laundry.

She studied graphics at New York's High School of Industrial Arts. Not yet a focused student, she spent only a year and a half at Nashville's Tennessee State University. Back in New York, she decided to learn simply how to make money. She was determined to escape poverty, and so she took jobs and courses of study to acquire the basics of accounting, marketing, advertising, and management. Then Edwards found a field—broadcasting—to which she shrewdly applied them. Working in bookkeeping and ad-layout jobs, she took business classes at Pace College and more at the State University of New York's Empire State College, where she earned a B.S.

In the early 1960s, Edwards was hired at seventy dollars a week as assistant controller of WWRL, a radio station owned by Sonderling Broadcasting, and in three months was named controller. After a year she became assistant general manager, then corporate liaison.

She left WWRL in 1971 to be a partner in an advertising firm, which failed. The next year she invested in and became corporate vice president then general manager of WLIB-AM, an Inner City Broadcasting-owned New York station with a $1 million debt. Running five broadcast divisions, Edwards cut a staff of thirty-five to eight and erased the debt. Then she acquired for Inner City WBLS-FM and aired a highly profitable crossover mix—about 80 percent black artists liked by whites and 20 percent white artists liked by blacks.

When she left Inner City in 1979 despite a $100,000 salary, Inner City's sales had risen from $189,000 to more than $22 million. The company was now worth around $50 million and owned seven radio stations.

At twenty-six, Dorothy Edwards had married James Brunson. They had two sons, Daniel James and Edward Ross. Edward would later be a host and computer operations overseer for her television station. The marriage lasted twelve years. "The first time I made more money than he did," she has said, "he hit the ceiling."

After leaving Inner City, Edwards formed Brunson Communications, Incorporated, and, with $3 million in loans, bought Baltimore's badly declining radio station WEBB. She poured $250,000 into its recovery, quickly raising profits and ratings. In the early 1980s she spent $400,000 for each of two radio stations—WIGO in Atlanta, Georgia and WBMS in Wilmington, North Carolina—and eventually doubled the Atlanta station's revenues.

Edwards divested the three stations in 1986 in order to be the licensed owner of Channel 48, a bankrupt and off-the-air UHF television station in Philadelphia that also served Burlington City, New Jersey and northern Delaware. The station cost between two and two-and-one-half million dollars. Legal opposition delayed licensing, and a recession delayed the station's capitalization. It finally reached the airwaves in 1992, offering old movies, sports, musical shows, and series reruns—whatever Brunson, heading at first a low-rated station, could afford. But expansion, both in programming and in corporate holdings, was to come. The next year she was

Having grown up in poverty, Dorothy Edwards Brunson studied accounting, marketing, advertising, and management because she was determined to make money. She became not only the first black woman in America to own a radio station but also the first to own a television station. (CHANNEL 48, PHILADELPHIA)

able to project earnings up to $70 million by 1998.

Ambitious, determined and smart, Dorothy Brunson broke new ground for black women in this difficult but rewarding area of business.

GARY HOUSTON

C

Cadoria, Sheridan Grace (1940–)

In 1985, when Sheridan Grace Cadoria was promoted to brigadier general, she was the first black woman in the regular U.S. Army to achieve this rank and the second black female in history to earn the honor. The year Cadoria made first lieutenant and became a platoon officer in Company B of the Women's Army Corps Training Battalion at Fort McClellan, Alabama, a series of events occurred that had a major impact on U.S. history. The year was 1963. During that year violence threatened the core of America as racism sparked riots around the country, and President John F. Kennedy was assassinated. The feminist movement emerged with Betty Friedan's *The Feminine Mystique.* The death of civil rights activist Medgar Evers and the unprecedented march on Washington, where Dr. Martin Luther King, Jr., gave his "I Have a Dream" speech, renewed widespread support for the black revolution. Meanwhile, not far from Fort McClellan, Governor George Wallace physically blocked a black student from entering the University of Alabama.

Throughout the turbulent 1960s, while the United States waged war at home and abroad, Sheridan Cadoria fought a personal battle that would eventually take her to the top. The military, perhaps more than any other institution, was a male dominion. Although initially Cadoria was in the Women's Army Corps (where racism was prevalent), after the women's corps was dissolved in 1978, she moved into the male-dominated regular army. She excelled as an executive officer in Europe, during a tour in Vietnam, at the U.S. Army Command and General Staff College, and as a regional commander of a criminal investigation division in Maryland.

Born January 26, 1940, the Marksville, Louisiana, native also had career-building assignments in military schools such as the Adjutant General School (advance course) and U.S. Army War College. She received a B.S. in Business Education from Southern University and A&M College in Baton Rouge, Louisiana (1961) and an M.A. in social work from the University of Oklahoma in Norman (1974).

From 1985 to 1987, General Cadoria, as director of Manpower and Personnel, J-1, Organization of the Joint Chiefs of Staff, in Washington, D.C., was responsible for the placement of personnel in all branches of the armed services, including the army, air force, navy, marines, and reserve components.

After a successful campaign against double discrimination—racism and sexism—Cadoria retired from military service in 1990. Her outstanding military record was signified by the Defense Superior Service Medal, the Distinguished Service Medal, the Bronze Star with two oak leaf clusters, a Meritorious Service Medal with an oak leaf cluster, an Air Medal, the Joint Chiefs of Staff Identification Badge, and an Army Commendation Medal with three oak leaf clusters.

LINDA ROCHELLE LANE

Cardozo Sisters

As the owners and founders of the Cardozo Sisters Hair Stylists, Margaret Cardozo Holmes and her sister, Elizabeth Cardozo Nicholas, were entrepreneurs and innovators who turned hardship into opportunity. In many ways they were a case study in progressive management and financial savvy.

Born in Washington, D.C. at the turn of the century, the sisters were the daughters of Francis Lewis Cardozo, Jr. and Blanche Warrick Cardozo. Margaret was the eldest of seven children. Her father was a principal in the Washington public schools; her mother was a schoolteacher. Her maternal grandparents owned successful barbering and hair styling salons in Atlantic City and Philadelphia, catering to a wealthy Quaker clientele. While the pay was not always good, the elder Warricks often got stock and investment tips from the Quakers. Following this advice left them quite well-off over the years. When they died in the early part of this century, they left an estate of $90,000, a very large sum of money in those days.

The Cardozo children often visited their grandparents in Atlantic City, where they helped in the salon. Their grandmother, Emma Warrick, taught them how to make hair-care products such as brilliantine and hair grower. Young Margaret was helping to fan client's hair dry by the age of nine and helping her grandmother make wigs by the age of ten.

Another early influence was the Cardozo girls' aunt, **Meta Warrick Fuller**. She was one of the most renowned black sculptors of the era, and she early recognized Margaret's creative talents. However much Margaret admired her aunt, she realized that she was not cut out to be an artist.

One summer, Margaret's mother fell ill in Atlantic City, and Margaret stayed behind to nurse her while the rest of the family returned to Washington. Margaret was only eleven. The other children fell under the care of Elizabeth, who was only nine. Their mother died in 1911, and Margaret returned to her family in Washington.

Francis Cardozo decided that the older girls were better off at boarding school and so sent Margaret, Elizabeth, and Emmeta to St. Francis de Sales Convent School in nearby Rock Castle, Virginia. The younger children were sent to another Catholic school in Pennsylvania. After graduation, Margaret Holmes went on to Armstrong High School in Washington, D.C., which had a respected art department. Margaret and Emmeta went to Paris in 1927, where Emmeta studied beauty culture. Later, Emmeta joined the Ziegfeld Follies.

Meanwhile, Elizabeth Cardozo had married and separated from her husband. Living in Washington with two small sons to support, she opened a hairdressing salon in her house in September, 1929. It was two short months before the stock market crash that signaled the start of the Great Depression. But Elizabeth Cardozo Nicholas kept the business alive. After a few years, in 1933, she asked her sister Margaret to join her in the business. Margaret, a milliner in Philadelphia, accepted the offer.

Holmes had been "hair conscious" as she put it, from an early age due to her grandparents' influence. While her grandparents mostly worked on white people's hair, Holmes and Nicholas decided to work on all types of hair. As Holmes later stated, "In view of the fact that historically humans have never been satisfied with their hair, forever changing color and styling, it is not surprising that the hair business prospered, along with related cosmetology."

The Cardozo sisters did especially well. In 1937, they moved the shop to its own location, naming it the Cardozo Sisters Hair Stylists. It was one of the best equipped shops, for whites or blacks, in the city.

The Cardozo sisters were ahead of their time in management practices. Today, at the end of the twentieth century, employers are considering advanced notions such as flex time or "the Mommy track," which allow a woman to progress in her career while still acknowledging the reality of her growing children. Amazingly, the Cardozo sisters promoted these practices in the 1930s. Both sisters saw the importance of balancing work and family duties and specifically made arrangements so that their employees would not have to sacrifice their home lives to earn a living.

The sisters continually innovated and improved their salon work as well. Both sisters could pass for white, and so they went to trade shows where African Americans were forbidden, to bring back new techniques. They referred to this as "scouting." By the 1950s, they were so successful and such valuable customers of the hair care companies, that they could insist that their beauticians also gain access to the trade shows.

By the 1940s, hair care became more a matter of scientific processes than the home-made products of previous decades. The Gillette Company approached the Cardozo Sisters for advice in their attempt to create a hair-straightener for blacks.

Holmes became the technical specialist, experimenting with different relaxants. This venture, however, was not successful, and Gillette gave up the effort.

In 1949, Catherine Cardozo Lewis, a younger sister, joined the business as general manager, staying until 1965. The original Cardozo sisters decided to retire in 1971. They sold the business to Camilla Bradford Fauntroy, a long-time, employee. By this time the business employed about twenty people and grossed more than $325,000 per year.

Even though the shop's location was no longer as fashionable as it had been when the Cardozo sisters first opened in the area in the 1930s, customers remained loyal over the years. In fact, after the riots of the 1960s caused many people to avoid the area, the Cardozos' customers still returned.

The Cardozo sisters not only practiced good management, they avoided the infighting that plagues so many family businesses. Honored and respected in their old age, they remained valuable assets to their community.

ANDRA MEDEA

Clayton, Xernona (1930–)

The first black woman to host a prime-time television talk show, Xernona Clayton is now corporate vice president for urban affairs in the Turner Broadcasting System. Paralleling her broadcast career is her work in civil rights. Not only did she toil for the Southern Christian Leadership Conference (SCLC) alongside Martin Luther King Jr. and Coretta Scott King, she seemed to achieve a miracle in 1968 when she persuaded the Grand Dragon of the Ku Klux Klan to renounce his affiliation with that group. She believes in gentle persuasion rather than confrontation, which is one reason she has won the esteem of many in and outside her profession.

Clayton and her twin sister Xenobia were born on August 30, 1930, to Baptist minister James M. Brewster and his wife Lillie in Muskogee, Oklahoma. She earned her B.S. with honors from Tennessee Agricultural and Industrial State University (now Tennessee State University) in 1952. Then Clayton and her sister continued their studies at the University of Chicago. Securing housing through the Chicago offices of the Urban League, the sisters, when not studying, worked for the League investigating job discrimination. They were later hired by a liquor distribution firm they had investigated.

A Chicago teacher in the 1950s, in 1957 Clayton married journalist Ed Clayton, who would write the Martin Luther King, Jr., biography, *The Peaceful Warrior*. They moved to Los Angeles, where she continued teaching and, in the early 1960s, volunteered in answer to the Kennedy Administration's call for increased efforts to prevent youngsters from dropping out of school. Soon the Claytons moved to Atlanta in response to another call, that of the SCLC, and in 1963 Clayton was organizing fund-raisers and traveling widely with Coretta King.

Clayton's husband died in 1966, also the year she coordinated the Doctors' Committee for Implementation, a project resulting in the desegregation of all Atlanta hospital facilities. Around the same time, Clayton became a columnist for the *Atlanta Voice*.

She began her broadcasting career in 1967 with the Atlanta CBS affiliate, WAGA-TV. The next year she hosted "Themes and Variations," a talk show with such guests as Lena Horne, Mahalia Jackson and Harry Belafonte. The show became popular, and the following season was renamed "The Xernona Clayton Show." Within months it went into syndication, ending in 1975.

While Jimmy Carter was Georgia governor, he appointed Clayton to the State Motion Picture and Television Commission. She was the first black and woman to serve on the commission.

Clayton joined Turner Broadcasting in 1979, first producing documentary specials, then as host of a weekly public affairs program titled "Open Up." In 1982 she was named Turner's coordinator of minor-

Xernona Clayton, a Turner Broadcasting System executive, was the first black woman to host a prime-time TV talk show, in 1967. A civil rights activist, she persuaded the Grand Dragon of the KKK to renounce the Klan in 1968. (TURNER BROADCASTING)

ity affairs and became the company's liaison with minority communities and organizations.

Many of the productions Clayton created won awards, and she has been singled out for such honors as an Emmy (1987), the SCLC's Drum Major for Justice Award, the President's Award from the National Conference of Black Mayors, Woman of the Year Awards from both the Black Woman Hall of Fame and Chicago's Bethune-Tubman foundations, and the American Spirit Award of the U.S. Air Force Recruiting Service—the highest military honor awarded to a civilian. Not the least honor is a scholarship that bears her name, each year enabling a gifted high school student to live and study abroad.

In 1974, Clayton married Paul L. Brady, a federal judge, and has two stepchildren. In the years since her first husband's death, she has contributed to the later, widely distributed and translated editions of his King book. Her autobiography, *I've Been Marching All the Time,* was published in 1991.

GARY HOUSTON

Coleman, Bessie   (1896–1926)

I knew we had no aviators, neither men nor women, and I knew the Race needed to be represented along this most important line, so I thought it my duty to risk my life to learn aviation and to encourage flying among men and women of our Race who are so far behind the white Race in this modern study.

Bessie Coleman, 1921

Elizabeth (Bessie) Coleman, aviator, barnstormer, parachutist, and activist, was born in Atlanta, Texas, on January 20, 1896, the twelfth of thirteen children. Her mother, Susan Coleman, was an African American. Her father, George Coleman, was three-quarters Choctaw Indian and one-quarter African. While Bessie was still a toddler, the Coleman family moved to Waxahachie, Texas, an agricultural and trade center that produced cotton, grain, and cattle. The town was about thirty miles south of Dallas and was recognized as the cotton capital of the West.

Here, the Coleman family made a living from picking cotton. George Coleman built a three-room house on a quarter acre of land, but by the time Bessie was seven years old, he had returned to Choctaw country in Oklahoma. Susan Coleman continued to raise nine children alone as she also continued to harvest in the fields, pick cotton, and do domestic work to make ends meet. When the children became old enough, usually about age eight, they too went to work in the cotton fields to supplement the Coleman family income. Recognizing Bessie's excellent mathematical skills, Susan Coleman exempted her daughter from working in the cotton fields and assigned her the family bookkeeping responsibilities.

The Colemans were religious Baptists, and each child was expected to demonstrate literacy skills by reading aloud from the Bible every evening. When Bessie was old enough to take in laundry, her mother permitted her to save her earnings for a college education. She was enrolled in the elementary division of the Colored Agricultural and Normal University in Langston, Oklahoma. The school was popularly known as Langston, named for the great-uncle of poet Langston Hughes. After graduating from high school, Coleman attended the teachers college for one year, until her finances were depleted.

Coleman, like many African Americans of the period, migrated to Chicago, where two of her brothers lived, sometime between 1915 and 1917. Just as she had avoided the backbreaking work of cotton picking in Texas, she also eschewed conventional women's labor in Chicago—she sought neither domestic nor factory work, the usual occupations of African-American women migrants of the day. She took manicuring classes at Burnham's School of Beauty Culture and obtained a job as a manicurist in the White Sox barbershop. In the masculine environment of her workplace Coleman listened to men who had returned from World War I, including her brother Johnny, discuss the war and the fledgling field of aviation. Coleman developed an intense interest in aviation, quit her job as manicurist, and focused her attention on becoming an aviator. Because Coleman was an African-American woman, her initial pursuit of a formal education in aviation met with rejection from the administration of newly established aviation schools in the United States. These schools were conforming to Jim Crow laws that stipulated separation between the races.

Upon advice from Robert Abbott (1870–1940), founder and editor of the *Chicago Defender,* and with financial support from him and Jesse Binga, founder and president of the Binga State Bank—both African-American philanthropists—in 1920, Coleman temporarily eluded this discrimination by registering in an aviation school located in France. She specialized in parachuting and stunt flying, and upon completion of her program of study, she received the first international pilot's license granted

One of hundreds of black aviators encouraged by Chicago Defender *publisher Robert Abbott, Bessie Coleman had to travel to France to receive her training. But she enjoyed a spectacular career in the United States as a barnstormer in air shows for circuses, carnivals, and fairs until she died when she fell from a plane at the age of thirty.* (ELIZABETH FREYDBERG)

to an American aviator from the Fédération Aeronautique Internationale, on June 15, 1921. Armed with a license that allowed her to fly in any part of the world, she returned to the United States as a barnstormer.

After Coleman received recognition as a top-flight barnstormer from predominantly white audiences and press in the northern and midwestern regional air shows, she concentrated her performances in the South toward primarily African-American audiences. Many of her southern appearances were at circuses, carnivals, and county fairs on the Theatre Owners and Booking Association (TOBA) circuit, which also included black theaters where documentary film footage of Coleman's achievements in Europe were shown between acts. She lectured at African-American schools, churches, and recreation facilities in an attempt to encourage African Americans to become involved in aviation and to raise money to launch an aviation training school for African Americans.

Although Coleman needed larger sums of money to establish her aviation school, she would not compromise her integrity. She refused to perform in her childhood town at the Waxahachie airport until the authorities desegregated the audience. In March 1926, she turned down the Orlando Chamber of Commerce when she learned that African Americans would be excluded from her performance. Although the white businessmen relented, Coleman did not agree to perform until "the Jim Crow order had been revoked and aviators had been sent up to drop placards letting the members of our Race know they could come into the field."

Shortly after the Orlando engagement, Coleman was hired by the Negro Welfare League in Jacksonville, Florida, to perform at their annual First of May Field Day. Coleman had trouble, however, locating an airplane in Florida because local dealers would not sell, rent, or loan an airplane to an African American. She summoned William D. Wills, her white mechanic in Dallas, Texas, to fly a plane to her in Jacksonville for the performance. During a dress rehearsal, Coleman was catapulted out of the airplane at about 2,000 feet when the plane somersaulted in several revolutions; she was not wearing a seatbelt or a parachute. Her body was crushed by the impact.

In spite of her untimely death, Coleman influenced other African Americans to pursue aviation as a profession. Several generations of African-American pilots still honor her during an annual memorial service by flying over her gravesite and dropping a wreath. In Atchison, Kansas—Amelia Earhart's birthplace and location of the International Forest of Friendship, which honors pilots from around the world—Coleman's achievements are commemorated by a plaque bearing her name. A biography by Doris L. Rich, *Queen Bess: Daredevil Aviator,* was published in 1993.

ELIZABETH HADLEY FREYDBERG

Coston, Julia Ringwood   (18??–?)

The vibrations of our silent suffering are not ineffective. They touch and communicate. They awaken interest and kindle sympathies.

Majors, *Noted Negro Women: Their Triumphs and Activities,* 1893

Julia Ringwood Coston was concerned about the long-suffering black women in the South, and she argued that press editorials could be effective in protesting their barbarous treatment. She supported women writers because she felt they had broad appeal and were excellent role models for young girls. She deplored the absence of black topics in ladies' fashion magazines of the time and so, in 1891, she began publishing the pioneering *Ringwood's Afro-American Journal of Fashion.* In various departments edited by black women, the journal contained illustrations of the latest Paris fashions, fashion articles, biographical sketches of prominent black women and promising young ladies, instructive messages to women and their daughters, witty passages, and love stories. It was then the only illustrated journal for black women in the world. From 1893 to 1895, she published a second journal, *Ringwood's Home Magazine.*

Coston was a pioneer among the black periodical press publishers in the United States. She distinguished herself as a journalist and addressed the interests of black women of her day.

Julia Ringwood was named for Ringwood Farm in Warrenton, Virginia, where she was born. Her birth date is unknown. When she was an infant, her family moved to Washington, D.C. She was educated in the public schools there and had almost completed school when her mother's health failed and she had to withdraw. She became governess for the family of a general in the U.S. Army while continuing her studies. In spring 1886, Julia Ringwood married William Hilary Coston, a student at Yale University and later a minister. They had two children—a daughter, Julia R., born in 1888, and a son, W. H., born in 1890.

In 1884, William Hilary Coston had published an eighty-four-page pamphlet, *A Freeman and Yet a Slave.* The work was expanded and published in book form in Chatham, Ontario, in 1888. The Costons settled in Cleveland, Ohio, where William Coston became pastor of Saint Andrew's Episcopal Church. His tenure there was fairly short, for he was deposed for reasons unknown, on May 14, 1894.

Husband and wife were mutually supportive of each other's work; Julia Coston fulfilled her household responsibilities as well as her duties for the church's congregation, while William Coston encouraged her to write and offered wisdom and guidance from his own experiences as a writer. Since white journals ignored black interests and excluded black faces and black themes, Coston was spurred to found *Ringwood's Afro-American Journal of Fashion* in 1891. The subscription rate was $1.25 per year.

The initial edition noted the journal's aim "to satisfy the common desire among us for

Love stories and the latest Paris fashions took their place beside biographical sketches of prominent black women in the pages of Ringwood's Afro-American Journal of Fashion, *edited and published by pioneer journalist Julia Ringwood Coston.* (SCHOMBURG CENTER)

an illustrated journal of our own ladies." It immediately found an audience and received high praise from its subscribers and from other publications. **Sarah G. Jones** wrote on March 1, 1892, that she was pleased with the journal and noted that men and women of considerable literary ability who were unknown beyond the locality in which they lived should "not be encouraged to remain in obscurity." She believed that the journal should make their works known.

Mary Church Terrell, author, women's rights and civil rights activist of Washington, D.C., edited the biographical section of the first issue, and immediately brought distinction and stature to the journal. Departments within the publication included "Plain Talk to Our Girls," edited by journalist Susie I. Lankford Shorter; "Art Department," edited by journalist Adina White; and "Literary Department," edited by journalist M. E. Lambert. Later women who were in charge of the departments were referred to as associate editors and managed their respective departments with ability and literary tact. **Victoria Earle Matthews**, a social worker and freelance writer for leading black newspapers, wrote on May 22, 1892, in praise of the journal. She wished Coston "positive and permanent success in establishing it . . . it is so pure, so womanly—positively agreeable in every feature as reading for private home, instruction, and guidance."

Bishop Theodore Holly of Haiti received a sample copy of the journal and noted with pleasure its contents as well as "the peculiar characteristics of its engravings." *Ringwood's Journal* was the first ladies' fashion journal in Haiti—a predominately black country. Bishop Holly marveled that it was introduced "by a lady of our race."

An unnamed friend wrote of Julia Ringwood Coston's femininity and modesty. She called Coston a lovable woman whose primary concern was to serve the highest interests of women at that time. She wanted to give them modest publicity to highlight their lives and present them as role models for "our growing womanhood."

Julia Ringwood Coston's life after 1895 is undocumented. Although there was a circulation of thousands of copies monthly of both her journals, no copy of either is known to exist.

William Hilary Coston wrote other works and was still publishing in 1899 when he issued the *Spanish-American War Volunteer: Ninth U.S. Volunteer Infantry Roster, Biographies, Cuban Sketches.*

Julia Ringwood Coston was one of several black women journalists of the nineteenth century and is known primarily for her work as editor and publisher of the world's first fashion magazine for black women. It was popularly received not only for its fashions but also because it celebrated black women and girls through biographical sketches and timely articles that addressed matters of interest to black women and their families.

JESSIE CARNEY SMITH

D

Day, Carolyn Bond   (1889–?)

"I should state at the outset," stated anthropologist Caroline Bond Day about the interracial families she studied in the early 1930s, "that however the achievements of this group may seem to argue for the advantages of race-crossing, it is my firm belief that Negroes who are of unmixed blood are just as capable of achievement . . . as those who are mixed."

Day herself was a light-skinned woman of black, Native American, and white ancestry, and that personal history may well have prompted her scientific curiosity about others who shared a similar heritage.

The daughter of Georgia and Moses Stewart, Caroline was born in Montgomery, Alabama, in 1889. The family lived in Boston for several years, but after her father's death Caroline and her widowed mother moved to Tuskegee, Alabama, where Georgia taught. Following her mother's remarriage, Caroline took the name of her new stepfather, John Bond. The Bonds subsequently lived in Birmingham, Selma, and then Washington, D.C., and the family was completed by the birth of Caroline's half-sister and half-brother.

Caroline earned a bachelor's degree from Atlanta University. A few years later, she wanted to pursue graduate study, but Radcliffe College of Harvard University refused to accept all of her Atlanta University credits. She went to Radcliffe for two additional years of undergraduate study, earning a second bachelor's degree in 1919. Following World War I, she worked briefly in New York City in relief and support services for black soldiers and their families. She then served with the **Young Women's Christian Association** (YWCA); taught at Prairie View College in Texas, where she married another teacher, Aaron Day; and became an instructor of English, drama, and anthropology at Atlanta University. She also wrote short stories, essays, poetry, and plays, her work appearing in magazines and anthologies.

In 1927, Day received the funding needed to pursue her long-delayed studies and was admitted to Harvard's graduate school of anthropology. For several years she collected material for a multigenerational study of interracial families, but she was frequently debilitated by recurring problems from a rheumatic heart condition. Day was probably the first person of African-American ancestry to earn a higher degree in anthropology when she acquired an M.A. in 1932. That same year, Harvard University's Peabody Museum of Archeology and Ethnology published her master's thesis, *A Study of Some Negro-White Families in the United States.*

Day's work goes beyond the physical anthropology that was her central academic focus. She touches on complex political, socioeconomic, and historical issues as well. The study includes descriptions of skin color, anthropomorphic measurements, hair samples, and numerous photographs of interracial families—sometimes going back five generations. Her thesis has provided scholars with details about the lives of hundreds of individuals but has been criticized by some later anthropologists for its unsophisticated methodology.

Day's poor health necessitated a sedentary life, and with the exception of intermittent teaching assignments and some unpublished writings, she went into semi-retirement following the publication of her book. She lived with her husband in Durham, North Carolina, where he had become an executive with North Carolina Mutual Life Insurance Company. The Days adopted a teenage boy, and most of her remaining time was spent with her family. She died in the late 1940s of complications from her chronic heart condition.

ADELE LOGAN ALEXANDER

A dynamic woman who believed profoundly in the healing power of books, Sadie Delaney served for thirty-four years as chief librarian of the U.S. Veterans Administration Hospital in Tuskegee, Alabama. She did pioneering work in what she called bibliotherapy, "the treatment of a patient through selected reading." (SCHOMBURG CENTER)

Delaney, Sara "Sadie"   (1889–1958)

Sara "Sadie" Marie Johnson Delaney was for thirty-four years the chief librarian (1924–58) of the U.S. Veterans Administration Hospital in Tuskegee, Alabama. Known for her determination, energy, and magnetism, Delaney became an outstanding practitioner of bibliotherapy in the twentieth century. Delaney defined bibliotherapy as "the treatment of a patient through selected reading." She began providing library services to thousands of physically and mentally disabled patients in a small enclave in the South, but knowledge of and need for her work spread, leading to worldwide recognition for her practice of bibliotherapy.

Born on February 26, 1889, in Rochester, New York, to James and Julia Frances Hawkins Johnson, she attended City College of New York, 1919–20, and

received a certificate from the New York Public Library School. She married Edward Louis Peterson in 1906. In 1907, they had a daughter, Grace Hooks, at present a retired social worker in Tuskegee. Her marriage ended in divorce in 1921, and in 1928 she married Rudicel Delaney of Jetersville, Virginia.

Sadie Johnson Peterson began her professional career at the 135th Street Branch of the New York Public Library in 1920. She lived in the Strivers' Row section of Harlem. As the neighborhood changed from native-born and European whites to African Americans migrating from other parts of the country, the library responded by hiring "colored assistants," according to its 1920 annual report. In this post, she was in the thick of the literary, artistic, and social ferment of Harlem in the 1920s. She worked with children and the blind (learning Braille and Moonpoint, another system of embossed writing), and arranged many concerts, art exhibitions, and lectures, at which figures such as W. E. B. DuBois and James Weldon Johnson spoke in 1921–23. She left New York in December 1923 after accepting a position as librarian at the Veterans Administration Hospital in Tuskegee.

She opened the veterans' library two days after she arrived, on January 3, 1924, with one table and 200 books. At year's end she had acquired larger quarters filled with plants, maps, photographs, and 4,000 books; she also set up a library for the medical staff. As the years went on she established a literary society, unique in veterans' hospitals, and encouraged discussion groups. Through these activities and consultations with doctors and psychiatrists, she pioneered her empirical practice of bibliotherapy.

Although books were recognized as healing devices by the Greeks, the word *bibliotherapy* was not coined until 1919, and the American Library Association (ALA) did not have a committee on bibliotherapy until 1939. Delaney used bibliotherapy with patients maimed in body and mind from both World War I and the pervasive racism of the time in order to reunite them with a broad community of ideas and to add significance to their experience. Her methods served as the model for other hospital librarians and students.

Sadie Johnson Delaney also was active in national and international professional organizations, representing American hospital librarians in Rome in 1934 and serving as councillor for the ALA's Hospital Library Division in 1946–51. She held memberships in, among other groups, the **National Council of Negro Women**, the Tuskegee Women's Club, and the New York **National Association for the Advancement of Colored People**, where she served seven years on the advisory board.

For her pioneering work as a bibliotherapist, Delaney was cited more than fifty times in library, medical, and black publications. She was named Woman of the Year in 1948 (Iota Phi Lambda), in 1949 (Zeta Phi Beta), and in 1950 (National Urban League). Atlanta University bestowed an honorary doctorate on Delaney in 1950. She died on May 4, 1958, in Tuskegee. The Alabama Library Association inducted her into its Roll of Honor in 1982.

BETTY K. GUBERT

de Passe, Suzanne (1946–)

In Hollywood, it may appear that the most important people are the stars in front of the camera. But movie stars come and go, often in rapid fashion. The real powers in Hollywood are the people behind the scenes—the producers who decide who is going to be a star and what films those stars will work on. Suzanne de Passe, past president of Motown Productions and currently head of de Passe Productions, is one of the starmakers responsible for those decisions.

Born in Harlem in 1946, de Passe is descended from West Indians. Her parents divorced when she was three, but her father remarried six years later. Her reconstituted family provided a strong, supportive foun-

Suzanne de Passe went to work as creative assistant to Motown president Berry Gordy in 1968. By 1981, de Passe had become president of Motown Productions, the television, movie and theater arm of the company. She now heads her own production company, de Passe Entertainment, which produced the 1989 award-winning and critically acclaimed mini-series Lonesome Dove. *(DE PASSE ENTERTAINMENT)*

dation for her. De Passe attended school in Harlem and modeled clothing for well-to-do families in Harlem while a child. She attended New Lincoln School, a private, integrated school in Manhattan, and later attended Syracuse University. Wishing to be a writer, she majored in English when she transferred to Manhattan Community College.

In 1967, while still in college, de Passe became talent coordinator at a popular Manhattan night spot called Cheetah. As talent coordinator, she watched performers audition and chose those who would perform. She also learned about negotiating contracts and booking schedules. Later, she was hired as a talent consultant by the Howard Stein organization.

It was while working at Howard Stein that de Passe first had contact with Berry Gordy and Motown. She was having trouble scheduling Motown performers for Howard Stein and made it a point to meet Gordy when he came to New York in order to work things out. Soon, she was going out of her way to meet all of the Motown artists when they came to New York, which they often did. After a second meeting with Gordy in 1968, de Passe was hired to be his creative assistant at Motown in Detroit. That same year, de Passe moved with Motown to its new home in Los Angeles.

By 1970, de Passe was working in talent acquisition. Some of the Motown stars that she helped sign or develop were Michael Jackson and the Jackson Five, Lionel Ritchie and the Commodores, The Four Seasons, Thelma Houston, and Billy Preston.

By this time, Motown was expanding into television and movie production. De Passe's responsibilities continued to grow with the company. Now she tried her hand at writing and producing. She wrote the script for **Diana Ross'** solo television special *Diana* (1970) and was head writer for the Jackson Five special *Goin' Home to Indiana*. She then co-wrote the screenplay for Motown's first feature film, *Lady Sings the Blues*. It was a commercial and box office smash and won de Passe an Oscar nomination for best screenplay.

From this point de Passe primarily worked on television and films within Motown. Writing, producing and directing, she was involved in *The Wiz*, a black musical version of *The Wizard of Oz*, and *Mahogany*. She was rapidly promoted from director to vice president of Motown's Creative Division to vice president of Motown Industries. In 1981, de Passe became president of Motown Productions—the television, movie and theater arm of the company.

As president of Motown Productions, de Passe was responsible for a number of projects. There was *Berry Gordy's The Last Dragon*, a highly successful theatrical film release, and two television movies, *Callie and Son* and *Happy Endings*. She received an Emmy as executive director for the acclaimed television special *Motown 25: Yesterday, Today, Forever*. She received the **National Association for the Advancement of Colored People** (NAACP) Image Award for the same project. She later won a second Emmy for a three-hour television special, *Motown Returns to the Apollo*, which also won the NAACP Image Award.

In 1988, de Passe left Motown Productions after twenty years and opened her own production company, de Passe Entertainment. She continued to work in many of the same areas, with many of the same people. De Passe was executive director for the television mini-series, *Small Sacrifices*, which won a Peabody Award. Additional Motown specials included *Motown 30: What's Goin' On!* and *The Jacksons: An American Dream*. A later work, *Motown on Showtime*, included a segment that became a best-selling home video, *Michael Jackson: The Legend Continues*.

Showing her range and versatility, de Passe's work not only included Motown showcases, but highly successful western movies. In 1989 she was executive producer of the critically acclaimed mini-series *Lonesome Dove*. This outstanding production gathered a collection of Peabody, Golden Globe and Emmy awards. Another western mini-series, *Buffalo Girls*, was nominated for an Emmy. She followed up her success with a sequel, *Return to Lonesome Dove*, and was later the executive producer of the successful television series *Lonesome Dove*. She is also producer of the popular ABC television series *Sister, Sister*.

De Passe was inducted into the Black Filmmakers Hall of Fame in 1990 and into the Legacy of Women in Film and Television in 1992. She is a board member of the American Film Institute and the New York City Ballet and a former board member of the Hollywood Radio and Television Society.

Part of the significance of de Passe's success is that talented new black and/or female performers, writers, and directors can now present their projects to black and female producers. After a life of tremendous success, de Passe declares that her current goal is to put an end to the long-standing Hollywood system of "convincing a white man that this is a good idea."

ANDRA MEDEA

Diggs, Ellen Irene   (1906–)

Anthropologist Ellen Irene Diggs is best known for her research on Afro-Latin American culture and society, and the history of the African diaspora. Diggs was born in 1906 in Monmouth, Illinois, a small college town located in the state's agricultural belt near the Iowa border. She was raised in the supportive environment of an industrious but poor, working-class, nuclear black family. At a very young age, Irene Diggs became aware of and disturbed by poverty, social inequality, and inequitable wages.

Diggs' family saw education as a way to improve oneself and as a means to upward social mobility. Graduating at the top of her high school class, Irene Diggs spent one year at local Monmouth College before transferring to the University of Minnesota, where she received her B.A. in economics and anthropology in 1928. Soon after her graduation, Diggs moved to Atlanta and enrolled in the graduate school at Atlanta University, a historically black institution. There, she studied under the foremost black scholar of the day, W. E. B. DuBois. Diggs received Atlanta University's first master's degree in sociology in 1933.

For the next eleven years, Irene Diggs remained at Atlanta University, serving as DuBois' research associate. With DuBois, Diggs founded the journal *Phylon: A Review of Race and Culture*. During this period, Diggs developed an interest in the African diaspora and African historiography. Her research focused on the contributions of peoples of African descent in the physical, cultural, and social construction of the Americas, as well as on the continent of Africa.

In 1942, following an exciting summer holiday in Cuba, Irene Diggs decided to leave Atlanta and return to the Caribbean. As a Roosevelt Fellow of the Institute of International Education at the University of Havana, Irene Diggs began her research on Afro-Cuban culture. From 1942 to 1944, Diggs traveled throughout Cuba studying the impact and continuities of African cultural elements in Cuban society. Her mentor was the distinguished Cuban ethnographer Fernańdo Ortiz. In 1944, Irene Diggs was awarded a doctorate from the University of Havana.

After the end of World War II, Irene Diggs spent a year in Montevideo, Uruguay, doing archival and participant observation field work on the African presence in the Plantine region of Uruguay and Argentina. Shortly after her return from South America, she joined the faculty of Morgan State College. For twenty-nine years, Diggs was a member of the department of sociology and anthropology, retiring in 1976. She was a prominent teacher and taught sociology to countless students, fifteen hours per week and seven courses per year.

Diggs also produced numerous articles, reviews, and lengthy monographs on the African-diaspora cultures and histories and African history that appeared in the *Crisis, Phylon: A Current Bibliography on African Affairs, Negro History Bulletin,* and the *American Anthropologist.* Irene Diggs has been honored with the Distinguished Alumni Award from Monmouth College and a Lifetime Achievement Award from the Association of Black Anthropologists.

A. LYNN BOLLES

Dunnigan, Alice (1906–1983)

Alice Allison Dunnigan, educator and journalist, had to struggle for her education, for jobs, and for economic and professional security. In the end, it was struggle and determination that allowed her to break through a major journalistic barrier and become the first African-American woman to obtain Congressional and White House press credentials.

Alice Allison was born to a tobacco-growing sharecropper, Willie Allison, and a laundress, Lena Pittman Allison, near Russellville, in Logan County, Kentucky, on April 27, 1906. A passion for learning framed her early life: "I always wanted to go to school, even when I was only three or four years old. . . . When I had to stay home, I cried all day." Allison's determination paid off. She graduated as valedictorian from the county's black high school.

Following graduation, Allison resolved to attend Kentucky State College in Frankfort, one of the state's two publicly supported black colleges. Her parents, especially her father, dismissed the notion, until a dentist, one of the area's few black professionals, intervened and persuaded the Allisons to give their daughter a chance. Alice Allison supplemented her family's financial support by working in the college dining hall. In 1926, despite poor health and intermittent elementary school teaching, Allison completed the intermediate teachers' training course, which qualified her to teach in the state's elementary and secondary public schools.

That fall she began teaching in a one-room school in rural Todd County. There she met and married her first husband, Walter Dickinson, a sharecropper, who she quickly discovered did not intend for his wife to continue teaching. She was equally determined not to work in the fields and take in laundry. They divorced in 1930 and she married Charles Dunnigan, a childhood friend, a year later. He fathered her only child, Robert William Dunnigan. This marriage also ended in divorce, though not until her son was an adult. After Dunnigan

In 1948, Alice Dunnigan became the first black woman journalist to travel with a president, joining Harry S. Truman on his famous cross-country campaign trip. (RODGER STREITMATTER)

completed her undergraduate degree in 1932 at West Kentucky Industrial College in Paducah, she taught for ten years in Logan County schools.

Despite her training, Alice Dunnigan found it hard to make ends meet on a teacher's salary. In 1942, tired of the economic struggle and of the humiliating summer jobs available to her in Russellville, Dunnigan took a federal civil service examination and headed to Washington, D.C.

There she found that, as in Kentucky, jobs were not distributed or promotions awarded without regard to race. By the end of World War II, she had advanced from entry-level clerk to first-rung professional in the Office of Price Administration, but with the war's end the government scaled down its operation and Dunnigan soon found herself unemployed.

Her job search, even with the aid of a government placement office, met with one disappointment after another, each, in Dunnigan's opinion, tied to race discrimination. Dunnigan turned hopefully to journalism. While teaching in Russellville, she had gained some experience by writing for several of the state's black newspapers, including the *Owensburg Enterprise* and the *Louisville Defender*. In 1946, she applied to the Associated Negro Press (ANP) for a position as the news service's Washington, D.C., correspondent. Claude Barnett, ANP's founder and director, rejected Dunnigan's application for correspondent, but offered her employment on a space-rate basis, rather than pay her a salary. Dunnigan, desperate for a job and hopeful that she might eventually impress Barnett, accepted his terms—five dollars per column of a thousand words.

From the beginning, her relationship with Barnett and the ANP proved frustrating, and she often felt that she and the ANP worked at cross-purposes. It was practically impossible to support herself in Washington, D.C., as a piecework journalist and Dunnigan engaged in a more or less continuous battle to establish and protect her professional standing. Notwithstanding formidable barriers, Dunnigan managed to obtain Congressional and White House press credentials. As a White House correspondent, in one of the highlights of her career, she accompanied Harry Truman's 1948 campaign train from Washington, D.C., to California.

In 1960, Dunnigan left the ANP to work on the Kennedy-Johnson campaign. Vice President Lyndon Johnson rewarded her efforts the following year by appointing Dunnigan as a consultant to the President's Committee on Equal Employment Opportunity. She continued working for the Equal Employment Opportunity Commission, established by the Civil Rights Act of 1964, and later became a Department of Labor information specialist. By her own analysis, with the changing political tides signaled by the 1968 election of Richard Nixon, her opportunities for retention as a federal employee receded and she turned back to various writing projects. Among them, she published a massive autobiography in 1974, and a rambling history of African Americans in her native state in 1982. Alice Dunnigan died in Washington, D.C., on May 6, 1983.

VIRGINIA SHADRON

E

Early, Charity Adams   (1918–   )

In military jargon, "riding point" means being at the very front of an advance guard; it is a position of responsibility and vulnerability. Charity Adams "rode point" during World War II as the first black commissioned officer in the Women's Army Auxiliary Corps (WAAC; renamed Women's Army Corps [WAC]), and she commanded the only organization of black women to serve overseas during that war. Her determined leadership gave black women the opportunity to serve their country. When she left the army with the rank of lieutenant colonel—the highest possible rank except for WAC commander—Charity Adams went from serving her country to serving her community. She flourished equally in both capacities.

Charity Adams was no stranger to discipline before entering the WAC. Born on December 5, 1918, in Kittrell, North Carolina, she was the daughter of Reverend Eugene Adams and Charity A. Adams. Her parents, a minister and a teacher, expected exemplary behavior and educational achievements from their four children, and Charity, the eldest, set an example for her siblings by graduating from high school as valedictorian. She earned a scholarship to Wilberforce University in Ohio and, after graduating in 1938, became a math and science teacher in the Columbia, South Carolina, segregated school system.

In 1942, the dean of women at Wilberforce recommended her for the Women's Army Auxiliary Corps. After completing the necessary applications, she was selected for membership in the first officer-candidate class. After training at Fort Des Moines, she was commissioned on August 29, 1942.

Having experienced segregation in the South, Major Adams was determined to gain respect in the segregated army. While she was in command of the 6888th Central Postal Directory Battalion in Europe, a general reviewing her troops found fault, and when she protested he responded by saying that he would find a white junior officer to

After World War II, Charity Adams Earley (saluting, right), the first black commissioned officer in the Women's Army Auxiliary Corps, continued to serve her country by serving her community.   (CHARITY ADAMS)

show her how to do her job. She replied, "Over my dead body, sir," and he promised a court martial. When Major Adams and her staff began filing court-martial charges against the general for violating policy that forbade racial "emphasis" in any verbal or written commands, reports, or any type of communications between personnel, the general dropped his charges. On other occasions, Major Adams organized boycotts of segregated recreational facilities and military housing in Europe.

After leaving the army in 1946, she completed the requirements for a master's degree in vocational psychology at Ohio State University. She then worked as a registration officer for the Veterans Administration and as educational director at Miller Music Academy, both in Cleveland; as director of student personnel at Tennessee A & I University in Nashville; and as director of student personnel and assistant professor of education at Georgia State College in Savannah. In 1949, she married Stanley A. Earley, Jr., a medical student at the University of Zurich, and moved with him to Switzerland. After gaining proficiency in German, she began taking courses at the University of Zurich and the Jungian Institute of Analytical Psychology.

After the Earleys' return to the United States and the birth of two children, Stanley and Judith, Earley became involved in community affairs. She served on committees, task forces, and corporate boards encompassing all areas of human and social services, civic affairs, education, and business, from the United Way to the Black Leadership Development Program to the Dayton Power and Light Company board of directors. In 1982, she was honored by the Smithsonian Institution in a salute to 110 of the most important women in black history. Also in that year, the Atlanta chapter of the **National Association for the Advancement of Colored People** presented her with the Walter White Award for her pioneering service in the military. In 1989, her book, *One Woman's Army: A Black Officer Remembers the WAC,* was published, and she was a guest on the National Public Radio program, *Morning Edition.* In 1991, she was awarded an honorary doctorate in humanities by Wilberforce University and an honorary doctorate in humane letters by the University of Dayton. Upon her retirement from the Dayton Power and Light board of directors, a scholarship at Wilberforce University was established in her honor.

Earley and her husband currently make their home in Dayton, Ohio. Their son is a senior budget analyst for the city of Dayton, and their daughter works for the Department of Publications at the University of Southern California.

Charity Adams Earley entered an army segregated by both race and gender during World War II. By 1992, the fiftieth anniversary of women's membership in the military, those barriers were broken down, largely due to the efforts of Charity Adams Earley and her peers.

MAUREEN CREAMER

F

Fisher, Ruth Anna   (1886–1975)

Ruth Anna Fisher was a researcher and manuscript archivist for the Library of Congress from 1928 to 1956 and supervised the compilation of documents relating to American history that were in British archives. Born in Lorain, Ohio, on March 15, 1886, into the family of realtor David Crockett Fisher, she graduated from **Oberlin College** in 1906. She then taught at Tuskegee Institute but was fired by Booker T. Washington because she refused to cooperate with his philosophy of industrial education and would not teach Sunday school.

After teaching in Lorain and Indianapolis and working with a recreation center in New York, Fisher was sent by patrons to study in England. When she finished her program at the London School of Economics, she began work as a researcher with American historian J. Franklin Jameson, director of historical research for the Carnegie Institute of Washington, D.C. His research project included making copies of documents relating to American history in British repositories. Fisher soon became supervisor of this "foreign copying" project, reproducing documents from the Public Record Office, the British Museum, and the libraries of the House of Lords and the House of Commons, as well as various other repositories. She continued in that role when Jameson became chief of the Division of Manuscripts at the Library of Congress.

In 1940, when London was being bombed, Fisher's apartment was destroyed and she returned to the United States. After another three-year stint in London, she returned to the United States to work in the Library of Congress preparing calendars of the British documents she had accumulated. She retired in 1956 and died in late January 1975.

DEBRA NEWMAN HAM

Florence, Virginia   (1903–1991)

The first African-American woman to receive professional training in librarianship in the United States, Virginia Proctor Powell was born to Socrates Edward Powell and Caroline Elizabeth Proctor Powell on October 1, 1903, in Wilkinsburg, Pennsylvania. Her early education was in the public schools of Wilkinsburg. Following the death of both parents, she moved to Pittsburgh to live with an aunt. A 1915 graduate of Pittsburgh's Fifth Avenue High School, Powell received a bachelor's degree in English literature from **Oberlin College** in 1919.

Following her graduation from Oberlin, Powell worked for a brief time in St. Paul, Minnesota, as a secretary in the Girl Reserves of the Colored Girls Work Section of the **Young Women's Christian Association** (YWCA). After a year, she returned to Pittsburgh to work in her aunt's beauty parlor. She sought a teaching position in the Pittsburgh public school system, but because the schools had no African-American employees, she was forced to consider other professional options or continue to work in her aunt's salon.

Her fiancé, Charles Florence, introduced Powell to the notion of a career in librarianship. Aware of her love of children and books, Charles obtained the necessary applications for the Carnegie Library School. She was admitted to the school in 1922 and completed the course of study within one year. However, because school officials were uncertain about placement of their first African-American graduate, she did not receive her diploma until several years later.

She began her professional career with the New York Public Library in 1923 and continued there until 1927. In that year she became the first African American to take and pass the New York high school librarian's examination and was appointed librarian at the Seward High School in Brooklyn. She remained in that position until 1931.

Following her marriage to Charles in 1931, Florence spent the next eight years as the "First Lady" of Lincoln University in Jefferson City, Missouri, where her husband served as president. When the couple moved back East in 1938, Florence returned to librarianship. Charles became chairman of the English department at Virginia Union University in Richmond, and Florence was librarian at Cardoza High School in Washington, D.C., until 1945. Following a five-year period of recuperation from illness, Florence became librarian at Richmond's Maggie L. Walker Senior High School until her retirement in 1965. Widowed in 1974, Florence lived her remaining years in Richmond.

ARTHUR C. GUNN

The first African-American woman to receive professional training in library science in the United States, Virginia Florence graduated from Oberlin College in 1919, the year this photograph was taken, and then attended Carnegie Library School. (ARTHUR C. GUNN)

Fudge, Ann Marie (1951–)

One year Shake N' Bake was a dinosaur, the very name evoking thoughts of the 1960s and housewives in frilly aprons. The next, it was the latest entry in the low-fat, health-conscious food sweepstakes. The marketing genius behind this and other major successes of recent years—Kool Aid, Stove Top Stuffing, Minute Rice—is Ann M. Fudge. As president of Maxwell House Coffee, within the giant conglomerate of Philip Morris, Inc., Fudge is one of the most successful black women in corporate America. After twenty years of meeting corporate challenges, she broke the glass ceiling that confines most women to middle management. And what of the rumors that she will someday be CEO? She replies, "That's nice," and changes the subject.

Born in Washington, D.C. on April 23, 1951, Fudge is the daughter of Malcolm R. Brown and Bettye Lewis Brown. While middle-class, Fudge was not born to corporate power. Her father was an administrator with the Postal Service, while her mother was a manager at the National Security Agency. Fudge went to Catholic schools through grammar school and high school, where she appreciated the nuns insisting that she always do her best. Fudge started working in high school. One job involved serving on the Hecht department stores Teen Board, where she helped advise on teenage fashions.

Fudge attended Simmons College, a women's school in Boston. While only a sophomore, she married Rich Fudge, and had a baby before she graduated. Like most college students, they were strapped for cash. When they could not be home with the baby, they hired other students to babysit and sometimes paid them with food. Fudge got her B.A. in 1973, graduating with honors.

From 1973 to 1974, Fudge was a manpower specialist in the human resource department of the General Electric Company. Though many black women end up at less-than-promising jobs in human resources, Fudge decided that there were better career choices to be had. So she went to Harvard Business School, getting her M.B.A. in 1977.

After graduate school, Fudge joined General Mills. She began working in marketing, where she proved to be a particularly astute manager. Her field was brand management—how to present a product so that consumers will want to buy it. One of

Ann Fudge is the marketing genius who came up with the Shake N' Bake concept. One of the most successful black women in corporate America, Fudge, when she was marketing director at Maxwell House, was also the marketing genius behind the recent successes of Kool-Aid, Stove Top Stuffing, Minute Rice, and the new Maxwell House product, Cappio. She is now the president of the company.

her biggest successes came as part of the team that developed Honey Nut Cheerios.

Fudge's family helped her keep her success in perspective. She came home jubilant one day after being promoted to marketing director, the first African American and first women to hold that job at General Mills. Her young son Kevin was unimpressed. He said, "What's the big deal, mom? So now instead of one brand, you have four. You can do that." She did.

In 1986, Fudge left General Mills to become associate director of strategic planning at General Foods, a division of Philip Morris Foods. Philip Morris had a good record on affirmative action, and Fudge saw that, as a black woman, she could have a future there.

Fudge's particular gift is to take over a product that is having trouble and revitalize it in the marketplace. In 1987, she stepped in as marketing director when Kool-Aid sales were dropping off and revived its popularity. Two years later, she took on Shake N' Bake, a product that was on its way to being dead and forgotten. Consumers, who tended to look on the product as a 1960s throw-back, were won back by Fudge's emphasis on ease and low-fat cooking. The slogan was "Why Fry?" and sales jumped from $85 million to $140 million.

Fudge took over at Maxwell House Coffee in 1994, also becoming Executive Vice President at Kraft Foods. (Maxwell House is a Division of Kraft Foods, which is, in turn, a division of Philip Morris). Maxwell House was another brand in trouble.

Maxwell House Coffee is a $1.5 billion enterprise, but its customers are aging. New coffee drinkers are turning to more sophisticated brands. Fudge is the one who must win them back.

American coffee-drinking tastes have changed mightily since Maxwell House started a century ago. When the Baby Boomers came of age, they turned away from American coffees, preferring soft drinks. Later, Starbucks of Seattle revived American's taste for coffee by offering sophisticated, top quality products on the European model. By capitalizing on quality, Starbucks became the largest coffee retailer in North America.

An earlier management team at Maxwell tried to join in the coffee revival but missed their opportunity. As one analyst put it, "General Foods did not give enough credence to the consumer's ability to tell the difference between fresh and stale coffee." In short, the old managers were not as careful about quality as they might have been, and customers noticed.

Fudge is not likely to make that kind of mistake. Taking over at Maxwell House, she oversees the company's three coffee processing plants and even keeps tabs on the teams of workers who select the original coffee beans. She intends to keep quality high. And she is turning to Generation X, who are now developing tastes which will last a lifetime.

General Foods focuses on grocery store rather than café sales, but Fudge has the grocery store shelf looking like a coffee house. One new product that Fudge has premiered is the bottled cappucino drink Cappio.

Fudge is described as a gentle but tough manager. "Ann wears nice kid gloves that mask an iron fist," says a colleague. She believes in giving her team direction and then getting out of the way while they do their jobs. But make no mistake. She hires quality people and expects quality results.

Aside from her work at Maxwell House, Fudge also sits on the corporate boards of Liz Claiborne, Inc., and Allied Signal, Inc. She is vice president of the Executive Leadership Council, a not-for-profit organization of prominent black executives. Since 1981, she has been a member of the National Black MBA Association.

From her headquarters in White Plains, New York, Ann Fudge is making corporate decisions that affect everyday consumers in grocery stores around the nation. Fortunately, she has her eye on quality. She expects the best from herself and from her team, and is changing the face of corporate America.

ANDRA MEDEA

G

Gillespie, Marcia Ann (1944–)

When Marcia Ann Gillespie became editor in chief of *Ms.* magazine in 1993, she broadened the scope of an already valuable publication. The world's most read feminist periodical had been founded in 1971 to correct history's neglect of women's rights, opportunities, and contributions. This is surely still the case. However, to that agenda Gillespie works to add what she calls "a willingness to grapple with issues of race and class and disability, age and sexual difference, both within and outside our movement."

The daughter of Charles M. and Ethel Young Gillespie was born in New York City on July 10, 1944. She received her B.A. with honors in 1966 from Lake Forest College in Lake Forest, Illinois, having majored in its American Studies program. Seven years later, Lake Forest bestowed on her an outstanding alumni award.

For the next four years Gillespie worked in the New York division of Time-Life Books. This led to her being hired, in 1971, to be editor in chief of the newly formed *Essence* magazine, whose readership was African-American women. Conceiving the magazine's editorial philosophy and policy, she gained further authority when in 1975 she was named vice president of Essence Communications, Inc.

Under Gillespie's leadership the magazine's circulation grew from less than 50,000 to 750,000, with an estimated overall readership exceeding two million.

During her *Essence* years, advertising increased ten-fold and the publication won the National Magazine Award for editorial excellence. She left the editorship in 1980 and the vice-presidency two years later.

In her nine years as editor in chief of Essence *magazine, Marcia Ann Gillespie increased that publication's circulation from less than 50,000 to 700,000 and its advertising tenfold. Now editor in chief of* Ms. *magazine, Gillespie is writing a history of the women's movement to be used as a high school textbook.* (MS. MAGAZINE)

In 1980 Gillespie became a *Ms.* contributing editor while beginning a freelance career as consultant, lecturer and writer. With clients and connections in the U.S. and the Caribbean, she created a publishing seminar series for the University of the West Indies and advised the university's vice chancellor on a North America outreach program. She has since remained a guest lecturer for the institution's School of Communications.

She began writing a column for *Ms.* in 1987 and was named its executive editor the following year, overseeing staff, editorial strategy, and cover designs. From 1990 to 1992 she edited a Ms. Foundation book for the United Nations Development Programme on the global impact of the HIV epidemic before resuming her executive editorship and then becoming editor in chief.

As the top *Ms.* editor, Gillespie monitors all phases of the editorial process, plans budgetary and circulation strategies and is the magazine's number one spokesperson. It has been written that what Gillespie wants to bring about "is a movement of committed energies that goes beyond charity and isolated good deeds."

Currently at work writing a history of the women's movement to be used as a high school textbook, she also serves on the board of directors of the Arthur Ashe Institute for Urban Health and participating in a New York-based dialogue group of black and Jewish women.

GARY HOUSTON

Gleason, Eliza Atkins (1909–)

Eliza Atkins Gleason, librarian and educator, was the first dean of the School of Library Service at Clark Atlanta University (formerly Atlanta University) and the architect of a library education program that trained more than 90 percent of all African-American librarians in the United States. She was born in Winston-Salem, North Carolina, on December 15, 1909, to Simon Green Atkins and Oleona Pegram Atkins.

Following graduation Phi Beta Kappa from Fisk University in 1930, Gleason received a B.S. from the library school of the University of Illinois in 1931. In 1936, she received an M.A. in library science from the University of California at Berkeley. She studied at the University of Chicago Graduate Library School and in 1940 became the first African American to receive a doctorate in library science. She married Maurice F. Gleason, a physician, in 1937.

Gleason's professional career was distinguished, varied, and productive. Between 1931 and 1936, she held positions at Louisville Municipal College and Fisk University. From 1936 to 1937, she was director of libraries at Talladega College, where she became aware of the lack of public library services for African Americans throughout the South. Because of this concern, she opened the college library resources to black citizens in the surrounding communities. Her interest in the availability of public libraries to African Americans is reflected in her dissertation, "The Southern Negro and the Public Library."

Following her tenure as dean of the School of Library Service at Atlanta University from 1940 to 1946, Gleason moved to Chicago. In 1953, she became head of the reference department of the Wilson Junior College Library. From 1953 to 1954, she was associate professor and head of the reference department of the Chicago Teachers College Library. She returned to library education in 1954 as associate professor of library science at Illinois Teachers College, serving until 1963. From 1964 to 1967, she was assistant librarian at John Crerar Library. She served as professor of library science at the Illinois Institute of Technology from 1967 to 1970, when she became assistant chief librarian in charge of regional centers of the Chicago Public Library. During the 1974–75 academic year, Gleason was professor of library science at Northern Illinois University.

Active in professional associations, Gleason served as the first African-American member on the American Library Association Council (ALA) from 1942 to 1946. In 1964, she received the Fisk University Alumni Award for outstanding accomplishments.

In addition to writing *The Southern Negro and the Public Library: A Study of the Government and Administration of Public Library Service to Negroes in the South* (1941), she authored *A History of the Fisk University Library* (1936) and numerous journal articles.

In the fall of 1978, Gleason was appointed executive director of the Chicago Black United Fund. Retired, she continues to make her home in Chicago.

ARTHUR C. GUNN

H

Hare, Maud Cuney   (1874–1936)

Maud Cuney Hare dreamed of racial integration in the world of the performing arts—a seemingly impossible dream in the rigidly stratified and segregated Boston of the 1920s. Born in Galveston, Texas, in 1874, she was the daughter of Adelina Bowie and Norris Wright Cuney, a prominent businessman and leader in state and national politics. Maud Cuney Hare's goal was to propel young black talent into the mainstream of art and music. "I abhor the segregated districts," she confided in a letter dated September 25, 1927, to the African educator and feminist Adelaide Casely. Surviving playbills suggest that Hare's dream was indeed realized in the form of the Allied Arts Center, which sponsored productions of black playwrights' work.

In her own artistic right Maud Cuney Hare was a pianist trained at the New England Conservatory of Music in Boston and a musicologist who did research on black musical expression in the Caribbean. Like contemporary **Zora Neale Hurston**, she traveled to Mexico, the Virgin Islands, Haiti, Puerto Rico, and Cuba in search of African survivals—instruments, rhythms, and popular dances—in the New World.

Hare was also a playwright, as revealed in the four-act romantic drama entitled *Antar of Araby* that appeared in 1930. This play tells of a legendary Arab, or perhaps Persian, desert poet who romances the daughter of an Arab chieftain. The issue is color, for Antar is a slave whose dark pigmentation and low social status are a barrier to winning her hand. It is more than likely that Antar is a metaphor for the tragedy of black Americans, barred from the enjoyment of equality and privilege by a senseless color code.

In all of her writing, Hare expressed an unfailingly optimistic outlook. She believed that, as in the denouement of *Antar of Araby,* black talent would succeed on its own merits and be accepted into the American mainstream. Records show that she died of cancer in Boston in 1936.

LORRAINE ELENA ROSES

Harris, Marcelite   (1943–   )

Marcelite Jordon Harris, a graduate of **Spelman College** in Atlanta, Georgia, served as a White House aide to President Jimmy Carter. She is also the first and only black woman to earn the rank of general in the U.S. Air Force. While the native Texan may not yet be eligible for the title of Georgia's "favorite daughter," Atlanta Mayor Andrew Young was impressed enough to declare a Marcelite J. Harris Day on May 30, 1988; she was presented with the key to the city of Detroit in 1990; and the city of Houston designated February 11, 1991, as Marcelite J. Harris Day. Marcelite J. Harris has made it to the top of her field, and in the process she has accumulated a succession of firsts.

Harris earned a B.A. in speech and drama from Spelman College in 1964 and a

B.S. in business management from the University of Maryland, Asian Division in 1986. After teaching in the Head Start program in 1964–65, Harris joined the air force. Her initial assignments in administration were unchallenging, so she applied for the occupational specialty of maintenance. After two unsuccessful attempts, Harris was admitted into maintenance. She was the first woman aircraft maintenance officer in the U.S. Air Force. Then, in December 1988, Harris became the first female wing commander of the Air Training Command at Keesler Air Force Base in Gulfport, Mississippi. The air force school at this command trains thousands from all branches of the military in highly technical fields such as computer science, communications, avionics, electronics, and air traffic control. To continually update her own training, she has attended Central Michigan University, the University of Maryland, Harvard University, and the National Defense Institute, among other schools.

General Harris is married to Air Force Lieutenant Colonel Maurice Harris and has a teenage stepson, Steven, and a nine-year-old daughter, Tenecia.

LINDA ROCHELLE LANE

Eulogized as "the historian who never wrote," Vivian G. Harsh succeeded in building, within the Chicago Public Library system, one of the most important research collections on black history and literature in the United States. (VIVIAN HARSH COLLECTION, CHICAGO PUBLIC LIBRARY)

Harsh, Vivian Gordon   (1890–1960)

She was called "The Lieutenant" by some of her colleagues and a taskmaster by many of the youths who did their research at the Chicago Public Library branch she headed. Yet Vivian G. Harsh was revered by a generation of prominent black writers and scholars. She was eulogized as "the historian who never wrote," yet she succeeded in building one of the most important research collections on black history and literature in the United States.

Born in Chicago on May 27, 1890, to Fenton W. Harsh and Maria L. (Drake) Harsh, Vivian Gordon Harsh grew up in the world of Chicago's Old Settlers, the tightly knit community of pioneer black families. Both of her parents were graduates of Fisk University; her mother was one of the first women to graduate from Fisk

Normal School. The year after she graduated from Wendell Phillips High School on Chicago's South Side, Harsh began working for the only employer she would ever have, the Chicago Public Library. She started as a junior clerk in December 1909, rising slowly through the ranks during her first fifteen years of service. By 1921, she had graduated from Simmons College Library School in Boston, and on February 26, 1924, she became the first black librarian for the Chicago Public Library.

In the late 1920s, George Cleveland Hall, then chief of staff at Provident Hospital and one of the founding members of the Association for the Study of Negro Life and History, headed by Carter G. Woodson, began pressing the Chicago Public Library to open a branch in the rapidly expanding South Side black community. Hall convinced philanthropist Julius Rosenwald to donate land for the branch, but Hall died before construction was completed. On January 18, 1932, the building, now named the George Cleveland Hall branch, was opened to the public, with Vivian G. Harsh as its first head librarian.

Opening day created a sensation in the community, as thousands flocked to see the new library. Included among its holdings was a small but significant collection of books on black history and literature, which Harsh called the Special Negro Collection. Even before the opening of the library, Harsh had received a fellowship from the Rosenwald Foundation to supplement her studies at the Graduate Library School of the University of Chicago with travels to other black history collections. Harsh began to collect rare books, pamphlets, and documents on her journeys.

Aided by the Hall branch children's librarian, **Charlemae Hill Rollins**, Harsh tirelessly expanded the collection through subsequent Rosenwald Foundation grants, donations from supportive patrons, and her own purchases. The work continued throughout the 1930s, despite persistent antagonism from the Chicago Public Library's administration, which did not believe that public funds should be expended on such a project.

As the collection's reputation spread, the library became a meeting place for young black writers and artists. The Works Progress Administration's (WPA) Federal Writers Project launched a study called "The Negro in Illinois," headed by Arna Bontemps; the library served as its unofficial headquarters.

Many young scholars were attracted to the library's book review and lecture forum, begun by Harsh in 1934. Its bimonthly meetings featured an impressive array of black speakers, including Richard Wright, Langston Hughes, **Zora Neale Hurston**, Arna Bontemps, **Gwendolyn Brooks**, Horace Cayton, William Attaway, **Margaret Walker**, Alain Locke, and St. Clair Drake.

Harsh encouraged these writers to help build the Special Negro Collection. Langston Hughes, a regular visitor to the collection in the 1940s, donated the typescripts and galley proofs of his autobiographical work *The Big Sea*. When Richard Wright's *Native Son* was published, he returned to the library to present Harsh with an inscribed copy, and he credited the collection with enriching his knowledge of the black experience. Arna Bontemps, faced with the shutdown of the WPA Federal Writers Project in 1942, turned over nearly 100 boxes of research from "The Negro in Illinois" study to Harsh.

Throughout the 1930s and 1940s, Harsh was active in community and professional organizations. She served on the board of the Parkway Community Center and participated in the work of the **National Association for the Advancement of Colored People,** the Young Men's Christian Association, and the **Young Women's Christian Association,** and was a member of the influential Sixth Grace Presbyterian Church. After a serious illness, Harsh retired on November 10, 1958. She had never married and had no children, yet when she died two years later, on August 17, 1960, her funeral was crowded with friends and former library patrons.

In 1970, the Chicago Public Library renamed the Special Negro Collection as the Vivian G. Harsh Collection of Afro-American History and Literature. By 1975, it had been moved to the new Carter G. Woodson Regional Library, where a large photograph of Harsh hangs adjacent to one of Woodson. The collection has grown to some 70,000 volumes, with important holdings of rare black journals and newspapers, and an outstanding collection of archival materials on Illinois black history.

As a black bibliophile and collector, Harsh's achievements complement the work of Arthur Schomburg, Jesse Moorland, and other pioneers in the field. Even in the face of bureaucratic opposition and tight Depression-era finances, she was able to institutionalize her collection. Her greatest legacy is the extraordinary milieu she created, a meeting place that helped develop the work of so many black writers and scholars.

MICHAEL FLUG

Haynes, Elizabeth Ross (1883–1953)

Elizabeth Ross Haynes was a pioneering analyst of black domestic and women workers, a writer, and a leader in the **Young Women's Christian Association (YWCA),** black women's clubs, and the Democratic party. Born July 30, 1883, in Lowndes County, Alabama, to Henry and Mary Carnes Ross, prosperous farmers and freedpersons, Elizabeth Ross was valedictorian of the State Normal School in Montgomery, received an A.B. from Fisk

Elizabeth Ross Haynes was a pioneer advocate of black urban women workers.
(SCHOMBURG CENTER)

University in 1903, and an M.A. in sociology from Columbia University in 1923. Ross married George E. Haynes, a sociologist and cofounder of the National Urban League, in 1910. Their interests in racial uplift, women's rights, and survey research were closely matched. Haynes had one child, George Haynes, Jr., in 1912. W. E. B. DuBois published her first book, *Unsung Heroes,* a collection of inspirational biographies for black children.

Elizabeth Ross Haynes was a persuasive advocate of job training and improved social services for black urban women workers, and was a skilled organizer with a pragmatic approach to improving race relations. She accepted segregated social agencies if black professionals were hired to staff them. This stance occasionally placed her at odds with more militant leaders, but it also made Haynes a vital link between white and black reform groups such as the YWCA and the **National Association of Colored Women** (NACW). From 1908 to 1910, Haynes was the YWCA's student secretary for work among colored women, and the number of black YWCA branches increased because of her efforts. Appointed to the YWCA's new Council on Colored Work in 1922, Haynes served as the first black person on its national board from 1924 to 1934. She also assisted her husband, who was head of the Federal Council of Churches' Department of Race Relations, from 1922 to 1946.

A dollar-a-year worker for the U.S. Department of Labor during World War I, Haynes took part in some of the first systematic studies of black women workers. After her husband's federal appointment was terminated, Haynes was hired as domestic service secretary in Washington, D.C. for the U.S. Employment Service. Her 1923 Master's thesis was the most comprehensive study of black domestic workers until the 1970s. Haynes was a founder and officer of the National League of Republican Colored Women, but spoke out against the racist tactics used by the GOP against Al Smith in the 1928 president campaign. She was among the first black women leaders in the NACW to become a New Deal Democrat and was active in Harlem politics. Haynes became coleader of Harlem's Twenty-first Assembly District in 1935, was a member of the colored division of the national Democratic speakers' bureau by 1936, and in 1937 was the first woman appointed to the State Temporary Commission on the Condition of the Urban Colored Population.

In 1952, at age sixty-nine, she finished *The Black Boy of Atlanta,* a biography of Major Richard Robert Wright, college president and banker. Haynes died on October 26, 1953, in New York City.

FRANCILLE RUSAN WILSON

Houston, Drusilla Dunjee
(1876–1941)

Drusilla Dunjee Houston is the earliest known black woman to author a multivolume study of the history of ancient Africa and its people. A teacher, journalist, and self-trained historian, she was the daughter of John William Dunjee and Lydia Taylor Dunjee. In her father's expansive library, she first read and began to master what she would later call "the dry bones of history." At twenty-two, she married Price Houston, a storekeeper, and they had a daughter. With her brother Roscoe Dunjee, she helped establish the *Black Dispatch,* a weekly Oklahoma City newspaper. As a columnist, she frequently researched and wrote articles of historical interest.

She is best known as the author of *Wonderful Ethiopians of the Ancient Cushite Empire* (1926). Beginning with the origin of civilization, *Wonderful Ethiopians* examines the links among Egypt, Ethiopia, and the ancient black populations in Arabia, Persia, Babylonia, and India. Two other volumes written on similar themes were completed but never published. Both are now lost.

Drusilla Houston approached world history by first recognizing the blood and cultural ties that connect African people the world over. In this sense, she anticipates and shares views articulated by today's Pan-Africanist scholars.

Drusilla Houston was a significant and unique writer of ancient history. Her contribution to black historiography and women's history has yet to be adequately appraised, in part because information on Drusilla Houston and her work is difficult to locate. An introduction to her life and work, along with a commentary and an afterword, can be found in the republished edition of *Wonderful Ethiopians*.

W. PAUL COATES

Hunter-Gault, Charlayne (1942–)

"Whatever I have faced as a woman," Charlayne Hunter-Gault said, "is probably a lot more subtle than what I have faced as a black person." By the time she and Hamilton Holmes became the first black students to enter the University of Georgia, Athens, in January 1961, Charlayne Hunter had endured two years of legal maneuvering and bureaucratic delays.

After the riots and unrest that followed, many journalists interviewed the two black students, and Hunter's interest in becoming a journalist grew. She joined the staff of the *New Yorker* in 1963 as a secretary. Her writing talent enabled her to advance rapidly at the *New Yorker*, at the *New York Times*, and in other news positions, to become a leading journalist.

The eldest of three children, Charlayne Hunter was born on February 27, 1942, in Due West, South Carolina, to Charles S. H. Hunter, Jr., a Methodist chaplain in the U.S. Army, and Althea Hunter. In 1954, the Hunters moved to Atlanta, Georgia, where her mother was secretary in a real estate firm. Her father's long tours of duty abroad left the rearing of Charlayne and her two younger brothers to her mother and grandmother.

From 1954 to 1959, Hunter attended Henry McNeal Turner High School, where she was an honor student and editor of the student newspaper. She became a Roman Catholic at age sixteen. Her ambition to be a reporter led Hunter to seek admission to the University of Georgia. A group of prominent civil rights activists supported Hunter and Holmes in the fight to integrate the university. While waiting for the court order, she studied at Wayne State University in Detroit, Michigan. At the University of Georgia she worked on weekends for the *Atlanta Inquirer*, founded by Georgia college students, including Julian Bond.

She received a B.A. in journalism from the University of Georgia in 1963, became secretary at the *New Yorker*, and the next year was promoted to staff writer. After receiving a Russell Sage Fellowship in 1967 to study social science at Washington University, St. Louis, she left the *New*

Yorker. In St. Louis she edited articles for *Trans-Action* magazine, which sent her to cover the Poor People's Campaign in Washington, D.C. Later that year she became investigative reporter and anchorwoman of the local evening news broadcast of WRC-TV, and in 1968 she joined the metropolitan staff of the *New York Times.* In the early 1970s, she took a leave of absence to become codirector of the Michele Clark Fellowship program for minority students in journalism at Columbia University, returning later to spend a total of nine years with the *Times.* Hunter-Gault joined *The MacNeil/Lehrer Report* on PBS in 1978 and was named national correspondent in 1983, when the show was expanded to *The MacNeil/Lehrer NewsHour.*

Hunter-Gault has received numerous major journalism awards: the *New York Times* Publisher's Award, the National Urban Coalition Award for Distinguished Urban Reporting, two national news and documentary Emmy Awards, and the George Foster Peabody Award for Excellence in Broadcast Journalism.

In addition to her print and broadcast work as a journalist, she has written articles for *Change, Essence, Life, Ms., Saturday Review, The New Leader,* and other magazines. She married Walter Stovall, a white student, while in college. They had one daughter, Susan, born a few years later. In 1971, she married Ronald Gault, a black Chicagoan, and they have one son, Chuma. She published her autobiography, *In My Place,* in 1992. In 1988, she became the first black person in the 203-year history of her alma mater, the University of Georgia, to deliver the commencement address. [Hamilton Holmes, her fellow student, was then a member of the Georgia Foundation, the governing board of the University.]

Charlayne Hunter-Gault set a goal early in life, which, coupled with her talent and tenacity, led her to become a leading journalist. The University of Georgia, though it once denied her admission and was the site of violent protests against her presence on campus, now accepts and honors Hunter-Gault.

JESSIE CARNEY SMITH

Hutson, Jean Blackwell (1914–)

One of the foremost librarians in the country and a noted authority on black life and culture, Jean Hutson was born in Summerfield, Florida, on September 4, 1914, to Paul O. Blackwell and Sarah Myers Blackwell, but spent much of her early life in Baltimore. An exceptional student, she was always ahead of her classmates because of her love of reading. She graduated from high school at the age of fifteen and enrolled in the University of Michigan with the intention of studying psychiatry. However, because of the Great Depression and the high cost of medical school, Hutson, on the advice of her mother, who was a strong influence, transferred to Barnard College in New York City, where she received a B.A. in 1935. A year later she received a B.S. from the Columbia University School of Library Service.

Her first professional assignment following graduation was as a high school librarian in Baltimore. Later she worked for the New York Public Library system in Manhattan and in the Bronx. While in the Bronx, she observed that the Spanish-speaking people in the neighborhood had difficulty making use of library services.

She subsequently began ordering materials in Spanish, which resulted in greater use of the library by residents of the neighborhood. These efforts did not go unnoticed by the administrators of the library system and led them to consider her when efforts were made to increase services to other underserved populations in the city.

In 1955, Hutson became curator of the Schomburg Collection of Negro Literature and History at the New York Public Library (now called the Schomburg Center for Research in Black Culture). The author of many short stories and introductions to books, Hutson's proudest accomplishment was overseeing the development of the Schomburg's *Dictionary Catalog,* which has made it possible for scholars and researchers around the world to review the collection's holdings and more easily pursue their own research interests.

During 1964–65, Hutson was assistant librarian at the University of Ghana. After her return to New York, she served as chair of the Harlem Cultural Council and lectured at City College of the City University of New York. She belongs to numerous organizations that promoted the study of the heritage of Africa. Hutson retired from the Schomburg in 1984.

She was honored by Barnard College in 1990, by Columbia University's School of

One of the foremost librarians in the country and a noted authority on scholarship about blacks, Jean Blackwell Hutson was curator of the Schomburg Center for Research in Black Culture for nearly thirty years. She is shown here with Langston Hughes. (SCHOMBURG CENTER)

Library Service in 1992, and by the Schomburg Center in an extensive public ceremony in 1995.

ARTHUR C. GUNN

J

Jefferson, Lucy C. (1866–1953)

One of the first African Americans to own and operate a business in the state of Mississippi, Lucy Crump Jefferson was an entrepreneur and community leader. With her husband, William Henry Jefferson, she opened the W.H. Jefferson Funeral Home in Vicksburg, Mississippi in 1894. Described as "the family matriarch," Jefferson went on to become a philanthropist and civic leader.

Jefferson was born on November 3, 1866 in Jackson, Mississippi. Her mother was Alice Reynolds Crump. Jefferson attended public schools in Vicksburg. In 1889 she married William Henry Jefferson, the son of a prosperous Virginia freedman. For a time she taught schools in the Vicksburg public school system.

Before the 1890s, black-owned businesses were unknown in Mississippi. W. H. Jefferson worked in a white-owned funeral home until he and his wife decided to open their own establishment in 1894. Many friends did not believe they could succeed. The Jeffersons had to educate the black community to patronize a black business.

In the beginning Jefferson's husband had to work a second job on the railroad in order to help the business through the lean years. His job kept him traveling, leaving Jefferson to manage the business. In five years the business had become a success. Later, Jefferson helped a niece establish herself as a funeral director in Chicago.

In 1914, the Jeffersons founded the Jefferson Burial Society. Burial societies were a sort of insurance that were popular in that era. Good funerals were expensive and beyond the reach of people struggling day-to-day to make a living. A burial society gave people a chance to put away a small amount of money each week, perhaps just a few pennies. In return members were guaranteed a proper funeral when they died. Burial societies were usually organized by people regarded with trust and admiration in the community. It was fitting that the Jeffersons organized a burial society for the black community of Vicksburg.

Jefferson became sole owner of the funeral home when W.H. Jefferson died in 1922. The business is still family-owned more than 100 years later.

Jefferson's success in business was matched by her leadership in civic affairs. She was generous in her support of the Margaret Murray Washington Home for Delinquent Boys and Girls, which was founded during her years of leadership at the Mississippi Federation of Colored Women's Clubs. She was president of the federation from 1928 to 1934. She also created the Lucy C. Jefferson Scholarship, given to a graduating high school student every year for forty years, and was trustee of Campbell College in nearby Jackson, Mississippi.

Jefferson worked for the construction of a black junior high school and, many years

92

after her death, it was finally built. In the same year, 1966, a high school was named in her honor.

A tireless clubwoman, Jefferson was part of the Camille Art and Literary Club and vice president of the National Association of Colored Women's Clubs. She was also a member of the first Interracial Council of Vicksburg, Southern Regional Council. In keeping with her religious beliefs, she was steward, trustee and president of the Missionary Society of Bethel AME Church. She died as she lived, a respected and beloved leader.

ANDRA MEDEA

Jemison, Mae C. (1956–)

Because of her background, education, talent, and interests, Mae C. Jemison would be a valuable asset to any private corporation. That she has chosen instead to build a career in public service, as the first black female astronaut in the National Aeronautics and Space Administration (NASA), is America's good fortune.

Born on October 17, 1956, in Decatur, Alabama, to Charlie and Dorothy Jemison, Mae moved to Chicago with her parents at an early age. A graduate of Morgan Park High School in Chicago, she earned a

The first black woman in space, Mae C. Jemison qualified as a mission specialist on space shuttle crews in August 1988. She is shown here (far left) with the crew of the NASA STS-47 Spacelab-J. Mission. (NASA)

One hopes that Patricia Cowings' [see the Science, Health, and Medicine *volume in this encyclopedia] training works as Mae Jemison floats in zero gravity.* (NASA)

National Achievements Scholarship to Stanford University. She graduated from Stanford in 1977 with a B.S. in chemical engineering while at the same time fulfilling all requirements for a B.A. in African and Afro-American Studies. From Stanford, she went on to Cornell University Medical School, earning her M.D. in 1981. Along the way, Jemison received a host of awards for involvement in such uncommon activities as working in a refugee camp in Thailand. She completed her internship at the University of Southern California Medical Center in Los Angeles.

In January 1985, after a brief period spent in private practice, Jemison joined the Peace Corps. Until 1985, she served as the area Peace Corps medical officer in Sierra Leone and Liberia in West Africa. Then she took a position managing the health care delivery system for both Peace Corps and U.S. Embassy personnel as well as developing self-help information for local constituents.

In 1987, NASA selected Jemison as an astronaut candidate. She completed her one-year training and evaluation program in August 1988, qualifying as a mission specialist on space shuttle crews. Jemison was then a mission specialist on STS-47, Spacelab-J, a cooperative mission between the United States and Japan. As part of her training for work in space, Jemison helped prepare space shuttles for launch. Her responsibilities included preparing launch payloads and thermal protection systems as well as verifying the integrity and performance of shuttle computer software.

On September 12, 1992, she was aboard the space shuttle *Endeavour* when it was launched on a one-week mission to study the effects of zero gravity on people and animals. The first black woman in space took with her an Alvin Ailey American Dance Theater poster depicting the dance *Cry,* explaining to **Judith Jamison**, the director of the company, that the dance was created for Jemison and "all black women everywhere."

Jemison resigned from NASA in March of 1993 to form her own company, which specializes in adapting technology for use in underdeveloped nations. That same year she made a guest appearance on *Star Trek: The Next Generation,* stating that she was originally inspired to be an astronaut by the black Lieutenant Uhura on the original *Star Trek,* played by **Nichelle Nichols**.

CHRISTINE A. LUNARDINI

An Emmy-winning television news anchor, Carol Jenkins has covered events ranging from the collapse of a bridge to national political conventions to Nelson Mandela's release from prison in South Africa.   (CAROL JENKINS)

Jenkins, Carol   (1944–   )

In February, 1996, Emmy Award–winning television news anchor Carol Jenkins joined New York's Fox 5/WNYW as co-anchor of "Fox Midday News." In April of the same year, her role was expanded to include her own daily talk show, "Carol Jenkins Live," New York's first interactive talk show.

Before joining Fox 5, Jenkins was a news anchor with WNBC, the flagship NBC station in New York City. Notable for her coverage of national political events, Jenkins has interviewed President Bill Clinton and First Lady Hillary Clinton, and Vice President Al Gore. She has also done global news, filing live reports from South Africa on the release of Nelson Mandela, and hosting a one-hour primetime special, "South Africa: Steps Toward Freedom," which was nominated for an Emmy.

Born on November, 30, 1944 in Montgomery, Alabama, Jenkins' family moved to Jamaica, New York, when she was three years old. She attended Boston University, graduating with a bachelor of arts degree in 1966. She went on to get her master of arts degree from New York University in 1968. She is the mother of two children.

Jenkins began as a reporter and anchor for WOR-TV in 1970. By 1971 she had moved up to become a moderator on the *News Report with Bill Ryan,* at the same station. In 1972 she moved to ABC-TV to become a network correspondent with the *Reasoner-Smith Report* and *Eyewitness News.* There she stayed until she moved to WNBC in 1973.

When Jenkins moved to WNBC-TV in New York, she began as a general reporter. In time she contributed reports to the evening and late evening newscasts, became co-anchor of *Weekend News Channel 4* at 6 and 11 P.M., and rose to become co-anchor of *News Channel 4* at 6 P.M. Jenkins has also anchored news reports for NBC's popular daytime program, the *Today* show.

Aside from working the New York beat, Jenkins has covered a range of important stories in national and international arenas. Her coverage of the release of Nelson Mandela culminated in a one-hour prime time special titled "South Africa: Steps Toward Freedom." She also handled a story on returning POWs, as well as going to Israel to report on the Middle East.

On the national front, Jenkins has covered several Democratic National Conventions for WNBC, as well as the 1988 Republican National Convention. She also covered the 1992 Presidential election, as well as Clinton's inauguration.

In New York City Jenkins has covered the heated mayoral election in 1989, in which the first black mayor was elected there. Jenkins has interviewed a number of New York mayors, dating back to John Lindsay who served in the 1970s, as well as New York governors and senators.

Jenkins has been honored by a wide range of news and professional organizations. In 1983 she won an Emmy award for her report on the collapse of the Mianus Bridge. She also

won a United Press International award for spot news reporting on the collapse of a building in the Bronx. She won an Associated Press Award for spot news reports on Gorbachev's sudden departure from New York City in 1988. In 1990 Jenkins earned the New York Association of Black Journalists Lifetime Achievement Award, in honor of her long-standing excellence in the field of journalism. She has also been granted an honorary doctorate from the College of New Rochelle, New York.

A seasoned television anchor who has covered the news for more than twenty years, Carol Jenkins has become a newsmaker in her own right.

ANDRA MEDEA

Johnson, Eunice Walker   (19??–   )

Not only is she one of *the* Johnsons of Johnson Publishing—the dynasty which publishes *Ebony, Jet,* and its own line of books—Eunice McAlpine Walker Johnson is also the producer and director of the Ebony Fashion Fair. This eminently successful traveling fashion show has toured the United States since the mid-1950s, raising millions of dollars for black charities.

Johnson was born in Selma, Alabama, the daughter of Ethel McAlpine Walker and Nathaniel D. Walker. Her father was a prominent doctor in Selma. Her mother was an instructor at Selma University, as well as a high school principal. Her maternal grandfather, William H. McAlpine, was born in slavery but rose to become founder and second president of Selma University.

Johnson grew up in Selma and went to Talladega College in Talladega, Alabama. She graduated with a B.A. in sociology from the college that would later benefit from her success. After moving to Chicago, she received her M.A. in social service administration from Loyola University. She later went on to graduate studies in journalism at Northwestern University.

In the late 1940s, Johnson and her husband, John Johnson, founded Johnson Publishing Company in Chicago, Illinois. She became secretary-treasurer of the company and, later, fashion editor of *Ebony* magazine. As the magazines flourished, Johnson Publishing was asked to sponsor a fund-raiser in New Orleans for the Women's Auxiliary of Flint-Goodrich Hospital. The year was 1956, and Jessie C. Dent, wife of the president of Dillard University, proposed a fashion show. The show was a great success, and the publishers decided to take the project on the road. The fashion show would visit various cities for fund-raisers and sell subscriptions to *Jet* and *Ebony* along with the tickets.

The idea was a savvy combination of fashion, social event, marketing, and community relations. The shows themselves were a tremendous success, with proceeds going to local charities. By the end of 1995, Johnson Publishing estimated that the Ebony Fashion Fairs had raised more than $45 million for churches, hospitals, schools, and other organizations.

In 1958, Frieda DeKnight, who was then fashion and food editor for *Ebony,* produced the first national tour. Five years later Johnson took charge of the tour, a position she has maintained to the present. The event showcases black models and black designers such as Willi Smith, Patrick Kelly and Stephen Burrows, as well as fashions from the famous European designers.

As part of her role as fashion scout, Johnson travels yearly to the great fashion capitals of the world—Paris, Rome, Milan, Florence, and New York. She chooses the fashions to be showcased, identifies each year's theme, and personally selects and supervises the models and photographers.

Part of the appeal of the Ebony Fashion Fair is that it does not focus solely on high fashion. Casual, everyday clothing is also represented, as well as fashions for larger women. On a typical tour, the fashion show appears in more than 160 cities, in itself a major logistical undertaking.

Johnson has also been active in cultural and charitable causes. She is on the women's board of the Art Institute of Chicago, is a member of the National Foundation for the Fashion Industry, and is on the board of directors of Selma University. She is also on the advisory board of Harvard University and has been a major donor to her own alma mater, Talladega College.

Combining good business sense with a flair for fashion, Eunice Walker Johnson has created a lasting institution in the Ebony Fashion Fair. In the process, she has deeply enriched the black community.

ANDRA MEDEA

Jones, Clara Stanton (1913–)

The year 1976 was an eventful one for black librarians. As the American Library Association (ALA) celebrated its centennial and the country celebrated its bicentennial, a black woman, Clara Stanton Jones, became the first black president of the ALA.

She was born in St. Louis, Missouri, in May 1913, to Ralph and Etta Clara Stanton. She received a B.A. from **Spelman College** and an A.B.L.S. in Library Science from the University of Michigan. She married Alfred Jones in 1938 and they had three children. Her library career began at a historically black college, Dillard University in New Orleans. Her next position was at Southern University in Baton Rouge, Louisiana, where she served as associate librarian and instructor in library science.

She took a position in 1944 at the Detroit Public Library, where she was first a children's librarian and then rose through the ranks to become a library neighborhood consultant in late 1968. In 1970, she was elected director of the Detroit Public Library, the fifth largest public library in the United States, by the Detroit Library Commission. After her appointment Jones later commented: "You might say that in a sense I was the dark horse candidate, both figuratively and literally. My appointment was unconventional because I am black, I am a woman, and I come from middle management in our own system."

As director of the library, she was instrumental in creating the Information Place, commonly known by public librarians as TIP, a pioneering information and referral service that was established as an integral part of every branch. As director, she continued to use creative leadership to maintain a viable library service for the people of Detroit in a period of fiscal problems. She became a well-known speaker in Detroit and a champion of that city's revitalization and cultural development.

She has received numerous awards including the Distinguished Alumnus Award of the University of Michigan School of Library Science. She has also been associated with the **National Association for the Advancement of Colored People,** Women's International League for Peace and Freedom, and the American Civil Liberties Union.

She served as acting president of the American Library Association in 1975 and served as president from 1976 to 1977. As the first African-American president of the ALA, Clara Stanton Jones provided sterling leadership in the development and promotion of appropriate activities for the centennial celebration of the association.

JOYCE C. WRIGHT

Jones, Virginia Lacy   (1912–1984)

Among library educators, Virginia Lacy Jones was known as "the Dean of Deans." Diminutive in stature, Dean Jones was a giant in library education. A wise counselor, inspired teacher, patient mentor, and demanding scholar, she was a courageous leader who pointed the way to achievement and success against barriers that most would have considered insurmountable.

Born in Cincinnati, Ohio, on June 25, 1912, the daughter of Edward Lacy and Ellen Louise Parker Lacy, Jones grew up in Clarksburg, West Virginia, where she had an early exposure to books at home and at the library. Her school years were spent first in Clarksburg and then in St. Louis, Missouri, when her family relocated.

While a student at Summer High School, in doing research for an essay contest, Jones came into contact with a reference librarian at the St. Louis Public Library whose knowledge, resourcefulness, and dedication made a lasting impression. Although she had earlier intended to enroll in Stowe Teachers College after graduation in 1929, fired with the desire to become a librarian, she entered Hampton Institute in Virginia. During her fourth year at Hampton, she met Florence Rising Curtis, director of the library school. Curtis' personal interest in her professional advancement had a lifelong impact on Jones.

After graduation from Hampton in 1933, she began her professional career at Louisville

Municipal College in Kentucky as assistant librarian. In 1935, she returned to study at Hampton. During 1935–36, she worked part time in the Hampton Institute Library and accompanied Curtis to the American Library Association (ALA) Conference in Richmond, Virginia. At the meeting, she and other African-American librarians experienced the degradation of institutional racism in the South during that era. As a result of protests about the humiliating treatment of black librarians at the Richmond conference, ALA made it a policy not to convene in cities where all librarians could not participate fully in all facets of the meeting.

Returning to Louisville Municipal College in the fall of 1936, after receiving a bachelor's degree in education at Hampton, Jones became head librarian. Later, with a fellowship from the General Education Board and with a leave of absence from the college, she studied for and received an M.L.S. from the University of Illinois in 1938. After a year at Louisville again, she became catalog librarian at Atlanta University's Trevor Arnett Library in 1939, where she remained for two years. When the Atlanta University School of Library Service opened in 1941, Jones was one of the original faculty members, teaching cataloging and classification, school library service, and children's literature. In the same year, she married Edward Allen Jones, professor of French and chairman of the Department of Modern Language at Morehouse College.

In 1943, Jones was awarded a fellowship from the General Education Board to study at the graduate library school of the University of Illinois, and in 1945 she became the second African American to receive a doctorate in library service. She was named dean of the School of Library

Service at Atlanta University, a position she held until December 1981, when she became the first director of the Atlanta University Center Robert W. Woodruff Library.

Jones was a prolific contributor to library literature. Believing that ethnic and racial barriers should be broken down from within professional organizations, she worked untiringly in the ALA to make it an organization responsive to all its members. She held various offices within the ALA, including posts on the ALA Council in 1946–69 and on the executive board in 1970–76. Her 1976 honorary membership award citation from the ALA stated: "In your pursuit of excellence for librarianship, you have conducted institutes, persuaded foundation officials, pressured state library associations to drop discriminatory practices, and insisted that your students demonstrate both commitment and scholarship." She also won the Melvil Dewey, Joseph E. Lippincott, and Beta Phi Mu awards, among others. In 1967, President Lyndon B. Johnson appointed Jones a member of the President's Advisory Committee on Library Research and Training Projects, where she served until 1970.

For her contributions to American librarianship, Jones received an honorary doctorate of humane letters from Bishop College and an honorary doctorate of letters from the University of Michigan, both in 1979. She retired from active service to the profession in 1984. She died December 3, 1984.

ARTHUR C. GUNN

Julian, Anna Johnson   (1904?–1994)

Sociologist, entrepreneur, and policy advisor, Dr. Anna Johnson Julian participated in a wealth of social changes that spanned the century.

Julian was born in Baltimore, Maryland to Charles Speare Johnson and Adelaide Scott Johnson. Julian attended the University of Pennsylvania, earning a B.S. with majors in sociology and English in 1923. She went on to receive her M.A. in sociology in 1925 and a Ph.D. with honors in sociology in 1937. Julian was the first black woman to earn a Ph.D. in sociology from the University of Pennsylvania and the first black to join the prestigious Phi Beta Kappa society.

From 1925 to 1928, Julian was a case worker for Family Services in Washington, D.C. From 1928 to 1929 she taught English at the Bordentown Industrial Institute in Bordentown, New Jersey. She then returned to Washington, where she spent the next ten years in the department of research of the Washington, D.C., public schools. In 1937 she authored the sociological study *Standards of Relief: A Study of One Hundred Allowance Families in Washington, D.C.*

On Christmas Eve, 1935, Anna Johnson married Percy Lavon Julian, a successful chemist and researcher. From 1948 through 1953 Julian served as vice president and treasurer of Suburban Chemical Company in Franklin Park, Illinois, one of her husband's ventures, and in 1953 became vice president of Julian Associates and Julian Research Institute. She remained vice president of Julian Associates until the family sold the company to a large pharmaceutical firm in 1962. Julian kept her position as vice president of Julian Research until that company closed in 1976, following the death of her husband.

As successful professionals and entrepreneurs, Julian and her husband purchased a home in nearby Oak Park, Illinois, a prosperous white suburb. Their home was firebombed. The event was covered by the national news. Refusing to be intimidated, the Julians hired bodyguards to protect their home. Oak Park is now peacefully integrated.

Though working in the family business, Julian remained active and influential in social programs. She was a founding member of the board of directors of the widely respected Family Institute of Chicago, which later became affiliated with Northwestern University. She received an appointment from the British ambassador to serve on the advisory council for the Marshall Scholarships, enabling American students to study at British universities.

In 1963, after retiring from Julian Associates, Julian was appointed by the governor of Illinois to the Commission on the Study of Birth Control. After a two-year study, this commission recommended that the state of Illinois make it legal to distribute birth control information.

Julian also served on the women's board of the University of Chicago, as well as two terms as chair of the board of trustees of Rosary College in nearby River Forest. She was elected to the national board of the NAACP Legal Defense and Educational Fund in 1977. In addition, she was on the women's advisory board of the Chicago Foundation for Women and on the advisory board of the Chicago area Phi Beta Kappa. She also founded the Percy L. Julian Scholarship Fund at DePauw University, along with other scholarship funds.

A woman who was a success in several fields, Julian influenced social policy in numerous ways. Over almost a century, she saw remarkable changes in the lives of African Americans and participated in many of them.

ANDRA MEDEA

K

King, Reatha Clark (1938–)

Black women in America have a remarkable tradition of service to their communities, equalled only by their commitment to education. Reatha Clark King has been a remarkable contributor to both those areas.

King was born Reatha Clark on April 11, 1938, in Pavo, Georgia. She attended Clark College, where she received a bachelor's degree in 1958. In 1960, she was awarded a master's degree from the University of Chicago and, in 1963, a doctorate in chemistry from that institution.

King began her career as a research chemist for the National Bureau of Standards, a position she held for five years. Then, in 1968, she became assistant professor of chemistry at York College in New York State. She moved up at York until she was professor of chemistry and associate dean of academic affairs. Then, in 1977, she received her master's in business administration from Columbia University. That same year, she was appointed president of Metropolitan State University in St. Paul, Minnesota.

During the eleven years she was at Metropolitan State, King was very active in serving the community. In addition to work with such charitable organizations as the St. Paul United, of which she was board chair, she was appointed to head governmental commissions and task forces.

King's record as an administrator, combined with her exceptional work with non-profit, governmental, and corporate organizations, led the General Mills Foundation to choose her as its president and executive director. At the same time, she became a vice president of General Mills, Incorporated. At the Foundation, she is responsible for grants made to organizations in the areas of education, health and social action, and arts and cultural affairs.

Reatha C. King's record as a university administrator, combined with her exceptional work with nonprofit, governmental, and corporate organizations, led the General Mills Foundation to choose her as its president and executive director. (GENERAL MILLS FOUNDATION)

In 1991, President George Bush appointed King to the United States Commission on National and Community Service, where she served for two years. In 1994, President Bill Clinton appointed her to the board of the Corporation of National and Community Service.

King has received a dozen honorary degrees, from such colleges and universities as Smith College and Seattle University. She is married to Dr. N. Judge King, Jr., and has two children.

KATHLEEN THOMPSON

L

Latimer, Catherine Allen

(1895?–1948)

In 1920, Catherine Allen Latimer became the first black professional librarian at the New York Public Library. She was assigned to the 135th Street branch, which is now the Schomburg Center for Research in Black Culture. In her twenty-six years there she created a clipping file that continues to be an important source of information on black Americans; she incorporated

The first black professional librarian at the New York Public Library, Catherine Latimer created and developed the famous Clipping File at the Schomburg Center for Research in Black Culture. She is seated fourth from the right (with crossed ankles) at the unveiling at the Center in 1936 of Pietro Calvi's bust of actor Ira Aldridge as Othello. Arthur A. Schomburg is standing, second from right. (SCHOMBURG CENTER)

Arthur Schomburg's personal library into the branch's Negro Collection; and she inspired many with her knowledge, competence, and professional methods.

Born in Nashville, Tennessee, about 1895, to H.W. Allen and Minta Bosley Trotman, Latimer grew up in Brooklyn. She attended Howard and Columbia universities, and worked as an assistant librarian at Tuskegee Institute in Alabama before returning to New York City. At the 135th Street branch of the New York Public Library during the Harlem Renaissance, when interest in and material about the New Negro was burgeoning, Latimer created and developed what is known as the Clipping File. It was maintained during the 1930s by Works Progress Administration (WPA) workers who mounted the clippings in scrapbooks that are still in use. She also actively sought periodicals that featured articles on aspects of the black experience. This file was never weeded, and so it grew into a most unusual resource. Latimer was an experienced reference librarian who was sought after by writers and researchers, and she was mentioned in the writings of Langston Hughes and Elise J. McDougald. She wrote for *Crisis, Looking Forward,* and the *Negro History Bulletin.*

Latimer was married to Benton R. Latimer and had one son, Bosley. She retired in 1946 because of poor eyesight and illness and died in 1948.

BETTY K. GUBERT

Lewis, Ida Elizabeth (1935–)

Ida Elizabeth Lewis loved reading throughout her childhood. But only after a high school teacher refused to believe a paper she had handed in was written without help did she resolve to be a writer. In years to come, she became the first financial columnist for the *Amsterdam News* in New York, a reporter for *L'Express* in Paris, a *Washington Post* correspondent, the first black female panelist on TV's *Meet the Press,* the editor of *Essence* magazine and the founder-editor-publisher of *Encore* magazine. In these roles, and as a freelance writer, she has strongly revealed at least two things. One is that she is more a journalist—one interested in the larger truths behind events—than she is a reporter of the smaller truths called facts. The other is that the press is a great instrument for black unity.

Lewis was born in Pennsylvania on September 22, 1935. The second eldest of six children, she was the daughter of Sam Lewis, a plumber and laborer, and Grace Lewis, who ran an employment agency. At the all-black Phillis Wheatley grammar school she found, she said later, "loving teachers." At the mainly white Swarthmore High School she "generally" found "indifference" or worse.

Upon receiving her B.S. degree in 1956 from Boston University's School of Communications, where she studied both journalism and economics, Lewis took the *Amsterdam News* position. To supplement its low pay, she held other jobs and briefly tried her hand as an East Side coffeehouse proprietor. In 1959, she began a year as financial editor of the newspaper *New York Age* before beginning her freelance writing career.

Living in Paris between 1963 and 1969, Lewis traveled annually throughout Africa. Her first trip resulted in a book of essays, *The Deep Ditch and the Narrow Pit,* published in 1964. Her second produced an article for *Life* magazine on a revolt in

Tanzania. She translated for *L'Express* readers the African-American response to Richard Nixon's 1968 Presidential campaign, covered the civil war in Nigeria for the *Post* and was a writer and broadcaster for the British Broadcasting Corporation's African Service. She contributed to the weekly magazine *Jeune Afrique* ("Young Africa") and continued to do so after returning to the United States.

Back in New York, in 1970, she became editor of the newly launched black women's magazine, *Essence,* and saw its circulation grow to 171,000 by its second year. Leaving after a conflict in 1971, she raised $40,000 and began *Encore* in May, 1972. Before the year ended, *Encore* went from quarterly to monthly publication, and Lewis remained with it until 1982. That year she also resigned the board chairmanship of *Eagle and Swan,* a magazine for African Americans in the military that she had founded in 1978.

Lewis has been president of the Port Royal Communications Network since 1978. In 1984, she began publishing and editing the wide-ranging *Five Fifteen,* which called itself "The First Black Women's Newspaper."

Not surprisingly, Lewis has often been a media consultant for African-American political candidates. Recipient of many awards and a woman with many professional affiliations, Ida Elizabeth Lewis has led a colorful, influential, and sometimes controversial life. She has had a major impact on the publishing world and the black community.

M

Major, Gerri (1894–1984)

She was the society writer for the black community, reporting on events from San Francisco to Harlem and across the sea to Europe and Africa. If there was an important black society occasion, Gerri Hodges Major was on hand to report the news for *Jet* magazine. Born to high society and at home in the social milieu, Major turned her natural inclination into a lifelong vocation.

Major was born in a prosperous part of the South Side of Chicago on July 29, 1894. Her mother died at her birth and she was raised by her mother's sister, Maude Powell Lawrence, and Lawrence's husband. Both her aunt and uncle were prosperous professionals, at home in society. Her childhood included dancing school, parties at fashionable clubs, and dining out in style.

Major attended Douglas School in Chicago, where she was one of two black students. She went on to Wendell Phillips High School, then the University of Chicago. She graduated in 1915 with a bachelor of philosophy degree.

Like many well-educated black women of her time, Major first took a job teaching. She had never received teachers' training, but in 1915 she taught at Lincoln Institute in Jefferson City, Missouri, a school founded by black soldiers of the Civil War. Her situation at Lincoln did not work out, so she returned to the city to pursue a teaching certificate at Chicago Normal School. She received certification in 1917.

At the end of 1917, Major married Binga Dismond. After summer study at Hampton Institute in Hampton, Virginia, she again returned to Chicago, this time to teach at her old elementary school, Douglas.

Major broke into society writing while living in New York City in 1925. She wrote an article titled "Through the Lorgnette," which was published in the *Pittsburgh Courier*. Her next article was "In New York Town," which appeared in *The Chicago Bee*.

In 1928, having found her calling in society writing, Majors founded her own business, the Geraldyn Dismond Bureau of Specialized Publicity. The same year she began to write a social column for the *Baltimore Afro-American* titled, "New York Social Whirl." She became managing editor of the *Interstate Tattler* from 1928 to 1931, covering society events, gossip, politics, sports, and entertainment.

In 1933, Major briefly edited the *Daily Citizen,* until that newspaper went out of business. In the depths of the Depression she took a job writing for the New York Bureau of Public Health. After a divorce from Dismond and a brief marriage to Gilbert Holland, she married John Major, who took her to Atlantic City. She moved back to New York after John Major died. Her next job was to edit and write for the women's pages for the *Amsterdam News*.

In 1953, Major was hired by Johnson Publishing as senior staff editor of *Ebony* and society editor for *Jet*. She worked in the firm's New York bureau, but also covered events in Europe and Africa. For a while she covered society events for the Paris bureau.

In a single *Jet* article Major might describe a wedding in New Orleans, an embassy reception in Nairobi, and a theater opening on Broadway. Naturally, Major could not attend all three in a single week, but her reports gave readers the opportunity to savor glittering black stars in a black social whirl.

As *Ebony* noted at the time of her death, "She was a 'jetsetter' before there were jets. She celebrated her birthdays in such romantic places as Nassau, Paris, and Cairo."

One of the oldest working journalists in the country at the time of her death, she wrote her last society column just two days before she was felled by a stroke at the age of ninety.

Malone, Annie Turnbo   (1869–1957)

Annie Minerva Turnbo Pope Malone was an early black entrepreneur who made her fortune creating and marketing black beauty products. As generous as she was successful, she used her wealth to support a wide variety of good works in black communities across America.

Malone was born in 1869 on a farm near Metropolis, Illinois, across the Ohio river from Kentucky. She was the tenth of eleven children. Her father was Robert Malone, and her mother was Isabella Cook Malone. Orphaned as a child, she was raised by a sister in Peoria, Illinois, in the northern part of the state.

In the late nineteenth century, cosmetics and hair care compounds were more likely to be home-made concoctions than prepackaged products that could be bought at the corner store. And there were very few products available for the black consumer. At the same time, grooming was a very high priority among black women who felt a strong desire to protect themselves against disrespect by presenting a proper image to the world.

Part of this image was straight hair. And it was this particular desire that Malone decided to address. Most products for straightening at the time were either heavy fats, such as goose grease, or acidic straighteners that could burn the hair and scalp. By the late 1890s Malone was experimenting with new products. By 1900 she

Specializing in black beauty products, Annie Turnbo Malone was one of the first black women to be successful at nationwide marketing to the black community. (MOORLAND-SPINGARN)

had developed hair oils, straighteners, and hair growing products.

Working in the little town of Lovejoy, Illinois, around the turn of the century, Malone made and marketed the Wonderful Hair Grower. She was also credited with creating and patenting the first pressing iron and comb, in 1900. Two years later she moved her business to the larger black community in St. Louis. There Malone and three assistants sold the products door-to-door, and provided free hair treatments to win new customers.

Malone opened her first establishment in time for the St. Louis World's Fair in 1902. Soon her products were available throughout the Midwest, marketed through individual black women who sold the products in their communities. She named her line Poro products, after a West African word referring to physical and spiritual masking.

Malone was one of the first black women to be successful at nationwide marketing to the black community. She personally toured the South to generate interest in her products. She took out ads in key black newspapers. She held press conferences to generate publicity. In this same period, she ended a brief marriage after her husband attempted to interfere in her business affairs.

One of Malone's early proteges was **Madame C. J. Walker,** who later became one of the first black millionaires in America. A former laundress, Walker became a Malone agent in 1905 and soon began experimenting with a similar hair straightening product. In 1906, Walker moved to Denver, Colorado, and struck out on her own. Walker's enterprise continued to expand rapidly across the country, until her death in 1919.

There is some debate over whether Walker or Malone was the first major black beauty entrepreneur. Many sources indicate that Malone was the original and Walker the imitator. In any case, in 1906, soon after Walker set out on her own, Malone copyrighted her Poro trade name, while assailing "fraudulent imitators."

In 1910, Malone moved her establishment to larger quarters in St. Louis, and in 1917 she built the Poro College complex. Here, new products could be created, tested, and manufactured, and agents trained in the use of new products. Equipment and furnishings were valued at over one million dollars, a very large sum in 1917.

Malone not only taught the business side of beauty culture, she also taught the personal side. African Americans were at this time moving north in record numbers and striving for upward mobility. A polished, cultured look was highly desirable. Poro College not only taught selling, but deportment. The white elite at this time had "finishing schools," where women could learn etiquette and deportment. Through her sales agents, Malone appealed to black women who wanted to acquire a polish similar to theirs.

St. Louis was segregated at this time, and so the Poro College complex became an important center for the black community. Local and national organizations used the complex for special events and office space. After the St. Louis tornado disaster in 1927, Poro Complex was an important relief station for the Red Cross. At its height, the Poro complex included classrooms, laboratories, barbershops, a cafeteria, dining room, ice cream parlor; and an auditorium, theater, and roof garden, all in a black environment that welcomed a black clientele.

At its peak in 1926, Poro College employed 175 people, while Poro products claimed 75,000 agents operating throughout the United States, the Caribbean Islands and other countries. This made Malone a major source of economic independence in the black community.

In the end, the problems at Poro came not from the product, but from management practices. Poro had expanded rapidly during the 1920s, a boom time for American business. However, rapid expansion requires careful management, and Poro didn't have it. Much of the management was in the hands of Malone's husband, Aaron Malone, and the couple began having problems in the early 1920s. While they were careful to appear happy in public, the marriage dissolved in a bitter divorce in 1927.

The divorce was a business disaster that eventually involved a number of local and national black leaders. Aaron Malone tried to persuade black leaders that Poro was a success because of his efforts; that the business contacts were his and he should claim the company. Annie Malone retaliated by lobbying black woman leaders, such as **Mary McLeod Bethune**. Since black women bought most of the products, and Annie Malone gave more money to causes than her husband, her side won. Annie Malone kept the company, but Aaron Malone received a $200,000 settlement.

Annie Malone kept the company out of bankruptcy in spite of the disruptions and appeared to win the overall case. In 1930, the base of operations was moved to a new complex in Chicago. However, the in-fighting and resulting public scandal seriously damaged Poro's image. Soon Malone was involved in another lawsuit brought by a local editor, which was dismissed for lack of evidence. Next she was sued by a former employee and had to make a settlement. As a result of these problems, she was forced to sell the St. Louis complex.

Malone was also hit with a series of tax problems. While generous in her support of the black community, she was reluctant to pay taxes, a serious fault in an entrepreneur. She was slow to pay the 20 percent federal excise tax on luxuries and cosmetics during the 1920s. By 1943 she owed almost $100,000 in taxes. She was repeatedly in court over unpaid taxes of one sort or another, until the government finally seized Poro for back taxes in 1951. Unpaid real estate taxes eventually led to foreclosure on most of the Poro buildings.

As eccentric as Malone was about taxes, she was remarkably generous to the black community. At a time when a working wage was often only a few dollars a week, Malone gave thousands of dollars to black orphanages and colleges. She was reported to have supported two students at every black land-grant college in the United States. She gave $25,000 to **Howard University**'s Medical School Endowment. Tuskegee Institute received numerous gifts of $1,000 and $2,000.

Malone gave enthusiastically, rather than wisely. With gifts of gold plaques and diamond rings to employees, Malone created cash flow problems that plagued the company for years. She died in Chicago several years after having lost her company to taxes, no longer a millionaire, but still possessed of $100,000. It was the end of a dynamic, extravagant, and generous career.

ANDRA MEDEA

Malveaux, Julianne (1953–)

A scathing and witty economist and commentator, Julianne Malveaux enjoys her life as columnist, radio and television host, economic consultant, and puncturer of inflated egos. She confronts the powers-that-be with humor and anger, making her point to many people who would never otherwise listen to an economist.

Born in San Francisco on September 22, 1953, Malveaux was the eldest of five children. Her parents were Paul Warren Malveaux and Protcone Alexandria Malveaux. Both her parents taught, but her father was also a realtor, while her mother was also a social worker.

Malveaux's first published work appeared when she was a teenager. It was a poem in the *Journal of Black Poetry*. While she was in college, she won a poetry contest sponsored by *Essence* magazine, with her poem "Black love is a bitter/ sweetness."

Malveaux went to Boston College where she studied economics, graduating magna cum laude in 1974. The following year she received a master's degree in economics at the same institution. She was soon holding some prestigious positions. From 1977 to 1978, she served on the staff of the Council of Economic Advisors under the Carter administration. From 1978 to 1980, she worked with the Rockefeller Foundation.

In 1980, Malveaux completed her Ph.D. in economics at the Massachusetts Institute of Technology. She then began teaching at the New School for Social Research in New York City. In 1981, however, she moved to San Francisco State University. She stayed on the faculty there until 1985. From 1987 to 1989, Malveaux worked with the Institute for Study of Research on Women and Gender, a project of Stanford University. She also taught economics at the University of California at Berkeley.

Malveaux briefly dabbled in electoral politics with an unsuccessful bid for the San Francisco City and County Board of Supervisors in 1984. While she did not win the election, that same year she successfully sponsored a ballot initiative that forced the city to remove more $300 million dollars in city pension funds from companies that were doing business in South Africa.

During this period, Malveaux began reaching out to regular citizens with her clear explanations of economic trends. In 1986 she co-edited, with Margaret Simms, *Slipping Through the Cracks: The Status of Black Women*. By 1990, Malveaux had begun her career as a newspaper columnist. Her columns are published in the *San Francisco Sun Reporter* and syndicated through the King Features Syndicate.

Malveaux also writes a regular column, "Economics and You," for *Essence* and another titled "The Left Coast" for *Emerge*. She is also a regular contributor to *Ms.* magazine, and her work has appeared in *USA Today*.

Malveaux's wide-ranging commentary is equally effective on the air. She has appeared on CNN's *CNN and Company*, as well as on *To the Contrary*, produced by PBS. She was an occasional talk show host on a local program in San Francisco until she was lured to Washington, D.C. to host her own radio show, *Malveaux in the Morning*.

Malveaux's latest book, a compilation of 150 of her columns titled *Sex, Lies and Stereotypes: Perspectives of a Mad Economist*, was published in 1994.

Along with her many other activities, Malveaux has served as vice president of the NAACP San Francisco branch, and president of the San Francisco Business and Professional Women's Club. She is also a board member of the Center for Policy Alternatives. Able to deliver economic insights with the quick wit of a born communicator, Julianne Malveaux is a voice well worth listening to.

ANDRA MEDEA

Matthews, Miriam   (1905–)

Miriam Matthews is a foremost authority on California black bibliography. She is also a dedicated librarian, a civil rights activist, a lecturer on race relations, a photographer, a collector of African-American art and literature, and a writer.

Miriam Matthews was born in Pensacola, Florida, on August 6, 1905, one of three children born to Reuben and Fannie (Elijah) Matthews. The family moved in July 1907 to Los Angeles, where Miriam received her early education.

Miriam Matthews received an A.B. from the University of California in 1926, a certificate in librarianship from the University of California in 1927, and an M.A. from the University of Chicago in 1945. The title of her Master's thesis was "Library Activities in the Field of Race Relations."

In 1927, Matthews was appointed to the Los Angeles Public Library system—the first black professional librarian hired by the library. From 1929 to 1949, she served as a branch librarian, and in 1949 she became a regional librarian for the Los Angeles Public Library, supervising twelve branch libraries. In this capacity, she served on top administrative committees, repre-

The first black professional librarian of the Los Angeles Public Library system, Miriam Matthews has been documenting the history and contributions of African Americans in California for decades. (MIRIAM MATTHEWS)

senting all the branch librarians in Los Angeles. She also served on numerous committees and boards representing more than fifty organizations, not only concerned with libraries and archives but also with civil rights, health, youth problems, education, race relations, history, and art. During her membership in the American and California library associations, Matthews, as a national councillor, played a prominent role in promoting the cause of intellectual freedom in California and throughout the United States. Significantly, she served as chair of the Committee for Intellectual Freedom of the California Library Association from 1946 to 1948. She served on numerous other committees.

In 1977, Governor Edmund G. Brown appointed Matthews to the California Heritage Preservation Commission and to the California State Historical Records Advisory Board, where she was active in the preservation and use of archives throughout California. In addition, she helped transmit evaluations of archival grant proposals from California institutions to the National Historical Publications and Records Commission for funding. In 1979, she was instrumental in securing a permanent archival program for Los Angeles. During this time, she served on the supervisory committee for the California Historical Records Educational Consultant Service.

While a member of the Los Angeles Bicentennial Committee, Matthews proposed and fought to have a monument erected honoring all the multi-ethnic founders of the city of Los Angeles. In 1981, a large monument was erected on the spot where the city was founded. A small plaque below the monument credits Matthews as the originator of the project.

Among the many committees Matthews has served on are the advisory board of the National Youth Administration, Los Angeles (1938–39); Youth Committee, Los Angeles (1938–40); and the executive board of the National Intercollegiate Christian Council, Asilomar area (1937–38). She is also a member of the American Association of University Women, the **National Association for the Advancement of Colored People** (life member), the University of California and University of Chicago alumni associations,

and the Southern California, San Diego and Western Historical Society.

Throughout her career, Matthews has accepted numerous city, county, state, and national awards. Most important is the Miriam Matthews Award, established in February 1988 by California State University, Dominguez Hills. It is presented annually to individuals who have made outstanding contributions in the field of African-American history and culture. Matthews was named Woman of the Decade in Literature in 1960 (*Los Angeles Sentinel*), Newsmaker of 1975 (National Association of Media Women), and Gran Dama of the City and County of Los Angeles in 1984 (City Council and County Board of Supervisors). In 1982, she received the Award of Merit (California Historical Society), and in 1988 she was appointed one of the first five Fellows of the Historical Society of Southern California. In 1984, she received the U.S. House of Representatives Award.

An interest in the history and contributions of African Americans to California led Matthews to research this subject back to 1781. As a result, she acquired a large collection of books, documents, historical photographs, and art over the years. She has shared her collection with researchers and writers of television documentaries. She has loaned her paintings and sculptures to museums for exhibitions, and she has made donations to many permanent collections in museums. She was the first person in Los Angeles to initiate an interest in the celebration of Negro History Week.

Matthews has lectured at educational institutions and meetings of organizations and appeared on radio and television. In March 1959, she presented a paper entitled

"Weeding and Replacement" at the University of Southern California workshop, "Improving the Book Collection."

DOROTHY PORTER WESLEY

McClain, Leanita (1952–1984)

Leanita McClain, the first black member of the *Chicago Tribune* editorial board, was born in 1952. Named by her parents, Lloyd, a factory worker, and Elizabeth McClain for her two elder sisters, Leatrice and Anita, she grew up in a public housing project named for the pioneer black woman journalist **Ida B. Wells-Barnett**. McClain was a high achiever in the public schools, and while a student at Chicago State University she decided to pursue a career in journalism. She received a full scholarship to the Medill School of Journalism at Northwestern University, completed her master's degree in 1973, and went to work as a general assignment reporter at the *Chicago Tribune*, where she met and married Clarence Page. The marriage ended in divorce.

McClain's superior journalistic abilities earned her frequent promotion. She moved from general assignment reporter to working on the copy desk, to the picture desk, to the Perspective department. Soon she was editor of the Perspective section and then a weekly columnist, the second black person to become a staff columnist in the 137-year history of the newspaper. And in fewer than ten years after joining the *Tribune*, she became a member of the editorial board. McClain was barely thirty years old.

Her writings and professional accomplishments have been honored outside the *Chicago Tribune*. She received the Chicago chapter of Sigma Delta Chi's Peter Lisagor Award, the 1983 Kizzy Award for an outstanding black female role model, and the Chicago Association of Black Journalists' top award for commentary, as well as being listed by *Glamour* magazine as one of the country's ten most outstanding career women.

After accomplishing so much so quickly, she painfully asked of herself and her friends: "I have made it, but where?" In an article that was an important catalyst to her career, she answered quite clearly by saying: "I have overcome the problems of food, clothing, and shelter, but I have not overcome my old nemesis, prejudice. *Life is easier, being black is not.*" As an accomplished black professional woman from the housing projects of Chicago's South Side, McClain was caught with one foot in each world. "Whites won't believe I remain culturally different. . . . blacks won't believe I remain culturally the same." Leanita McClain committed suicide in May 1984 at the age of thirty-two, and though she left a stack of suicide notes, including one labeled "generic suicide note," it is possible that her publications reveal some of the conditions of her life that led her to choose that end.

McClain began her professional career just after the pressures of the civil rights movement opened some doors for talented young African Americans, and she was extremely conscious of the privileges that the movement enabled her to enjoy. Her first major article, published in *Newsweek* in 1980, on the responsibilities and burdens of the black middle class, addressed the frustration that black professionals felt over being accused of having forgotten where they came from when she in fact had not. McClain was committed to her race as well as to her professional position. She was optimistic about her ability to bridge those two worlds, but she was not a romantic. She noted in that article:

> I am burdened daily with showing whites that blacks are people. I am, in the old vernacular, a credit to my race. I am my brothers' keeper, and my sisters', though many of them have abandoned me because they think that I have abandoned them. I run a gauntlet between two worlds, and I am cursed and blessed by both. I travel, observe and take part in both; I can also be used by both. I am a rope in a tug of war. If I am a token in my downtown office, so am I at my cousin's church tea. I assuage white guilt. I disprove black inadequacy and prove to my parent's generation that their patience was indeed a virtue. I have a foot in each world, but I cannot fool myself about either.

McClain also achieved prominence just before Chicago politics turned its ugliest—when Harold Washington won the Democratic primary in the mayoral contest. She was appalled and apparently shocked by the incessant virulent racist attacks, and the equally persistent efforts after Washington's election to prevent his governing effectively. Ultimately, her anger led her to write an article that was published in the *Washington Post* under the title "How Chicago Taught Me to Hate Whites" (so titled by *Post* headline writers). McClain's point was that until the 1983 campaign she had always believed that race relations were improving and that ultimately racism and bigotry would be eradicated, but the campaign and its after-math were so vile that she had to acknowledge that "an evilness still possesses this town, and it continues to weight down my heart"; the constant mean-spiritedness confounded her and led her to "begin that morning [after the election] to build my defenses brick by brick." She realized she could never trust even her own judgment as easily as she had before. Worse still, the campaign and its aftermath made her realize that she had the capacity to hate. McClain worked to reclaim her old working relationships and to shed her hate, but many Chicagoans never forgave her for exposing them in the national press.

In her essays for *Newsweek* and the *Washington Post,* as well as in her weekly and then twice-weekly columns for the *Tribune,* it is clear that Leanita McClain was a crusader, and she was a responsible one. She fought for better government, better schools, better housing. She worked to convince people that politics and race were inseparable, that privilege came with responsibility, that public schools could work, that public housing did not have to be a scourge, and that racism, sexism, and bigotry could and would destroy us all.

STEPHANIE J. SHAW

Morgan, Rose (1912–)

She was a businesswoman with a flair for living that she turned into a profession. Self-described as a homely child, Rose Morgan created a million-dollar beauty establishment and founded several banks along the way.

Born in Shelby, Mississippi, Morgan was one of thirteen children of Chaptle Morgan. Her father was a rare figure for his day—a successful sharecropper. He knew how to keep accounts, which helped him to afford to move his family to Chicago when Rose was six years old. She attended Chicago public schools, and with help from her father, set up her first business at the age of ten. She made artificial flowers and convinced her friends to sell them door to door. Her father approved. "He used to praise everything I did. And I'd work as hard as I could to please him. I believed I could do anything because he told me I could."

Her father could also be tough. Once, when Rose had to wake at 5:30 each morning to go to a grueling job in a laundry, she did not want to get up. Her father said, "You've made yourself a hard bed. Now lie in it." Morgan added, "I was determined from that point it would not be a hard bed all my life."

Morgan began styling hair when she was only eleven, and was picking up extra money by styling friends' hair by the age of fourteen. After finishing high school, Morgan attended Morris School of Beauty. She rented a booth in a neighborhood salon and had her start in life.

Through a friend in the theater, Morgan met **Ethel Waters** and styled her hair when she was in Chicago in 1938. Waters was so impressed she offered to take Morgan back to New York City with her. On the first vacation of her life, Morgan rode cross-country in Waters' car, and had a look at the New York of the 1930s. "I went on a boat ride and saw the most glamorous women, all dressed up. I wanted to stay." She returned to Chicago for her family's approval, got it, and returned to New York for good.

Morgan was soon a success. In six months she had enough business to open her own shop, in the converted kitchen of a friend's apartment. She was soon able to hire five more operators, but she needed more room. She joined another friend, Olivia Clark, and took a ten-year lease on a dilapidated mansion, which she renovated into the "Rose Meta House of Beauty." Not everyone had faith in her. She notes, "All the men I knew thought I was out of my mind—doomed to failure. They said I didn't know anything about renovation. But I'm in a business where a woman has to take care of herself. I've never been afraid to take the next step, to take on responsibilities." The place was a spectacular success.

Three years later, the Rose Meta House of Beauty had grown into the largest black-owned beauty shop in the nation. In the late 1940s, Morgan opened a line of Rose Meta cosmetics. It was well-marketed and priced just right—another natural success. Next, Morgan began staging elaborate fashion shows to expose the public to her beauty ideas. These were glamorous social events held at the Rockland Palace in Harlem, or the Renaissance Casino. Thousands of people came. Morgan had become the grand dame of Harlem fashion.

By the mid-fifties Morgan wanted to open a new, more chic establishment. She purchased the shell of a building, with plans to spend a quarter of a million dollars on renovation and decor. Able to raise most of the money herself, she only needed a $25,000 loan to finish the work. The bank where she had deposited three million dollars over twenty years refused her the loan. She got the loan from another bank, and later went on to found two banks of her own that weren't afraid to make loans to members of minorities.

When the Rose Morgan House of Beauty opened in 1955, women stood in line for blocks to enter. The mayor's wife cut the ribbon, and 10,000 attended. It was a hit from the beginning. Morgan made $200,000 the first year.

In 1955 Morgan married Joe Louis, who was then retired as heavyweight boxing champion. Although he had earned five million dollars before retiring as champion, he owed one million in back taxes, a debt that continued to haunt him. Morgan and he were the society couple of the season. Their wedding was mobbed by reporters. Count Basie played at the reception.

As a couple, Morgan and Louis tried several joint business ventures, most of which were successful. In one of the few ventures that didn't work, Morgan was merely ahead of her time. She packaged *My Man,* a cologne for men. Unfortunately, black men of the fifties were not ready for the concept. Although the marriage was annulled in 1958, Morgan and Louis retained a lasting respect for each other.

In the 1960s Morgan married Louis Saunders, an attorney. Together they founded Bethune Federal Savings and Loan in New Jersey. They separated after two years, although they never filed for divorce. Morgan left the savings and loan project, returned to New York, and soon joined the group forming the Freedom National Bank. She remained one of the bank's largest stockholders.

In 1972 Morgan opened a franchise business, Trim-Away Figure Contouring. In addition to her business ventures, Morgan also did a great deal to help others. She was the director of the Interracial Council for Business Opportunity, the vice president of the **National Council of Negro Women,** and a life member of the NAACP. She was on the Task Force Economic Advisors Committee to the Mayor of New York, on the board of directors of Kilimanjaro African Coffee, and a board trustee of several other institutions.

Morgan, who still cuts a glamorous figure, currently resides in New York City.

ANDRA MEDEA

Murray, Joan   (1941–)

She was the first black female news anchor on national television and, later, the owner of the largest black-owned advertising company in the United States. Joan Elizabeth Murray worked her way up against the odds and rose to success in two different, highly competitive fields.

Murray was born with her identical twin June on November 6, 1941, in Ithaca, New York. Her father, Isaiah William Hunter, was a Fulbright scholar, and later a construction worker and union executive. Her mother was Amanda Pearl Yates Murray.

Murray spent one year at Ithaca College in upstate New York before moving to New York City with her sister. Their intention was to go to school and break into television. Going to school was the easy part. She first attended Hunter College, then the New School for Social Research and the French Institute.

Breaking into television proved to be more difficult. It was during the early days of the civil rights movement, and African Americans were not readily accepted into this high-paying field. Murray first found work as a court reporter, then, in 1960, became a secretary-assistant in the press information department at CBS. In 1963, she was hired by Alan Funt as production assistant/script assistant on the weekly series "Candid Camera." She stayed at this job only six months. In the meantime, she had been pursuing her modeling career, and she and her sister June were been hired for the first series of television commercials to target black consumers.

Murray's first serious break in news reporting came when she was hired for the NBC daytime show "Women on the Move" in 1963. Murray was hired to write segments and also appear on the air to present light news features. The show was canceled two years later. Murray decided to write CBS suggesting that they hire her. CBS had no black reporters on the air at the time. The letter gained her an audition, and she was hired a week later. She thus became the first black woman correspondent for a major news show.

Murray also worked on special projects. She covered a number of historic events, such as Nikita Khrushchev's visit to the United States, the Kennedy-Nixon debates, and the assassination of Martin Luther King, Jr. She worked with famed newsmen such as Edward R. Murrow and Walter Cronkite. She also worked on documentaries of famous figures such as President Eisenhower and poet Carl Sandburg. In 1968, Murray published a memoir of her life in television titled *A Week with the News*.

In 1969 Murray left television reporting to found her own advertising agency, Zebra Associates. Once again she was a success. Zebra became the largest black-owned advertising agency in the United States at that time, acquiring clients that included Gulf Oil, General Foods, and Gillette. She continued to head the agency until 1976.

Murray has lectured at universities across the United States and overseas. She has won more than seventy-six major awards, including the Urban League's Certificate of Merit, the **Mary McLeod Bethune** Achievement Award, and Media Woman of the Year. She is also a board member of the Dance Theater of Harlem and a former member of the board of directors of the National Center for Voluntary Action.

Aside from her many other accomplishments, Murray is an avid amateur pilot and was the first black woman to enter the Powder Puff Derby.

ANDRA MEDEA

N

Nelson, Jill   (1952–   )

She was an activist, feminist and freelance writer who accepted a lucrative job with the *Washington Post*. The job was not exactly satisfactory, but the experience gave rise to Jill Nelson's first book, *Volunteer Slavery*. This book spoke to black women trying to earn a living in corporate America and earned Nelson a place as an author and essayist.

Born in Harlem in 1952, Nelson was the daughter of Dr. Stanley Earl Nelson and A'Lelia Ransom Nelson. Her father grew up under hard conditions in Washington, D.C., but as an adult developed a successful practice in reconstructive dentistry. By the time Nelson was twelve, the family had moved from Harlem to the upper-middle class world of West End Avenue.

Her father had to threaten a lawsuit to get the family into their building, but once there, they were determined to be upper-middle class. Her family had the good things in life, including a large New York apartment, and a vacation home on the beautiful island of Martha's Vineyard. Nelson received two strong messages during her growing up—be a good "race-woman" and be a material success.

Nelson attended private schools and then went to City College of New York. She gave birth to her daughter Misumbo at the age of twenty but stayed in college and graduated in 1977. From 1979 to 1980, she attended graduate school at the Columbia School of Journalism, earning her M.S.

Nelson and her daughter Misumbo made their home in Greenwich Village. Nelson was a freelance writer for such publications as *Essence*, the *Village Voice, USA Weekend, Ms.*, and the *New York Times*. She spent a year on Martha's Vineyard but otherwise called New York City home.

By 1986 the freelance lifestyle was starting to wear thin. She was paying her rent, but she wanted to provide something better for her daughter. When the *Washington Post* offered her more than double her income to move to Washington and become an employee, she took the offer.

It was not a good match from the start. The corporate culture was cold, competitive, and alien. Nelson had to fight for the black point of view. By late 1986, she and others had pulled together a women's caucus at the *Post*, and by 1988 she was challenging management about discriminatory hiring practices. Nelson and the union filed a discrimination complaint tracing discriminatory hiring and salary practices going back to 1988. In 1990, Nelson left the *Post* and went back to New York.

Once again a freelancer, Nelson decided to write about her years at the *Post*. Her book was titled *Volunteer Slavery: My Authentic Negro Experience*. The book was first published by Noble Press, a small African-American publisher in Chicago. After achieving success, it was picked up by

Penguin Paperbacks, one of the large publishing houses in New York.

Nelson now has a contract with G. P. Putnam to publish a collection of essays and commentary. Emphasizing humor and insight, this book will also be a view of the world through the eyes of a black woman. Nelson remains an activist, feminist, and writer in search of integrity.

ANDRA MEDEA

O

Oglesby, Mary (1915–)

"I've been fooling people for years," teacher, aviator, and community activist Mary Oglesby once said, "letting them think I've been working, but I've been having fun."

Mary Oglesby was born January 6, 1915, to Melinda (Dunham) and Charles Owings in Portsmouth, Ohio. Her mother's family came from Madagascar, and her father was a Cherokee Indian from Oklahoma. They met and married in Chicago when Melinda was fifteen and Charles was fifty-one. Mary's mother died on January 8, 1915, leaving behind an eleven-month-old daughter and two-day-old Mary. Charles Owings raised Mary and her sister during their early years with the help of a German woman who came in to cook, clean, and do the laundry.

As a Civil War soldier, Charles Owings had already contributed to history before his daughters were born. In 1865, he presented the flag to President Abraham Lincoln at the Appomattox Courthouse in Virginia during General Robert E. Lee's surrender to General Ulysses S. Grant, signalling the end of the Civil War.

By 1918, Owings had moved the girls to Glenellen, Indiana, where Mary began elementary school at age four because her sister was already in school and her father was at work—there was no one home to take care of her. When the school sent Mary home because she was too young to attend, her father took her to the school and insisted that they accept her because he would not leave her home unattended.

The family moved between Chicago and various sections of Ohio. The girls completed East High School in Xenia, Ohio, about three miles from Wilberforce. When their father died they moved back to Chicago and lived with the family of their first cousin, **Katherine Dunham**, the renowned choreographer, dancer, and anthropologist. Both Mary and her sister received scholarships for academic achievement and attended Joliet Junior College in Illinois. From there they completed their bachelor's degrees at **Howard University**, where Mary majored in physical education and her sister majored in home economics. Mary had the counsel of surrogate mother Mary Rose Reeves Allen at Howard, whom she addressed as "Lady Allen." Lady Allen was head of physical education at Howard and guided primarily Mary, but also her sister, toward their professional careers. While at Howard Mary studied African history with Leo Hansberry (**Lorraine Hansberry**'s uncle), dance with Violet Warfield, and studied anatomy, kinesiology, physical therapy, and physiology with Allen. Mary graduated from Howard in 1937 and accepted a teaching offer in Indianapolis, where she has remained ever since. She has continued her graduate work at Butler, Purdue, and the University of Michigan.

As a child Mary often "dreamed of jumping off a house and floating away."

She used to take umbrellas down to the barn and jump out of the hayloft window. She always wanted to fly.

Mary married in 1944, after which she and her husband began to travel the country by car. One day she suggested that they learn to fly. They located a training school at the Plainfield Airport in Plainfield, Indiana, that provided basic training, classroom work on the mechanics and the parts of an airplane, and hands-on experience in flying aircraft. Mary Oglesby received her student pilot's license on August 8, 1946, and her private pilot's license on October 27, 1946. She and her husband took lessons together. Oglesby's husband was jealous because on September 21, 1946, she soloed cross-country in an airplane before he did.

Oglesby was in one crash, on December 4, 1948. The plane was piloted by a third party and she and her husband were passengers. They were flying in inclement weather when the pilot descended too rapidly and hit a tree limb; her head hit the gyro-compass, resulting in a compound fracture of the skull. Oglesby had a cranial operation during which a permanent plate was placed in her head. She resumed flying in 1949.

Oglesby is a major in the Indiana Wing Civil Air Patrol, which participates in search-and-rescue missions for downed aircraft. She is a commandant for women cadets during drill competitions. For more than forty years she has flown a Cessna 150 on search-and-rescue missions.

Mary Oglesby has devoted her life to others. For approximately forty-eight years she has taught health classes, physical education, driver education, and safety at Crispus Attucks High School. She was a swimming coach for fifteen years and a basketball, track, and volleyball coach for three years. She taught swimming for fifteen years for the Fall Creek **Young Women's Christian Association** and still teaches swimming at Washington High School in Indianapolis. Retired and widowed, Oglesby is physically fit and continues to serve others. She drives daily up and down the roads of Indiana picking up food from farmers and merchants to donate to the homeless. She organizes volunteers who come to a church on Sundays to cook and serve a decent dinner to the homeless community. Her daughter Mona is an international flight attendant and interpreter for deaf travelers.

ELIZABETH HADLEY FREYDBERG

P

Payne, Ethel L.   (1911–1991)

Known as the "first lady of the black press," Ethel L. Payne built a reputation as a hard-hitting and insightful reporter for the *Chicago Defender,* covering and participating in the major events of the modern civil rights movement and becoming the first black woman journalist to specialize in international news.

Ethel Lois Payne was born in Chicago on August 14, 1911. Her father worked as a Pullman porter; her mother taught high school Latin. After briefly attending two colleges and working as a clerk at the Chicago Public Library, Payne, in 1948,

"The first lady of the black press," Ethel Payne was the Chicago Defender's *one-person Washington bureau during the 1950s. During the 1952 Democratic National Convention, she interviewed presidential candidate Adlai E. Stevenson.* (RODGER STREITMATTER)

became a hostess for an Army Special Services club in Japan.

Payne, who never married, was led into journalism by a diary she kept while in Japan. She showed her diary to a *Chicago Defender* reporter who had traveled to Japan on his way to cover the Korean war. The reporter took the diary back to Chicago, and the *Defender* ran excerpts on its front page. After the editor telephoned Payne and offered her a job, she returned to Chicago and began reporting full time in 1951. After two years in Chicago, Payne became the *Defender*'s one-person bureau in Washington, D.C.

Payne arrived in the nation's capital as the modern civil rights movement was beginning. She doggedly covered legislative and judicial battles on Capitol Hill and then presented the results—or lack of results—in her blunt, straightforward style. By 1954, Payne had established herself as a tough reporter and powerful writer. That same year black reporters named her their "newsman's newsman," the Washington reporter who best exemplified high journalistic standards.

Payne received national attention in 1954 when, during a White House press conference, she asked President Dwight D. Eisenhower when he planned to ban segregation in interstate travel. Eisenhower barked back that he refused to support any special interest. Front-page stories in the *Washington Post* and *Washington Evening Star* characterized Eisenhower as being "annoyed" by the question and described him as responding in "clipped words." After the incident, Eisenhower refused to recognize Payne during press conferences, but members of the White House press corps said her question helped move civil rights onto the national agenda.

Payne never claimed to be an objective reporter. Instead, she called herself an advocacy journalist. During an interview for an oral history project, Payne said:

> If you have lived through the black experience in this country, you feel that every day you're assaulted by the system. You are either acquiescent, which I think is wrong, or else you just rebel, and you kick against it. I wanted to constantly, constantly, constantly hammer away, raise the questions that needed to be raised.

Although Payne was assigned to Washington, she volunteered to traverse the Deep South in order to chronicle the historic events erupting there. In 1956, she reported on the Montgomery bus boycott and desegregation efforts at the University of Alabama. In 1957, she traveled to Arkansas to cover efforts to desegregate Central High School in Little Rock. She carried a sign during the 1963 demonstrations in Birmingham, and when 250,000 activists marched on Washington that same year, Payne was among them. Two years later, she joined 15,000 marchers who walked from Selma to Montgomery to demand voting rights, and when President Lyndon B. Johnson signed the Civil Rights Act of 1964 and the Voting Rights Act of 1965, he asked Payne to join him in the Oval Office for the historic occasions.

Because Payne both reported on and participated in history as it was being made, she suffered much verbal and physical abuse from segregationists. During her oral history interview, Payne recalled the angry mob that faced her in Selma:

You could just feel the hatred. It was just like an enveloping cloak around you. I'll never forget the faces, the contorted faces of housewives, standing out and screaming like they were just lunatics from the asylum: "Nigger! Nigger! Nigger!"

In the mid-1960s, Payne shifted her attention to international affairs and reported from thirty countries on six continents. In 1966, Payne traveled to Vietnam to report on black troops fighting in the war. In 1969, she covered the Nigerian Civil War. A year later, she joined Secretary of State William P. Rogers for a ten-nation tour of Africa, and two years after that traveled to Zaire to attend the First Ordinary Congress of the Popular Revolution Movement. Later in the 1970s, Payne visited the People's Republic of China, reported on the International Women's Year Conference in Mexico City, and accompanied Secretary of State Henry Kissinger on a six-nation tour of Africa.

Payne broke new ground for journalists of her race and gender by becoming the first black female commentator employed by a national broadcast network. Three times a week from 1972 to 1982, Payne shared her views with listeners and viewers of the *Spectrum* public affairs program on CBS, first on radio and later on television.

In 1973, at the same time that she worked part time as a network commentator, she was promoted to associate editor of the *Defender,* in charge of its Chicago news operation. Payne left the *Defender* in 1978 and wrote a syndicated column for black newspapers from Florida to California. She died in her Washington, D.C., home on May 28, 1991.

Throughout her forty years of covering the modern civil rights movement and international affairs, Payne was respected as a professional journalist of the highest caliber. Her pithy writing style and fearless reporting combined to raise the standard of black female journalists. After her death, the *Washington Post* on June 2, 1991, carried a tribute to Payne, stating:

> Her voice was low, but her questions were piercing, and her reports on the world were cherished by millions of readers. The proof of professionalism—fairness, straightforward accounts of all sides and independence of views—were in her writings.

RODGER STREITMATTER

Phinazee, Alethia (1920–1983)

A good library, to Alethia Phinazee, is as essential to the nourishment of the mind as food is to the nourishment of the body. Her single-minded dedication to this premise has had a lasting impact on the practice of librarianship in America.

Born on July 25, 1920, in Orangeburg, South Carolina, Phinazee received a bachelor of arts degree from Fisk University in 1939 and a bachelor of library science degree in 1941 from the University of Illinois. After teaching library science at Caswell County Training School in North Carolina, she returned to the University of Illinois, where she earned a master's degree in 1948. In 1961, she became the first woman to receive a doctorate in library science from Columbia University.

After receiving her doctorate, Phinazee taught at the Atlanta University School of Library Science from 1963 to 1969, when she resigned to found the Cooperative

College Library Center in Atlanta. She served as director of the center through 1970. She also held various nonteaching posts as librarian at Talladega College, Lincoln University (Missouri), Southern Illinois University, and Atlanta University.

In 1970, Phinazee became dean of the School of Library Science at North Carolina Central University. Working tirelessly to win accreditation for the school from the American Library Association (ALA), she eventually succeeded and established the school's program in early childhood librarianship. Having distinguished herself as a national leader in the profession, she distinguished herself in North Carolina when she was elected the first African-American president of the state ALA. In 1978, Governor Jim Hunt granted her the first two four-year terms on the Public Librarian Certification Commission. In the same year, she also served as chair of the Council of Deans and Directors of the Association of American Library Schools.

An ALA activist, Phinazee was cochair of an ALA-sponsored Institute on Use of Library of Congress Classification, served four years on the ALA Council, and was first chair of its Standing Committee on Library Education. In 1980, friends and colleagues throughout the country nominated her to run for the presidency of the ALA. She described herself at the time as a "possible-ist" seeking effective ALA continuing-education programs, equitable dues, and shorter conferences.

A prolific author and respected speaker, Phinazee was chair and editor of proceedings for two major library conferences: "Materials by and about American Negroes" in 1965 and "The Georgia Child's Access to Materials Pertaining to Negro Americans" in 1967.

She died on September 17, 1983.

ARTHUR C. GUNN

Pleasant, Mary Ellen   (1814–1904)

Mary Ellen Pleasant arrived in San Francisco during the Gold Rush heyday, probably sometime in 1849. In the next fifty years she worked as cook, accountant, abolitionist, and entrepreneur in the

A legend in San Francisco, where she was restaurateur, entrepreneur, labor boss, and possibly madam, Mary Ellen Pleasant also supported abolitionists around the country. She was the target of what one historian calls an "avid controversy" that sought to silence her, and it was said that she harbored the skeletons of San Francisco's elite in her closet. (SCHOMBURG CENTER)

bustling town on the bay. Histories of the West describe her as madam, voodoo queen, and prostitute. Pleasant herself requested that the words "she was a friend of John Brown's" be printed on her gravestone, indicating her own desire to be remembered as an abolitionist. She was the target of what one historian calls an "avid conspiracy" that sought to silence her, and it was said that she harbored the skeletons of San Francisco's elite in her closet.

Sources report conflicting stories of her background (some say she was from Georgia, others Virginia), but Pleasant herself claimed she was born on August 19, 1814, in Philadelphia. She described her mother as a free colored woman and her father as a wealthy planter. Pleasant was educated on Nantucket by the Hussey family. She appeared to have spent time in Boston where she met William Lloyd Garrison and other abolitionists, including Alexander Smith, whom she married. Smith was a wealthy Cuban planter and, upon his death, willed Pleasant a considerable sum that most sources estimate at $45,000. Smith intended her to use the money for abolitionist causes. Her second husband, John James Pleasant, joined Mary Ellen in San Francisco sometime between 1848 and 1852, but he does not figure prominently in the records of her California career. Pleasant had one child, Elizabeth Smith, but little is known of her beyond an 1866 report in the *Elevator*, a black newspaper, that Pleasant sponsored a lavish wedding for her daughter at the African Methodist Episcopal Zion Church in San Francisco.

Pleasant spent time in Canada in the late 1850s, working in the community of black abolitionists and fugitive slaves stationed near Chatham. She and John Pleasant, along with **Mary Ann Shadd [Cary]**, Martin Delaney, and others, were members of the Chatham Vigilance Committee, organized to aid escaped slaves after the passage of the 1850 Fugitive Slave Act. Pleasant also bought real estate in Chatham in 1858. She reported that she met John Brown in Chatham, where the raid on Harpers Ferry was planned, and that she gave him financial support for his activities.

By the 1860s, she had returned to San Francisco and become a restaurateur and investor. San Francisco's thriving elite provided an eager market for her elegant restaurants and boardinghouses, where she entertained some of the West's most famous financiers. Her best-known establishment, at 920 Washington Street (in the heart of today's Chinatown), was the meeting place for some of the city's most prominent politicians, including Newton Booth, elected as governor of California in 1871. In the private domain of Pleasant's kitchens and dining rooms, she was privy to information about San Francisco's most powerful businessmen and politicians.

Pleasant also ran laundries in which she employed black men and women. She operated an extensive employment network for the black population of the city, supplying the chief employers of African Americans—mining moguls turned hotel owners—with most of their labor force. In this way she functioned as a city boss, running an informal employment agency in black San Francisco. Her efforts to improve conditions for African Americans in the West extended beyond the workplace; she harbored fugitive slaves and fought for passage of an 1863 law guaranteeing black Americans the right to testify in court. Pleasant also challenged Jim

Crow laws in her landmark case against the North Beach Railroad Company in 1868. She was awarded $500 in damages after drivers refused to allow her to board the streetcar, but the case was appealed.

In 1884, Pleasant again appeared in court. This time it was as a witness in the highly publicized trial *Sharon* v. *Sharon*. Stories of the trial and Pleasant's testimony were common fare in national as well as local papers, indicating that Pleasant's entrepreneurial reputation was well known. Further, her role in the trial was pivotal as she testified to the authenticity of a marriage contract between mining mogul and Nevada senator William Sharon and Sarah Althea Hill. Pleasant reportedly funded Hill's case, which was eventually thrown out of court, and press coverage of Pleasant likened her to a scheming voodoo queen.

Pleasant was well aware of the distortions her character suffered in the press: "You tell those newspaper people that they may be smart, but I'm smarter. They deal with words. Some folks say that words were made to reveal thought. That ain't so. Words were made to conceal thought."

Pleasant died in San Francisco in 1904. All that remains of the mansion she had built, on the corner of Octavia and Bush Streets in San Francisco, are the eucalyptus trees she planted. Her legend—although tangled—reveals the financial genius of a nineteenth-century African-American woman whose power, at the very least, inspired mythology and imagination.

LYNN HUDSON

Procope, Ernesta G. (1929–)

In 1953, Ernesta G. Procope was selling low-cost homeowners insurance policies to

Ernesta Procope founded the E.G. Bowman Company in 1953, providing homeowners insurance to African-American families. By 1995, Bowman was a $30 million company, insuring universities, churches, and top corporations. Procope's success earned her the nickname "First Lady of Wall Street." (E.G. BOWMAN COMPANY)

residents of Brooklyn's Bedford-Stuyvesant neighborhood. Today, she is the president and chief executive officer of the nation's largest African-American-owned insurance brokerage company, with an estimated thirty million dollars in annual premiums. The business, E.G. Bowman Company, is Procope's creation, and she is the mighty force behind its growth from a small, neighborhood company to a giant in the industry, insuring universities, churches, and top corporations, including PepsiCo, IBM, Tiffany, and Time Warner.

Born in Brooklyn, New York, Ernesta G. Procope was one of four children born to Clarence and Elvira Lord Foster, immigrants of West Indian descent who moved to Brooklyn's Bedford-Stuyvesant neighborhood in the early 1900s. She studied music when a child, and showed talent on the piano, performing in a concert at Carnegie Hall at the age of thirteen. She graduated from the High School of Music and Art and attended Brooklyn College.

But it was not in music that Procope would make her real mark. Encouraged by her first husband—a real estate developer named Albin Bowman, whom she married in the late 1940s—Procope studied at the Pohs Institute of Insurance and Real Estate. She earned her real estate license, opening up a whole new world to her—the world of business.

Procope's career began with managing insurance coverage for the properties that her husband bought and sold. It was a challenge, but Procope's perseverance and meticulous attention to detail served her well. By the time of Bowman's death in 1952, her business acumen had developed, her skills were sharp, and she was determined to succeed on her own terms.

Procope founded the E.G. Bowman Company in 1953, providing homeowners insurance to African-American families. Her timing could not have been better. African Americans were making strong progress economically, and the demand for insurance was on the rise. Procope's business boomed.

But disaster threatened in the late 1960s, when urban rioting brought destruction to many American cities. Large insurance companies began the practice of "redlining" minority neighborhoods, making it impossible for property owners in high-risk areas to purchase insurance. In one day, one of Procope's fire insurers canceled insurance for eighty-eight accounts. Clearly this could not go on. Procope took it upon herself to lobby Governor Nelson Rockefeller personally on the redlining issue. She was instrumental in the establishment of New York State's Fair Plan in 1968, making insurance available to all New York State property owners.

For Procope, the redlining scare was a wake-up call, pointing out the need to diversify her business if the E.G. Bowman Company was to survive. So, in 1969, she began to seek commercial and government insurance accounts. New affirmative action policies provided a foot in the door toward steady income and increased profits.

In 1969, Procope wrote a letter to Philip Baecker, director of risk management at PepsiCo, explaining that she was a minority insurance broker who wanted to do business with "mainstream America." In short order, PepsiCo became E.G. Bowman Company's first large commercial account. According to Baecker, "The reality is that we talked to them because of that first letter, but we gave them a shot and they delivered. They had no inside track. They earned the right to grow."

And grow they did. In 1979, Procope moved the E.G. Bowman Company to new offices in the heart of New York City's financial district, bringing the firm into the mainstream of commercial brokerage. The E.G. Bowman Company became the insurance broker for the United States portion of the Alaskan Pipeline, the Fulbright Scholars of the U.S. Information Agency, and provided a pension plan for the employees of Conrail. The company also continued to garner commercial clients such as Avon Products, Pfizer, and Philip Morris. Procope's success earned her the nickname "The First Lady of Wall Street."

Procope has managed to ensure the survival of her company in the risky insurance industry through hard work, tenacity, and, above all, responsiveness to the needs of her clients. "If you're not responsive, something will fall between the cracks," says Procope. "That's my theme song." She makes it company policy to listen when clients express their views and to make changes when and where appropriate. Procope also believes in making sure that people know about her company's longevity. In 1993, the company letterhead trumpeted the company's forty-year track record with a special commemorative seal. "If you've been in business for forty years, you must be doing something right," she says.

Dynamic, ambitious, and energetic, Procope continues to set new challenges for herself. In 1991, she formed a partnership with her second husband, John Procope, and financier Alan Bond to found an investment company—Bond, Procope Capital Management. Says Procope, "We invested because we thought there is a market for pension funds to be managed by minority money managers." Indeed. In just two years, they managed to attract assets of $315 million dollars.

On top of all her other activities, she is on the boards of three Fortune 500 companies and has been a member of the Board of Trustees of Adelphi University for fifteen years, and chairperson of the Board from 1993 to 1997.

Procope's trailblazing efforts and notable success have not gone unnoticed. She was honored as Woman of the Year by First Lady Pat Nixon, appointed by President Ford as Special Ambassador to Gambia, and has received honorary doctor of law degrees from **Howard University,** Adelphi University, and Marymount Manhattan College.

CHRISTINE SUMPTION

Proctor, Barbara Gardner   (1933–)

The odds certainly seemed to be against Barbara Proctor, but she didn't see it that way. Turning disadvantage to gain is a reason she cites for her steady successes through life up to her multimillion-dollar business in the advertising world.

Even the name choice for the Chicago firm she founded in 1970 and of which she is chief executive officer and creative director—Proctor & Gardner Advertising, Inc.—showed pluck and cunning. The use of both her maiden name, Gardner, and her marriage name, Proctor, allowed potential clients to believe a man existed as her partner and equal. And she knowingly exploited the ring of respectability in a name not unlike Proctor & Gamble's.

Proctor was born November 30, 1933, in Black Mountain, North Carolina, the only child of a single mother but raised by her grandmother and her uncle. A scholarship took her to Talladega College in Talladega, Alabama, where she studied in the 1950s and graduated with B.A. degrees in English, education, and sociology. There she won, in 1954, the Armstrong Creative Writing Award.

She then moved permanently to Chicago, where her writing was devoted to jazz. Marriage to a road manager for **Sarah Vaughn** produced one son before the couple's divorce. Starting in 1958 Proctor was a *Downbeat* magazine critic and contributing editor and also wrote television specials, a column for a South Side Chicago newspaper, and snippets for jazz books.

Beginning in 1961, Proctor wrote liner notes for Vee-Jay Records International in Chicago. This work led to her becoming the company's international director. She held that position in 1963 when the company released the first Beatles single in the United States.

Soon, however, Proctor began to focus her special combination of writing and business skills on advertising— "the single most important way of reaching everyone in America," she would later say. She was a partner in Post-Keys-Gardner Advertising from 1965 to 1968, an employee of Gene Taylor Associates from 1968 to 1969, and copy supervisor for North Advertising Agency from 1969 to 1970. North fired her after she refused to work on a hair-product campaign parodying civil rights marches.

Concluding that white-controlled agencies were unable or unwilling to reach black consumers, or to know their needs and tastes, she formed Proctor & Gardner with an $80,000 loan from the Small Business Administration. Instead of seeking many small clients, which was usually the strategy of new agencies, she sought a few large ones and got accounts with Jewel Food Stores, Sears, Kraft Foods, and Gillette.

Proctor approached these companies with the idea that they should hire her firm, not in spite of the fact that she was a black woman, but because of it. She offered to help them target the black market. Within a year the company acquired new offices and increased its initial staff of three to twenty-three, and within a few years it became, despite odds and earlier skepticism, the world's largest black-owned advertising agency.

In the time since, she has retained her initial clients and gained many others. One is the G. Heileman Brewing Company, but she has steadfastly refused to take on accounts with alcohol, drug, or tobacco companies who, in her opinion, aim "dubious advertising pitches" at women and minorities. "I feel a deep responsibility for my work," she says.

GARY HOUSTON

Q

Quarles, Norma R. (1936–)

As the first woman in New York City to co-anchor a six P.M. news program, television journalist Norma R. Quarles is a pioneer in the field of broadcasting, paving the way for women in a traditionally male-dominated domain. She has won many awards for her incisive reporting, including an Emmy, and she was inducted into the National Association of Black Journalists Hall of Fame in 1990.

Norma Quarles was born in New York City on November 11, 1936. She is an alumna of Hunter College and City College of New York. She began her career first as a retail buyer and then as a real estate broker from 1957 to 1965, when she moved into the field of broadcasting as a reporter, disc jockey, and public service director for WSDM Radio in Chicago. The following year, Quarles transferred to television and attended a one-year news training program sponsored by NBC in New York. In 1967, she moved to Cleveland, Ohio, where she was news reporter and anchor for WKYC-TV for three years. She then went back to WNBC-TV in New York, this time as a reporter. While filling in as host of a women's show for three weeks, Quarles performed so well that the network offered her the position of anchor of the six P.M. newscast—the first time a woman had been given such a significant broadcasting position in New York.

In her work for WNBC over the next twenty-one years, Quarles was the recipient of many awards. In 1973, her news reporting about the documentary *The Stripper* won Quarles the Front Page Award. That same year she was awarded a Sigma Delta Chi Deadline Club Award. While working for WMAQ-TV, the NBC affiliate in Chicago, Quarles received an Emmy Award for outstanding reporting on her *Urban Journal* series. In 1984, she was chosen as a panelist for the League of Women Voters-

Emmy Award–winning reporter Norma Quarles was the first woman to anchor a six o'clock newscast in New York City. She is currently a correspondent and reporter for Cable News Network, based in CNN's New York office. (CNN)

131

sponsored vice presidential debate. Quarles is a member of the National Academy of Television Arts and Sciences and Sigma Delta Chi, and she is a member of the board of governors of the National Academy of Television Arts and Sciences.

Norma Quarles left NBC in 1988 to join Cable News Network (CNN), where she has served as co-anchor of the *Daybreak* and *Daywatch* programs. She also is a correspondent and reporter based in CNN's New York office. Divorced, she is the mother of two children, Lawrence and Susan. A notable success in her own right, Norma Quarles has also helped open doors for a new generation of women and black reporters.

FENELLA MACFARLANE

R

Randolph, Lucille (1883–1963)

Lucille Randolph was the wife of activist A. Philip Randolph and provided critical financial assistance for his publication, the *Messenger*. The youngest of seven children of William and Josephine Campbell, former slaves, Lucille Campbell was born April 15, 1883, in Christiansburg, a small town in western Virginia.

To enhance her skills as a teacher, she attended **Howard University**, where she met a law student named William Joseph Green. After he graduated in 1911, they married and moved to New York City, where he worked in the U.S. Customs Service, but he soon died.

Her life took a new turn. By 1914, she had gone into business with Amy E. Weddington, operating a Madam Walker beauty parlor on West 135th Street, and she had met and married another newcomer from the South, A. Philip Randolph. In 1915, after she met Chandler Owen at a party at Madam Walker's, she introduced her new friend to her new husband, and Owen became his partner and a central figure in his development.

When A. Philip Randolph and Chandler Owen began publishing the *Messenger* in 1917, Lucille Randolph's earnings at the beauty salon produced crucial financing for the enterprise. Speaking for himself and for Owen about those early years, A. Philip Randolph later said, "She carried us." More specifically, he declared that without his wife's money, "We couldn't have started the *Messenger*." It was the *Messenger* that brought him to the attention of the people who, in 1925, asked him to take the lead in organizing what became the Brotherhood of Sleeping Car Porters, the foundation for all his subsequent work.

By the mid-1920s, her beauty business had faded, and in subsequent years she spent much of her time in community work, particularly with the men and women in porters' families. For example, in the early 1930s she served as vice president of the Harlem Housewives League, a group in the incipient "Don't Buy Where You Can't Work" campaign that emerged in New York and elsewhere during the Depression decade. While A. Philip Randolph spent much of his time traveling about the country and she stayed in Manhattan, they kept in touch by mail, "Buddy" writing "Buddy," as their limited surviving correspondence from the 1940s and 1950s shows. They had no children. By the early 1950s, she was an invalid. She died in New York on April 12, 1963, just months before her husband led the great March on Washington.

PETER WALLENSTEIN

Rhone, Sylvia (1952–)

There have been many great black women recording artists—**Bessie Smith**, **Ella Fitzgerald**, and **Billie Holiday**, to name just a few. But there have been few black women recording executives, the ones who

After Sylvia Rhone graduated from the Wharton School of Finance and Commerce, she went into banking but hated it. Rhone found her niche in the music industry instead and would become the first black woman to be the CEO of a major recording company.
(EASTWEST RECORDS AMERICA)

make the decisions that affect the destinies of those recording stars. Sylvia Rhone has broken through the obstacles of race and gender prejudice and become the first black woman chief executive officer (CEO) of a major recording company.

Born in 1952 in Philadelphia, Rhone grew up in Harlem. She went to the famed Wharton School of Finance and Commerce at the University of Pennsylvania, and graduated with a bachelor's degree in economics in 1974. She returned to New York the same year and joined Bankers Trust, a prestigious—and conservative—institution. The job was all a well-trained economist could want, and Rhone hated it. After

a year she gave it up to become a secretary at Buddha Records, starting at the bottom of the ladder.

The recording industry turned out to be right for her. She was soon promoted to promotions coordinator at Buddha and then was asked to handle national promotions for a newly started label. She had never handled national promotions for anything before. It was a sink-or-swim situation, but she succeeded and was then asked to handle promotions for a series of other labels.

Apart from promotions, Rhone began to establish a reputation for discovering and developing black talent. In 1985, Atlantic Records hired her away from Buddha to become its director of national black music promotion. Atlantic had once had an outstanding line-up of black stars, but those stars were slipping away. **Aretha Franklin** left Atlantic in 1980 after twelve years of hits and went to a different label. The company was failing to secure new black stars. It wanted Rhone to reestablish their strength in black music and discover new talent for them. She did.

After being promoted to vice president and general manager of black music operations, Rhone was made a senior vice president in 1988. The same year, Atlantic Records was declared by *Billboard* magazine to have the number one black music division.

After being so successful at building divisions and labels, the next step for Rhone would be to head her own operation. In 1991, she was made co-president and CEO of EastWest Records America. Late that same year, Atlantic created Atco-EastWest Records, representing a broader range of music, from pop to blues to rap. Rhone was named chief executive officer and chair.

Rhone's next major coup was to be made chair and CEO of the Elektra Entertainment Group. This involved a delicate merger between her own music group, EastWest, and two other groups, Elektra and Sire Records. A consolidation of temperamental stars and equally temperamental managers can be fraught with hazards, but Rhone negotiated the merger successfully.

Aside from her corporate work, Rhone is on the board of directors of the Alvin Ailey American Dance Theater, the Studio Museum of Harlem, the Rock and Roll Hall of Fame, and the R&B Foundation. She has been honored with more than two dozen awards, including Sony's Soul of American Music Excellence Award, the Urban Network's Executive of the Year Award, and the 1995 Herbert H. Wright Award from the National Association of Market Developers.

ANDRA MEDEA

Rollins, Charlemae Hill (1897–1979)

When children ask baffling questions about life, parents and teachers must find answers that are honest and satisfying. Artists offer answers through their pictures, musicians through their music, and authors through honest portrayal of people in their books. This was the view of Charlemae Hill Rollins, librarian, author, and children's literature specialist, who led a lifelong crusade to change the image of black people in children's literature and promote the publication of books about the black experience in American life and culture. During the thirty-six years of her professional career, Rollins taught children's literature, lectured widely, and wrote articles about the importance of storytelling and the role of books in helping young people understand themselves and the people of other cultures.

Charlemae Hill was born in Yazoo City, Mississippi, on June 20, 1897, to Allen G. and Birdie (Tucker) Hill. The family moved to Oklahoma before it became a state. She was educated in her hometown of Beggs but later attended secondary schools in St. Louis, Missouri, and Holly Springs, Mississippi. Hill attended **Howard University** and taught school for a short period of time. She received her library training at the University of Chicago and Columbia University. In 1918, she married Joseph Walker Rollins. Shortly after the birth of their son, Joseph, Jr., the family moved to Chicago, where Charlemae lived until her death on February 3, 1979.

Rollins joined the staff of the Chicago Public Library as a junior assistant in 1926. When the George C. Hall Branch of the Chicago Public Library opened in 1932, Rollins was placed in charge of the children's room. At this branch, in the heart of the black community, Rollins became popular and widely known for her storytelling, which she believed helped children escape from hate, rejection, and injustice. For middle- and working-class families and their children, she emphasized planning programs and developing the book collection so that they could find information about their heritage.

Rollins decried the absence of books about prominent black Americans and their contributions to American history, and she disparaged the distorted images of black characters in books for children and young adults. With characteristic creativity and energy, she solicited help from publishers and worked with her colleagues at the Chicago Public Library to select those materials that presented realistic portrayals of black life. Later in life she published an anthology of black folklore about Christmas and wrote accurate and respectful biographies about black poets and entertainers as well as eminent black men and women.

Rollins gained national attention for initiating, coordinating, and revising *We Build Together,* a bibliography of acceptable children's books about black people. Published by the National Council of Teachers of English in 1941, the list was revised in 1948 and 1967, during the postwar years and the civil rights movement when there was growing concern about racial prejudice. The theme of the list, that black people are human beings and should not be depicted as stereotypes, gave tangible expression to Rollins' lifelong crusade. Acknowledged as an expert on intercultural relations and children's literature, she lectured widely on these topics, taught children's literature at Roosevelt and other universities, conducted workshops on storytelling, and contributed articles to professional journals.

A recipient of numerous awards for her humanitarianism, community service, and contributions to education, Rollins received the American Brotherhood Award from the National Conference of Christians and Jews (1952), the Woman of the Year Award, Zeta Phi Beta (1956), the Good American Award of the Chicago Committee of One Hundred (1962), and the Women's National Book Association Constance Lindsay Skinner Award (1970). She was awarded the Doctor of Humane Letters from Columbia College, Chicago in 1974. Her book *Black Troubador: Langston Hughes* won the **Coretta Scott King** Award in 1971.

During the 1950s, Rollins was an active member of the American Library Association (ALA). She was a member of the ALA Council for four years, held the office of treasurer for the Children's Library Association, and served as president of the Children's Services Division (1957–58). ALA honored her contributions to children's work and literature by awarding her the American Library Association Letter (1953), the Grolier Society Award (1955), and the Children's Reading Round Table Award (1963). ALA also extended its highest award, Honorary Membership, to Rollins in 1972.

BETTY L. JENKINS

S

Saunders, Doris (1921–)

From librarian to publicist, radio and television interviewer and finally professor, Doris Saunders has been a pioneer and guide in black media. Finding her true direction in the early years at Johnson Publishing, Saunders has organized black data, written black histories, interviewed black leaders, and is now teaching the black media makers of tomorrow.

Born in Chicago on August 8, 1921, Saunders was the daughter of Thelma Rice Evans and Alvesta Stewart Evans. Her father died while she was in her early teens, and the family had to move in with her mother's parents. Her mother went to work to help support the family. While still in high school, Saunders met a young man whose mother was the noted librarian **Charlemae Rollins**. Rollins took young Saunders under her wing. The young couple did not stay together, but Rollins remained as Saunders' other mother. Soon Saunders decided that she would be a librarian, too.

Saunders attended Englewood High School in Chicago, then went to Northwestern University in 1938. After two years at Northwestern, she transferred to Central YMCA College for 1940 and 1941. She completed the Chicago Public Library Training Class, and in May, 1942, joined the Chicago Public Library as a junior library assistant. She worked her way up, and by 1947 she became the first black reference librarian.

After encountering racist remarks from one of her colleagues, Saunders nearly walked out on her library job in 1949, but Rollins advised her to find another job first. About this time, John Johnson was in his early years as a publisher, building what would become the Johnson empire, encompassing *Ebony, Jet,* and other magazines. At Rollins' suggestion, Saunders wrote to Johnson suggesting that he create a reference library on black Americans for his clients and staff. Johnson accepted the suggestion and hired her to be librarian. She began to establish an outstanding reference library on blacks in the twentieth century.

In 1950, she married Vincent E. Saunders. In 1951 she received her B.A. from Roosevelt University, which she had been attending part-time for several years.

While developing the library, Saunders could see that a great many books on black Americans had yet to be written. She persuaded Johnson to create a book division to fill the gap and was appointed head of the division. The first book launched under her care was the classic *Before the Mayflower,* by Lerone Bennett, Jr. She personally compiled the *Negro Handbook,* published in 1966.

After a conflict with the owner, Saunders left Johnson Publishing in 1966 and opened her own public relations company, Plus Factor and Information. She also wrote society and food columns for the *Chicago Daily Defender.* From 1966 to 1968, she hosted "The Doris Saunders

Show" on WBEE. She then developed a television show for WTTW, Chicago's public television station, writing and producing "Our People" from 1968 to 1972.

During the same years Saunders was working in television, she was also director of community relations for Chicago State University. She then advanced to staff associate in the chancellor's office of the University of Illinois, Chicago Circle Campus. (The college was later re-named the University of Illinois at Chicago.)

In 1972 John Johnson asked Saunders to return as head of the book division for Johnson Publishing. Johnson had fired many people, but very few had been asked back again. During her second term as head of the book division, Saunders co-authored *Black Society* (with *Jet's* remarkable society editor, **Gerri Major**), which was published in 1976. She also edited *The Day They March* (1963), and *The Kennedy Years and the Negro* (1966).

Determined to return to school for an advanced degree, Saunders attended Boston University in 1975, commuting to her publishing job in Chicago. A year later, in 1976, she earned an M.S. in journalism and an M.A. in Afro-American studies.

While still keeping her job in Chicago, Saunders spent one semester in 1978 as writer-in-residence at Jackson State University, a traditionally black college in Mississippi. She stayed to become professor and coordinator of print journalism, finally leaving her job at Johnson Publishing. Saunders remains a Johnson admirer to this day.

Saunders became part of Jackson State University's Department of Mass Communications. She was named acting chair of the department in 1990 and pro-

moted to full chair in 1991. At the time, Mississippi had a mandatory retirement age of seventy, but Saunders was told not to submit her resignation. Later she again offered to retire, but again the administration asked her to stay.

Jackson State is only the second of the historically black colleges to offer an accredited degree in mass communication. Saunders currently teaches graduate classes in the department, and heads a department with five concentrations, with 208 undergraduate students and 20 graduate students. In 1994, her department acquired a low-power television station with state-of-the-art equipment.

Saunders is currently working on her memoirs, tentatively titled, *Hold My Hand*.

ANDRA MEDEA

Simmons, Judy   (1944–   )

Judy Simmons is an editor, essayist, commentator and poet—a critic-at-large of the modern scene. Whether encapsulating the human experience in a few short lines of poetry or introducing new black intellectuals in a national venue, Simmons uses her wit and style to change the world.

Born in Westerly, Rhode Island, on August 29, 1944, Simmons was the only child of Amanda Catherine Dothard and Edward Everett Simmons. Her father was in the air force, the son of prosperous caterers who supplied the millionaires of Newport. Her mother was from a small town in northeast Alabama. Her grandmother had earned a master's degree from Columbia and founded a rural school in order to have a place to teach. With few jobs at the time for well-educated blacks, the Dothard family had remained poor.

Both Simmons' mother and father were college educated. They married after a wartime romance and divorced when Simmons was five. After one year in Connecticut and another year in New York City Simmons and her mother returned to her roots in small town Alabama. It was a shock Simmons never forgot.

Going from New York City to rural Alabama in the 1950s was a cultural, social and political sea-change. Electrification was just reaching rural Alabama. Indoor plumbing was a luxury. Education without segregation was hard to come by.

After attending local schools, including one founded by her grandmother, Simmons was sent to Allen High School in North Carolina in 1956. She graduated from this boarding school in 1960. Allen was a descendant of the Freedman's Bureau schools, set up to educate freed slaves after the Civil War. It was, as Simmons points out, a domestic mission school. Many teachers were white missionaries returning from stations in Rhodesia. Much of black education in the South at that time was sponsored by philanthropy or church missions. Southern state and local governments did not make black public education a priority.

Simmons next attended Talladega College in Talladega, Alabama. After a year she switched to California State University at Sacramento, where her father had attended college. She earned her B.A. in psychology in 1967. Simmons soon moved to New York City, where from 1968 to 1974 she was a manager for AT&T. On her own time she explored language and politics and wrote poetry.

While Simmons was perfecting her art, she taught writing to others and shared her work with the community. From 1967 to 1968 she taught English and social studies at Rodman Job Corps Center, and was adjunct professor of English at Empire State College. From 1974 to 1992, when she left New York, she taught creative writing through the New York State Council on the Arts.

The late sixties and early seventies were the era of the new black consciousness, and Simmons became one of its poets. She has since published three volumes of poetry—*Judith's Blues* in 1973, *A Light in the Dark* in 1983, and *Decent Intentions* in 1984. Her work also appeared regularly in journals and anthologies.

Simmons' poetry can be startling, wise, and elegantly direct. The following is from the dedication of the collection *Decent Intentions*: "If you become the thing you kill / it exists still / and you are / what you wished to rid the world of."

From a poet of the new black consciousness, Simmons became a social commentator at large. In 1978, she had a weekly talk show at WBAI, New York's public radio station, titled "On the Real Side." From 1981 to 1984 she broadcast "The Judy Simmons Show" for a black news and information station, WLIB. Refusing to stick to mindless celebrities and stereotypical "black" issues, she booked left-wing intellectuals and doo-wop quartets and had a notorious row with then-Mayor Edward Koch on the air. She broadcast four hours each day, five days a week, and had a very good time.

Next, Simmons took her commentary to journalism, writing social criticism in national magazines. She was senior editor and business editor at *Essence* from 1980 to 1981. She then edited and wrote in a freelance capacity from 1985 to 1989. She was senior editor at *Ms.* from 1988 to 1990 and still contributes on a freelance basis. She was one of the early writers and editors at *Emerge,* from 1990 to 1993. From 1993 to the present she has contributed essays and reviews to *Quarterly Black Review of Books,* a general circulation quarterly from Manhattan. Simmons most recent essays appear in *Wild Women Don't Wear No Blues,* a sophisticated collection of sociological commentary.

In 1991 Simmons left New York to return to northeast Alabama to look after her aged mother. She became a columnist for the *Anniston Star* of Anniston, Alabama, writing social criticism masked under the title of arts and entertainment. Remarkably, she kept the column for two years. She noted that she probably made it hot for the managing editor, but that a great many people enjoyed a fresh point of view. While based in Alabama, Simmons also helped edit a U.N.-sponsored book on AIDS, with contributors from around the world.

Simmons is currently in Alabama, working on her latest collection of essays, *Collateral Damage.*

Simpson, Carole (1940–)

Broadcast journalist Carole Simpson was born on December 17, 1940, in Chicago, Illinois, to Doretha Viola Wilbon Simpson and Lytle Ray Simpson. She attended the University of Illinois from 1958 to 1960 and then transferred to the University of Michigan, where she graduated in 1962 with a B.A. She later did graduate work in journalism at the University of Iowa. From 1968 to 1970, Simpson worked as a news reporter at WCFL Radio in Chicago. She

One of this country's most respected broadcast journalists, Carole Simpson did graduate work in journalism before becoming Chicago's first black woman television newsperson. She was a Capitol Hill correspondent for NBC before moving to ABC, where she anchors World News Saturday *and hosts news specials and reports.*   (BRENT PETERSEN)

went from there to WBBM Radio, where she was special correspondent and weekend anchor.

Her move into television came while she was working at WBBM. She appeared as commentator on a minority affairs program on Chicago's public television station, WTTW, which led to a position as a news correspondent at WMAQ-TV. The next year, she also began teaching at Northwestern University's prestigious Medill School of Journalism.

As Chicago's first black woman television newsperson, Simpson quickly established her credibility and competence. Her on-the-air persona was likable but serious. In 1974, she moved to a Washington, D.C., public affairs show and then to the network. First she was substitute anchor for the *NBC Nightly News* and weekend anchor for *Newsbreak*; then, from 1978 to 1981, she was a Capitol Hill correspondent. Following her appearance as a perimeter reporter at the 1980 political conventions, she was lured away from NBC to become a general assignment correspondent for ABC, covering Vice President George Bush and his 1988 campaign for president.

In 1988, Simpson became anchor of ABC's *World News Saturday*. Along with her anchor duties, she has done three news specials and reports for other ABC news shows, covering a wide variety of issues, such as teen pregnancy, acquired immune deficiency syndrome, and battered women. While in South Africa to cover the release of Nelson Mandela from prison, Simpson was assaulted by a South African police officer and declared that she would not return to that country until apartheid had ceased.

Carole Simpson continues to be one of this country's most respected broadcast journalists.

KATHLEEN THOMPSON

Sims, Naomi (1949–)

Widely regarded as one of the foremost experts on black women's beauty, Naomi Sims was first a high fashion model, then a successful business woman. During the heyday of the civil rights movement, while still a teenager, she became a symbol of black beauty and turned her fame into a series of successful businesses attuned to the needs of the modern black woman.

Born in Oxford, Mississippi on March 30, 1949, Sims was the daughter of Elizabeth Parham Sims and John Sims. While Sims remembers little about her father, her mother instilled in her three children the belief that "nothing was impossible." Her mother had a nervous breakdown when Sims was eight years old, and she was then separated from her sisters. She grew up in Pittsburgh, eventually settling with a caring foster family.

After graduating from high school, Sims attended the prestigious Fashion Institute of Technology in New York. When she ran short of money for tuition, someone suggested that she make some extra money modeling. She was 5'10" tall and had wor-

Naomi Sims worried about being too tall when she was in high school. After achieving success as a fashion model, she went into business for herself, creating wigs, cosmetics, and perfumes specifically for black women, who, she says, are "the most exacting women in the world." (NAOMI SIMS, INC.)

ried about that in high school, but height was valued in a model. She gave it a try and, in an incredible stroke of luck, made the cover of the *New York Times* fashion section on her first paying job.

Her success was due not only to Sims' good looks, but to her innate elegance and presence. As the head of the modeling agency put it, "She could make any garment—even a sackcloth—look like a sensational haute couture." Sims was also fortunate to be eighteen in 1967, when the conviction that "black is beautiful" was sweeping the country. Before that year, there were virtually no jobs for black models. After that point, there were. Sims' timing could not have been better. Her success was also, almost certainly, a factor in the change.

In short order, Sims acquired a number of choice assignments. In 1968, she was featured on the cover of *The Ladies Home Journal.* In 1969, she was the first black woman on the cover of *Life.* She was the first black model to be featured in *Vogue* magazine.

A weaker woman might have been affected by the glamour and attention, but Sims kept a level head throughout her success. She was disturbed by the vanity she found in modeling. And she was reluctant to tell people she was a model, assuming that they would think she was empty-headed.

Sims quit modeling in 1973 at the age of 24, deciding to go into business for herself. Her first venture was to bring out a line of wigs for black women. It had been difficult for her to find high-quality wigs for herself, so she worked with Metropa, a wig manufacturer, to develop wigs that matched the hair of black women. On the basis of her

modeling success, Sims convinced eighty stores to carry her line. White store managers were reluctant, but the wigs sold by word of mouth. Her company has since become a multi-million dollar operation.

In 1976, Sims started writing for the black female consumer. Her series of books were all published by Doubleday. The first was *All About Health and Beauty for the Black Woman.* This was followed by *How to Be a Top Model,* in 1979. Next, in 1982, came *All About Hair Care for the Black Woman* and *All About Success for the Black Woman.* Those successful books launched a lecturing career. The book on success was written after Sims found that black women all around the country faced the same frustrations and roadblocks in their efforts to get ahead. Sims wanted to share her own secrets of success.

As Sims built a career for herself as a writer, she also expanded her product lines for black women. She realized that there were few cosmetics that suited the color tones and quality of black skin. In response to this, she brought out her own line of cosmetics, the Naomi Sims Skin Care, Hair Care, and Cosmetics Line. This project was ten years in development. In addition she brought out a line of perfume. Naomi Sims products are now sold in department stores and specialty shops across the United States, Europe, and Africa.

In 1995, Sims opened two beauty salons in Manhattan called the Naomi Sims Beauty Centers. These are projected as the beginning of a chain of beauty centers due to open across the United States.

Naomi Sims has made her mark by respecting the intelligence of her market and listening to the needs of her customers. While earlier black businesswomen designed hair and skin products for black consumers, they often tried to make black women look like white women. Sims found success by enhancing black women's natural gifts, while never underestimating the women she was serving. As Sims said, "Black women are the most exacting women in the world." By being as exacting herself, Naomi Sims moved far beyond being "just a pretty face," into being a high-fashion tycoon.

ANDRA MEDEA

Smith, Ida Van   (1917–   )

I believe that anything children do very young, they will probably be able to learn better and feel more at ease with than if they wait until they were my age to begin.

—Ida Van Smith, 1991

Ida Van Smith, a pilot and air flight instructor, has spent much of her adult life teaching others about the benefits of aviation and space. The youngest of three children, she grew up in a loving, sheltered environment in Lumberton, North Carolina. Her mother was an African American, and her father was of mixed ethnicity. The family was religious and attended church services often. Ida Van went to school in Lumberton, graduated from Redstone Academy in 1934 as valedictorian, and studied at Barber Scotia Jr. College in Concord, North Carolina, before attending Shaw University. She graduated from Shaw with a major in social studies and a minor in mathematics. She taught for two years in North Carolina; then she married Edward D. Smith and moved to New York City. She

Ida Van Smith was fifty years old and about to begin studies in a doctoral program at New York University when she decided instead to learn to fly. A few years later, she founded the Ida Van Smith Flight Clubs to introduce youngsters to careers in aviation and space. (ELIZABETH FREYDBERG)

taught in Queens, New York, and earned a scholarship to City College of New York. She received her M.S. from that institution in 1964.

Smith's love for airplanes began when, as a young child, she was delighted by barnstorming and wing-walking exhibitions in Lumberton. Her pursuit of her dream of piloting an airplane, however, was delayed half a century. Smith raised four children and taught for several years in the New York City public schools before she enrolled for her first flying lesson. She

Graduates of the Ida Van Smith Flight Clubs have become air force and navy pilots and officers, submarine navigators, and airline and private pilots. (ELIZABETH FREYDBERG)

was fifty years old and about to sign the final official papers to begin studies in a doctoral program at New York University when she drove to LaGuardia Airport and took her first lesson in a single-engine airplane. She later decided to study aviation at a small airport in Fayetteville, North Carolina, closer to her parents' home. She became a licensed pilot, instrument rated (allowed to fly during inclement weather), and ground instructor.

Smith founded the Ida Van Smith Flight Clubs in 1967 to introduce children from three through nineteen to the variety of careers in aviation and space. Adults are accepted by special request. Her students have become air force and navy pilots and officers, submarine navigators, and airline and private pilots.

Smith began teaching children about aviation using a stationary airplane instrument panel in her living room. She expanded her program into the public schools and started an introductory aviation class for adults at York College in Jamaica, New York. Volunteers from diverse areas of aviation give her classes tours of airplanes and airports, take her students flying, and give lectures and demonstrations that are tailored to each age group. Children in the club and their parents fly in small airplanes, seaplanes, and helicopters and visit aerospace museums and Federal Aviation Administration (FAA) installations. All members learn the controls, the functions of the instruments, and what makes a plane fly by actually sitting in the cockpit of Smith's Cessna 172.

Smith sponsors aviation workshops once a month at York College where children meet airline pilots, flight attendants, air traffic controllers, meteorologists, aircraft mechanics, and other people whose jobs are related to the aviation industry. Initially she used only personal funds to establish her flight clubs, but she now relies on corporate and private donations and volunteer efforts as well. There are now eleven Ida Van Smith Flight Clubs in New York, Texas, North Carolina, and St. Lucia.

Smith also designed an aviation-oriented coloring book for children and produced and hosted a weekly television program about aviation. Her photographs and story lines appear in the Smithsonian National Air and Space Museum with the Tuskegee Airmen's *Black Wings,* in the Pentagon, and in the International Women's Air and Space Museum in Dayton, Ohio. In 1978–79, the FAA funded aviation career programs designed by Smith for three high schools in New York and New Jersey. These programs were later adopted by the FAA.

In 1984, Smith became the first African-American woman to be inducted into the International Forest of Friendship, in recognition of her exceptional contributions to aviation. The forest was a bicentennial gift to the United States from the International Ninety-Nines (1929), an organization of women pilots, of which Amelia Earhart was cofounder and first president. The forest contains trees from the fifty states, several territories, and forty-one countries representing the location of more than 6,000 members worldwide. On special occasions a representative flag is flown next to each tree. Since her induction, Smith has sponsored the induction of **Bessie Coleman** (1896–1926) and **Janet Harmon Bragg** (1907–   ).

Smith and her clubs have won numerous awards for their work with inner-city youth. She has received many honors from national and international agencies in recognition of her outstanding work in aviation and her dedication to the education of children.

Over the years, Smith has produced and published five booklets on the history of the Ida Van Smith Flight Clubs. Ida Van Smith continues to speak about aviation at schools, churches, and museums.

ELIZABETH HADLEY FREYDBERG

Smith, Jessie Carney   (1930–   )

The work of a librarian is to organize information and to make it accessible. As such, Jessie Carney Smith has made her mark on contemporary America as one of its most activist librarians. Her work has made available essential information about African Americans on a hitherto unimagined scale. As a gatherer of information,

cataloguer, writer, and editor, she has contributed mightily to a broader understanding of the way we live together in America, especially through her most important works, *Ethnic Genealogy, Images of Blacks in American Culture,* and *Notable Black American Women.*

Smith was born on September 24, 1930, in Greensboro, North Carolina, to James Carney and Vesona Bigelow Carney. Her parents influenced her future choices profoundly. "I attribute my addiction to work to my father, who considered every

As a librarian and author, Jessie Carney Smith has a mission: to make more information about African Americans more available than it has ever been before. She is succeeding. (JESSIE CARNEY SMITH)

moment too precious to waste in unproductivity," she says. She notes that she learned "from my mother and maternal grandparents that one must share resources with others, that helpfulness is a gift to pass along." These were all qualities apparent in her eventual career.

Smith attended North Carolina Agricultural and Technical University, graduating in 1950 with a bachelor's degree in home economics. She followed that with the study of textile arts at Cornell and then married Frederick Douglas Smith in December of 1950. The couple had one son, Frederick Douglas Smith, Jr., and later divorced.

Smith earned her master's degree in child development at Michigan State University in 1956. She quickly followed that, in 1957, with a master's in library science at George Peabody College for Teachers. She then began working at Tennessee State University, first as head cataloguer and instructor of library science (1957–1960), and later as an assistant professor and coordinator of Library Service.

In 1965, she found her professional home at Fisk University in Nashville, Tennessee, when she was appointed university librarian and professor of library science. Of the chances for growth that her position afforded her, she says, "Librarianship offers tremendous opportunities for research and publication. . . . Fisk University Library and its notable collections on black themes have . . . influenced my writing, my consultant work, and my involvement in professional activities for librarians who needed to develop or enhance their expertise on black and ethnic themes."

Beginning with her *Bibliography for Black Studies Programs* in 1969, Smith has written for and edited a wide variety of books and articles aimed at sharing important resource information for and about black and minority experience in America. Perhaps her most influential and important work has been *Notable Black American Women,* the first volume of which was published in 1991, with a second in 1996.

Awards and honors she has gleaned include National Urban League fellowships in 1968 and 1976, the Martin Luther King, Jr. Black Author's Award in 1982, and the Distinguished Scholar's Award from the United Negro College Fund in 1986.

There is no sense of the cliché librarian about Jessie Carney Smith. No dust clings to her. Librarianship is a career that she views with warmth, insight, and an extraordinarily personal sense of satisfaction. In writing about her 1979 work, *Directory of Significant Minority Women in America,* she notes, "My research initiated a friendship with more than seven hundred minority women in America. As I prepared their biographies, I have come to know these women well, and to understand the sufferings that each endured as a minority and as a woman. The same double bind which they have known I have also endured."

RICHARD E. T. WHITE

Stewart, Pearl (1950–)

"Writers can make social and political changes. I don't think there's *anything* more fulfilling than that."

—Pearl Stewart, 1993

Pearl Stewart was born on November 16, 1950 in Camden, Alabama. Her family moved to Rochester, New York, when she was five years old. As a teenager she attended Nazareth Academy. After graduation she attended **Howard University,** graduating in 1971 with a B.A. in Afro-American Studies. The following year she received her master's degree in communications from American University. She worked as an award-winning reporter for United Press International and various magazines such as *Black Enterprise.* She began working at the *Oakland Tribune* in 1976 as a reporter and later as a features editor. In 1982, she left the *Tribune* to work as a reporter for the *San Francisco Chronicle.*

In 1992, the *Oakland Tribune* (118 years old, and—until its sale to the Alameda Newspaper Group—the oldest black-owned newspaper in America) brought her back, naming her their new editor, in charge of the direction of the paper's news and its editorial staff. Pearl Stewart was the first black woman to edit a major national daily American newspaper. At the time she said, "It's kind of jolting that in 1993 I'm the first to hold a position such as this. The only possible explanation is that it involves racism and sexism. There are *so* many highly qualified African-American woman journalists around."

Stewart stayed at the *Tribune* for only a year. She resigned in December of 1993 cit-

When Pearl Stewart was named editor of the Oakland Tribune, *she became the first black woman to edit a major American daily newspaper. She commented, "It's kind of jolting that in 1993 I'm the first to hold a position such as this. The only possible explanation is that it involves racism and sexism. There are* so *many qualified African-American woman journalists around."* (NICK LAMERS)

ing differences in style with the newspaper's rehired editor in chief , David Burgin. In 1994, Ms. Stewart moved to South Africa for a year to teach journalism. Now she is back in the United States teaching investigative journalism at Xavier College in New Orleans.

HILARY MAC AUSTIN

T

Taylor, Susan (1946–)

One day in May of 1970, Susan Taylor almost passed by a newsstand near her home in the Bronx, New York. But something caught her eye and made her stop. That "something" was the first issue of *Essence* magazine. By December of that

Under editor in chief Susan Taylor's guidance since 1981, Essence *magazine addresses issues of beauty, fashion, health, spirituality, politics—in fact, all the concerns of the modern, multi-faceted African-American woman. Each month, more than 5 million people read the magazine.* (ESSENCE)

same year, Taylor had joined the staff of *Essence* as a freelance beauty editor. That Taylor achieved this foothold without college and as a single mother only underscores her intelligence and exceptional determination. During eleven years, Susan Taylor earned the position of editor in chief.

Born in New York on January 23, 1946, Taylor grew up in Harlem and Queens. Her mother hailed from Trinidad, and her father came from St. Kitts. In 1967, Taylor married William Bowles. She was pursuing an acting career and was accepted into the Negro Ensemble Company. She left the company when she became pregnant.

After enrolling in cosmetology school, Taylor and her husband started Nequai Cosmetics, named after her daughter, Shana Nequai. When Taylor and Bowles were divorced in 1971, she lost the business. Taylor is now married to Khephra Burns, a co-writer of documentaries for PBS and NBC, in addition to the *Essence* Awards shows.

During her fourteen years at the helm at *Essence,* circulation has increased from 600,000 to 1 million. Approximately 5.2 million readers pick up *Essence* every month, making it the highest-circulation magazine for African-American women.

Under Taylor's guidance, *Essence* has become more stylish, providing a forum for the multi-faceted African-American female. Politics, fashion, spirituality, health, and healing are all welcome variations of blackness and femininity.

As *Essence* evolved, so did Taylor. In 1985, she began to pursue her B.A. degree by taking night classes at Fordham University. As editor during the day, student at night, and mother around the clock to her then fifteen-year-old daughter, Taylor truly embodied the "You Can" essence of *Essence*.

The magazine has served as a springboard for Taylor. Moving from page to spotlight, she served as host on the *Essence* television program from 1983 to 1988. Her monthly editorials, "In The Spirit," proved so popular that Taylor found herself on the lecture circuit, speaking at churches, campuses, corporations and drug rehabilitation centers. In 1993, a collection of her editorials was published under the title *In The Spirit: The Inspirational Writings of Susan L. Taylor.* Her latest book, *Lessons in Living,* was published by Anchor Books.

Never one to rest on her laurels, Taylor plans to pursue an M.B.A. In the meantime, she has added yet another prestigious position to her list of achievements. She is now a senior vice president of Essence Communications, a venture which includes Essence cosmetics and fashions as well as the magazine. Essence Communications also owns *Income Opportunities,* a magazine with a readership of 400,000 which targets individual entrepreneurs.

During one of her many appearances, Taylor told her audience, "The bottom line is we are human and divine. Life is a sweet struggle if you know that you are more than you seem, more than flesh and blood." The success of Susan L. Taylor is that she has remained true to her own words, thereby amplifying the words of those African-American women previously unheard.

ROSE WOODSON

The success of Ebony *magazine owes a great deal to one of its earliest editors, Era Bell Thompson, who once wrote a column for the* Chicago Defender *under the name Dakota Dick.* (LIBRARY OF CONGRESS)

Thompson, Era Bell   (1906–1986)

The success of *Ebony* magazine owes a great deal to one of its earliest editors, Era Bell Thompson. Thompson was born in Des Moines, Iowa, on August 10, 1906, and grew up in Driscoll, North Dakota, with her parents and her three brothers. She was a track star at North Dakota State University before attending Morningside College in Iowa. There she first discovered her bent for journalism. Her autobiography states that her teacher, Mr. Lewis, responded to her first theme by saying, "Well, Miss Thompson, there isn't much of yourself; there are many misspelled words; but the general impression is so good that I can't help it. 'A.'"

During her time at Ebony, *Era Bell Thompson wrote* Africa, Land of My Fathers *(1954).* Ebony *helped to promote the book.*

Thompson hardly needed the encouragement. She began writing with a vengeance. In no time she was writing for the *Chicago Defender.* She first tackled political issues, writing a feature that attacked Marcus Garvey's "Back to Africa" movement. Readers responded with fervor, for and against. Later, Thompson contributed an ongoing column about "the wild and woolly West" under the name Dakota Dick. Still, she remained more interested in acrobatics than writing until she sold an article to *Physical Culture* magazine. The three dollars she received tipped the balance from contortionism—her great ambition at the time—to journalism. She graduated from Morningside College in 1933 and went on to study at Medill School of Journalism at Northwestern University.

However, in Depression-era Chicago, journalism jobs were not easy to find. Thompson worked at Settlement House with Mary McDowell and got jobs through the Works Progress Administration, the Chicago Department of Public Works, the Chicago Relief Administration, the Chicago Board of Trade, and the Illinois State Employment Services Office. She also worked as a waitress, domestic worker, elevator operator, and office worker. In 1945, she was awarded a Newbery fellowship that supported her while she wrote an autobiography, *American Daughter* (1946).

Two years later, John H. Johnson hired Thompson to be managing editor of his new magazine *Negro Digest,* which was later called *Black World.* In 1951, she became co-managing editor of *Ebony,* a position she held until 1964. In that year, she moved to the position of international editor and spent another twenty-two years working for the world's most popular black magazine. She traveled all over the world and wrote stories for the magazine about her experiences.

During her time at *Ebony,* Thompson wrote *Africa, Land of My Fathers* (1954) and coedited, with Herbert Nipson White, the book *White on Black* (1963). She received numerous awards, was elected to the Iowa Hall of Fame, and was chosen, in 1978, by Radcliffe College as one of fifty women to be recorded and photographed for the Black Women Oral History Project. She was a member of the board of directors of Hull House, the Chicago Council on Foreign Relations, and the Chicago Press Club. Era Bell Thompson died in Chicago in 1986.

KATHLEEN THOMPSON

V

Villarosa, Linda (1959–)

Executive editor of *Essence* magazine, Linda Villarosa is a woman who speaks to other women about health, sexuality, and about what it means to be a woman or to grow up into one. Her two books on women's health can be seen as survival manuals—or owner's manuals—for women taking charge of themselves.

Born on January 9, 1959, Villarosa was the daughter of middle-class, professional parents. Her mother, Clara Villarosa, was a social worker, who went on to open a book store later in life. Villarosa was a cheerleader, president of the senior class, and captain of the track team. She was an honor-roll student, and candidate for prom queen. She suspected that other people found her annoyingly perfect.

Villarosa graduated from the University of Colorado and went to New York to make her living as a freelance writer. She contributed to many national magazines and newspapers, including *Ms., The New York Times Book Review,* the *Philadelphia Enquirer, Working Woman,* and *Glamour.*

Villarosa became senior health editor for *Essence* after writing for the magazine for a number of years. Pursuing her interest in women's health, she spent a year in residence at Harvard University from 1990 to 1991 as a journalism fellow at the School of Public Health.

Her articles on women's physical and emotional well-being have won her awards and national honors. In 1992, she won two awards for hard-hitting articles on women's health. The first was for "Emergency: The Crisis in Healthcare," which won the National Women's Political Caucus Media Award. The second was for "Showdown at Sunrise," an article on pollution in a small town in Louisiana, which won the Unity Award from Lincoln College. The same year, Villarosa and her mother together won the GLAAD Media Award for their jointly written article "Coming Out," about coming to terms with Villarosa's being a lesbian. The article, published in *Essence,*

Linda Villarosa is the author of books and articles on women's health and sexuality. After writing for Essence *magazine for several years, she became senior health editor, then, in 1995, executive editor.* (HARPERCOLLINS)

drew more letters than any other article in the history of the magazine.

Villarosa is in demand as a public speaker on issues relating to the health and well-being of women. She has lectured at Harvard, Oberlin, Ohio State University, Radcliffe, Swarthmore, Indiana University, and the University of California at Davis.

After so many honors, it was natural for Villarosa to acquire book contracts. *Body & Soul: The Black Women's Guide to Physical Health and Emotional Well-Being,* edited by Villarosa and sponsored by the National Black Women's Health Project, was pub-lished in 1994. Her next book, *Finding Our Way: The Teen Girls' Survival Guide,* was co-authored by Allison Abner and published in 1996. Villarosa was also the editor of the *Black Health Library Guide.*

In 1995 Villarosa was promoted to exec-utive editor of *Essence.* This gives her responsibility for the overall management of the editorial department.

Aside from being the perfect daughter, Linda Villarosa has gone on to make life better—and healthier—for women around the nation.

ANDRA MEDEA

W

Walker, Madam C. J. (1867–1919)

"I got myself a start by giving myself a start," Madam C. J. Walker often said. Madam Walker was an entrepreneur, hair-care industry pioneer, philanthropist, and political activist. At the 1912 National Negro Business League convention—after League founder Booker T. Washington had refused her request to be included on the program—she stood up on the last day of the assembly and addressed the body anyway.

"I am a woman who came from the cotton fields of the South," she began. "I was promoted from there to the washtub. Then I was promoted to the cook kitchen, and from there I promoted myself into the business of manufacturing hair goods and preparations. . . . I have built my own factory on my own ground." She so astounded and impressed the mostly male audience—and Washington—that she was invited back the next year as a keynote speaker.

Born Sarah Breedlove on a Delta, Louisiana, cotton plantation on December 23, 1867, she was orphaned by age seven. Her parents, Owen and Minerva Breedlove, had been slaves on Robert W. Burney's Madison Parish farm during the Civil War siege of Vicksburg when the property served as a battle-staging area for General Ulysses S. Grant's union troops.

In 1878, when the cotton crop failed and a yellow fever epidemic struck, ten-year-old Sarah and her older sister, Louvenia, moved across the river to Vicksburg to work as domestics. At fourteen, Breedlove married Moses McWilliams, in part to escape her sister's cruel husband. In 1887, when the McWilliamses' daughter, Lelia (later known as **A'Lelia Walker**), was two years old, Moses McWilliams died.

Businesswoman, philanthropist, and inventor, Madam C. J. Walker was the first self-made U.S. woman millionaire. Her Walker Company sent hundreds of agents into the field to promote her beauty care products. (A'LELIA BUNDLES)

To support herself and her daughter, Sarah McWilliams moved up-river to St. Louis. During the next seventeen years she eked out a living as a laundress, educated her daughter in the public schools and at Knoxville College, and joined St. Paul African Methodist Episcopal Church. Around 1904—the same year St. Louis hosted the World's Fair and a convention of the **National Association of Colored Women** (NACW)—there is evidence that she worked briefly as an agent selling hair care products for **Annie Turnbo Pope Malone**'s Poro Company.

She had used Malone's "Wonderful Hair Grower"—and some of the dozens of other commercially available hair and scalp conditioners—to remedy alopecia (baldness) that was brought on by poor diet, stress, damaging hair care treatments, dandruff, psoriasis, and other scalp diseases. The ailment was common enough among black women that Sarah Breedlove McWilliams decided she could make more money by developing her own line of products.

In July 1905, with $1.50 in savings, the thirty-seven-year-old McWilliams moved to Denver, where she joined her deceased brother's wife and four daughters. In January 1906 she married a newspaper sales agent, Charles Joseph Walker, adopting his name and—following a custom practiced by many businesswomen of the era—added the title "Madam." As her husband and business partner, Charles Walker helped her design her advertisements and set up a mail-order operation.

As Madam C. J. Walker, she tried her products first on friends, then canvassed door-to-door for customers. Her own "hair growing" formula had come in a dream where, she claimed, "a big black man

appeared to me and told me what to mix up for my hair. Some of the remedy was grown in Africa, but I sent for it, mixed it, put it on my scalp, and in a few weeks my hair was coming in faster than it had ever fallen out." She may also have discussed her ideas for a formula with Denver pharmacist E. L. Scholtz, for whom she worked as a cook for a short time.

While Madam Walker is often said to have invented the "hot comb," or steel straightening comb, it is more likely that she adapted metal combs and curling irons popularized by the French to suit black women's hair.

Acutely aware of the debate about whether black women should alter the appearance of their natural hair texture, she insisted years later that her Walker System was not intended as a hair "straightener," but rather as a grooming method to heal and condition the scalp to promote hair growth, to make the hair easier to comb once it grew back, and to help black American women find their own unique style.

"Right here let me correct the erroneous impression held by some that I claim to straighten the hair," she once told a reporter. "I want the great masses of my people to take a greater pride in their personal appearance and to give their hair proper attention."

In September 1906 Madam Walker and her husband began a year and a half of traveling to promote her products and train sales agents while her daughter ran the mail-order operation from Denver. From 1908 to early 1910 they operated a beauty parlor and training school called Lelia College for Walker "hair culturists" in Pittsburgh. Walker hair culturists learned a philosophy of inner and outer beauty, creating an atmosphere in their salons to pamper their clients. She considered her hot combing method more natural and an improvement over previous practices using a device called "hair pullers"—popularized by her competitor, Annie Malone—that flattened the hair strands.

In 1910, they moved the company to Indianapolis—then the nation's largest inland manufacturing center—to take advantage of the city's access to eight major railway systems. During this phase of development, Madam Walker assembled a talented and competent staff, including Freeman B. Ransom (Walker Company attorney and general manager for nearly forty years), Robert Lee Brokenburr (a graduate of Hampton College and Howard Law School and the first black Indiana state senator), Alice Kelly (a former teacher at Eckstein Norton Institute, Madam Walker's private tutor, and Walker factory forewoman), and Marjorie Stewart Joyner (founder of Alpha Chi Pi Omega sorority and national principal of Walker Beauty Schools).

In the midst of Madam Walker's success, personal and business differences with her husband resulted in divorce, though she retained his name for the rest of her life.

Meanwhile, Walker's daughter, A'Lelia, convinced that the company needed a base in New York City, persuaded her mother to buy a townhouse in Harlem on 136th Street near Lenox Avenue. In a letter to Attorney Ransom, Madam Walker pronounced the building—with its living quarters, beauty salon, and Lelia College— "a monument. . . . There is nothing to equal it, not even on Fifth Avenue."

After a dinner party there for board members of the National Equal Rights League, **Ida B. Wells-Barnett** wrote, "I was one of the skeptics that paid little heed to her predictions as to what she was going to do. To see her phenomenal rise made me take pride anew in Negro womanhood."

In 1912, A'Lelia Walker adopted thirteen-year-old Mae Bryant of Indianapolis. Initially Mae had run errands for the Walker women at company headquarters. After getting to know her, they decided Mae's long, thick hair would make her an excellent model for the Walker products, especially their "Wonderful Hair Grower." Mae's mother, Etta Bryant, persuaded that A'Lelia and Madam Walker would keep their promise to educate Mae, consented to their request to adopt her. Mae, later known as Mae Walker Perry, attended Spelman Seminary in Atlanta and was president of the Walker Company from 1931 to 1945.

From 1912 to 1916, Madam Walker crisscrossed the country and gave slide lectures promoting her business, as well as other black institutions, at conventions held by black religious, fraternal, and civic organizations. To expand her market internationally, she traveled to Jamaica, Cuba, Haiti, Costa Rica, and the Panama Canal Zone.

Madam Walker's reputation as a philanthropist was solidified in 1911 when, in response to a massive national drive led by Jesse E. Moorland to build Young Men's Christian Association branches in black communities across the country, she contributed $1,000 to the building fund of the Indianapolis branch. This was the largest gift given to the effort by a black woman.

In 1916, Madam Walker moved to Harlem, leaving the day-to-day management of her manufacturing operation in

To foster cooperation among the agents who sold her beauty care products and to protect them from competitors, Madam C. J. Walker created a national organization, the Madam C. J. Walker Hair Culturists Union of America, which held annual conventions. This group photograph was taken at the first convention, in 1917 in Philadelphia.   (A'LELIA BUNDLES)

Indianapolis to Ransom, Kelly, and Brokenburr. Madam Walker's business philosophy stressed economic independence for women. "The girls and women of our race must not be afraid to take hold of business endeavor and . . . wring success out of a number of business opportunities that lie at their very doors. . . . I want to say to every Negro woman present, don't sit down and wait for the opportunities to come. . . . Get up and make them!"

Helping to create those opportunities, Walker hired former maids, farm laborers, housewives, and schoolteachers to fill jobs at all levels from factory worker to national sales agent. One satisfied agent wrote to her in 1913, "You have opened up a trade for hundreds of colored women to make an honest and profitable living where they make as much in one week as a month's salary would bring from any other position that a colored woman can secure." By

1916, the Walker Company claimed 20,000 agents—women and men—in the United States, Central America, and the Caribbean.

To foster cooperation among the agents and to protect them from competitors, Walker created a national organization called the Madam C. J. Walker Hair Culturists Union of America, which held annual conventions. She also organized the first federation of black hair-care and cosmetics manufacturers.

When the United States entered World War I in the spring of 1917, Madam Walker was among those, like W. E. B. DuBois and James Weldon Johnson, who—though with reservations and caveats—encouraged black Americans to cooperate in the nation's war effort. Such a demonstration of loyalty, they believed, would be rewarded with long overdue equal rights. Madam Walker loaned her name—by now widely known in both the black and white communities—to the government's black recruitment and war-bond drives.

However, after the bloody East St. Louis riot during the summer of 1917, Madam Walker joined the planning committee of the Negro Silent Protest Parade. The event drew some 30,000 black New Yorkers, 10,000 of whom marched silently down Fifth Avenue on July 28 in a show of solidarity. Heartened by the response, Madam Walker, James Weldon Johnson, Harlem realtor John E. Nail, and *New York Age* publisher Fred Moore sought a meeting with President Woodrow Wilson to present a petition urging him to support legislation to make lynching a federal crime. When they arrived at the White House on August 1, Wilson claimed to be too busy to see them, dispatching his secretary, Joseph Tumulty, instead. Later that month, at the first annual Walker Hair Culturists' convention, Madam told the delegates, "This is the greatest country under the sun, but . . . we should protest until the American sense of justice is so aroused that such affairs as the East St. Louis riot be forever impossible."

Realizing that her wealth gave her visibility and credibility, Walker became increasingly outspoken on political issues. In early 1918 she was the keynote speaker at several **National Association for the Advancement of Colored People (NAACP)** fund raisers for the antilynching effort throughout the Midwest and East. That summer she was honored at the NACW convention in Denver for having made the largest individual contribution to the effort to save the Anacostia home of abolitionist Frederick Douglass.

After the official opening of her Irvington-on-Hudson, New York, estate in August 1918, guest of honor Emmett J. Scott (former private secretary to Booker T. Washington and special assistant to the Secretary of War in Charge of Negro Affairs) wrote to her, "No such assemblage has ever gathered at the private home of any representative of our race, I am sure." During the weekend, she and her guests discussed the status of black soldiers—especially Harlem's own Hellfighters of the 369th Regiment—and resolved to fight for the rights of returning black veterans. Madam Walker was emphatic that they be granted full respect.

Scott's message, and the gathering of black notables, especially delighted Madam Walker, who had intended her home not only as a showplace but also as a conference center for summits of race leaders. She thought of Villa Lewaro—designed by black architect Vertner Woodson Tandy, named by opera singer Enrico Caruso, and located near the homes of industrialists Jay Gould and John D. Rockefeller—as a monument to inspire other African Americans to pursue their own dreams.

During the spring of 1919, Madam Walker's long battle with hypertension exacted its toll. On Easter Sunday, while visiting friends and introducing a new line of products in St. Louis, she became so ill that she was rushed back to Irvington-on-Hudson in a private train car with her personal physician and a nurse.

Upon her return to Villa Lewaro she directed her attorney to donate $5,000 to the NAACP's antilynching campaign. News of the gift, announced a few days later by NACW president Mary B. Talbert at the group's antilynching conference at Manhattan's Carnegie Hall, brought a standing ovation from the 2,500 delegates.

During the final weeks of her life, Madam Walker revamped her will, contributing thousands of dollars to black schools, organizations, individuals, and institutions, including **Mary McLeod Bethune**'s Daytona Normal and Industrial School, Lucy Laney's **Haines Normal and Industrial Institute, Charlotte Hawkins Brown's** Palmer Memorial Institute, Tuskegee Institute and numerous orphanages, retirement homes, YWCAs, and YMCAs in cities where she had lived.

When she died at age 51 on Sunday, May 25, 1919, at Villa Lewaro, she was widely considered the wealthiest black woman in America and reputed to be the first black American woman millionaire. In some references she is cited as the first self-made American woman millionaire.

Her daughter, A'Lelia Walker (1885–1931), a central figure of the Harlem Renaissance, succeeded her as president of the Madam C. J. Walker Manufacturing Company.

Walker's significance lies as much in her innovative, and sometimes controversial, hair-care system as it does in her advocacy of black women's economic independence and her creation of business opportunities at a time when most black women were employed as servants and sharecroppers. Her entrepreneurial strategies and organizational skills revolutionized what has become a multibillion dollar black hair-care and cosmetics industry. She was a trailblazer of black philanthropy, using her wealth and influence to leverage social, political, and economic rights for women and blacks.

Madam Walker's friend and colleague, Mary McLeod Bethune, called Walker's life "an unusual one." She was, Bethune said, "the clearest demonstration I know of Negro woman's ability recorded in history. She has gone, but her work still lives and shall live as an inspiration to not only her race but to the world."

A'LELIA PERRY BUNDLES

Washington, Sarah Spencer (1889–?)

Black business leaders have been instrumental in bringing prosperity to the black community, and Sarah Spencer Washington opened many doors for many people. A leader in beauty culture, as well as a successful marketer and factory owner, Washington created a line of black beauty products that were sold all over the country. Her generous gifts also helped make the community strong.

Born on June 6, 1889 in Berkley, Virginia, Washington was the daughter of Joshua and Ellen Douglass Phillips. After attending public schools in Berkley, she went to the Lincoln Preparatory School in Philadelphia. Then she attended Norfolk Mission College in Norfolk, Virginia. As she became more involved with the vocation, she studied beauty culture in York, Pennsylvania, and did advanced work in chemistry at Columbia University.

Washington's family wanted her to use her education to teach school, not to become a beautician. While still a teenager, from 1905 through 1913, Washington earned her living as a dressmaker. Then, in 1913, she opened a small beauty shop in Atlantic City, New Jersey. Seeing that many beauty products did not effectively serve the needs to black women, she experimented with developing her own products. Getting started, she sold her wares door-to-door in the evenings. In 1919, she founded Apex Hair and News Company, which grew into a chain of Apex Colleges and supply stations in New York and New Jersey.

Washington was a resourceful businesswoman. As the Great Depression put African Americans out of work, she recruited people to sell her beauty lines. Her slogan was, "Now is the time to plan your future by learning a depression-proof business."

Ever the entrepreneur, Washington built her own laboratories in 1937 through 1939, while the black community was still hard hit by the Depression. Mindful of her responsibility to the community, she decided against automation in her factories in order to preserve the jobs of the line workers. In its prime, Washington's Apex empire employed 215 regular employees and more than 35,000 sales agents throughout the United States. All together, Washington created a product line of more than 75 beauty preparations. Her sales network provided an economic lifeline for many women, as well as affordable personal grooming products for thousands.

Washington also used her economic power to bring opportunity to people outside of her company. She awarded scholarships annually to black students throughout the country and donated twenty acres of farmland for a campsite for black young people. She also endowed an educational home for girls along the principles of the National Youth Administration. She donated large sums of money for other worthy projects. At the New York World's Fair of 1939, Washington was awarded a medallion for her many achievements.

Along with other early black female entrepreneurs such as **Madam C. J. Walker**, Sarah Washington took a field that she knew and turned it into an empire. By serving the black woman as consumer and believing in the black woman as an independent businesswoman, Washington helped make the community strong.

ANDRA MEDEA

Wattleton, Faye (1943–)

"My mother felt that I should be a missionary nurse," Faye Wattleton said in an interview for I Dream a World. "Her dream for me was to go abroad to Africa and other parts of the world to serve the suffering. I have been something of a disappointment to her ideal, but I think, from my own view, I have done missionary work nonetheless." Given the dedication with which she has worked for the reproductive rights of women in today's society, there must be tens of thousands of women who would agree with her.

Alyce Faye Wattleton was born on July 8, 1943, in St. Louis, Missouri. Her father,

George Wattleton, was a factory worker. Her mother, Ozie Wattleton, was a seamstress and a minister in the Church of God. The family was poor, but did not have, as Wattleton put it, "a poverty view of the world." After graduating from high school at age sixteen, she entered Ohio State University Nursing School. She graduated in 1964, the first person in her family to earn a college degree. For two years after graduation she worked as a maternity nursing instructor at the Miami Valley Hospital School of Nursing. While there, she learned about the consequences of illegal abortion and about the consequences—and lives—of unwanted children.

In 1966, Wattleton entered Columbia University in New York City. One year later, she received an M.S. in maternal and infant health care. Her time at Columbia had included an internship at Harlem Hospital, where again she confronted the problems of poor women.

From New York, she moved to Dayton, Ohio, to take a job as consultant and assistant director of Public Health Nursing Services in the Public Health Department. In Dayton, again faced with desperate women, neglected or abused children, and frightened teenage mothers, Wattleton began to volunteer her time to Planned Parenthood of Miami Valley. After serving on the board of directors for two years, she was asked to take over as executive director. She remained in that position for seven years. While she was in charge, the number of women served tripled, and the budget rose to almost $1 million a year. At the same time, right-to-life advocates began to attack the organization. In Miami Valley, the attacks were primarily verbal. In other places, such as Minnesota,

Nebraska, Virginia, and Vermont, and even in other Ohio cities, clinics were being firebombed.

In 1973, Wattleton married Franklin Gordon, from whom she was divorced in 1981. In 1975, while she was pregnant with her daughter, Felicia, she was elected to chair the national executive director's council of Planned Parenthood Federation of America (PPFA). Three years later, she was chosen president of PPFA. She was the first black person and the first woman to serve in that capacity. She was also the youngest president ever. "Even pro-life activists concede," *Glamour* magazine said about Faye Wattleton in 1990, "she is everything you don't want in an opponent—articulate, strikingly telegenic, bright, and most importantly, messianic on this subject. In short, she has star quality."

The star quality contributed to Wattleton's effectiveness in the battle for public opinion that has taken place in the years since her appointment. Yet in battling the Hyde Amendment of 1977, the Reagan administration's attempt to place restrictions on abortion, Wattleton proved to be an effective, hard-working, tenacious leader as well.

In 1986, Wattleton received the Humanist of the Year Award, an award that had once been given to Margaret Sanger, founder of the family planning movement in the United States. In accepting the award she said, "We must trust the people. We must trust each other. We must recognize that private morality should be taught in the home and preached from the pulpit, but must *never* be legislated by politicians. We must protect our own basic rights by protecting those of others. Most importantly, we must never be so convinced of the rightness of our position that we blind ourselves to the possibility that the realm of truth may lie in another person's vision."

In 1992, Wattleton resigned from Planned Parenthood to pursue other interests.

KATHLEEN THOMPSON

Wesley, Dorothy Porter (1905–1995)

In the fall of 1930, when Dorothy Porter was appointed "librarian in charge of the Negro collection" at **Howard University,** she discovered that the bulk of the books—donated in 1914 by businessman and Young Men's Christian Association general secretary Jesse E. Moorland—were stashed away in dusty boxes. "Nothing had been done in that collection, nothing had been brought together!" recalled Wesley. With pride, passion, and love, she ripped open the boxes and over the next forty-three years helped build the specialized library into what became the Moorland-Spingarn Research Center, one of the world's largest and most comprehensive repositories of materials on the history and culture of people of African descent.

Born on May 25, 1905, in Warrenton, Virginia, the first of four children of Dr. and Mrs. Hayes J. Burnett, Dorothy Burnett received her early education in Montclair, New Jersey. After she graduated from high school, she enrolled in Minor Normal School in Washington, D.C., in 1923. In 1926, she transferred to Howard University and began work as a student assistant in the Founders Library. She graduated from Howard in 1928 with an A.B. and a resolve to continue her education to become a librarian. After working

With pride, passion, and love, Dorothy Porter Wesley turned a stockpile of books in dusty boxes into the Moorland-Spingarn Research Center, one of the world's largest and most comprehensive repositories of the history and culture of people of African descent. (MOORLAND-SPINGARN)

at the Howard University Library as a cataloguer, Burnett enrolled in the Columbia University School of Library Science and in 1931 received a B.L.S. She received a scholarship to attend graduate school at Columbia from the Julius Rosenwald Fund and was awarded an M.L.S. in 1932, becoming the first African-American woman to do so.

Curator of the Moorland-Spingarn Research Center from 1930 to 1973, she was also a scholar. Dorothy Porter was the author of several works on nineteenth-century abolitionists. In addition, she published many bibliographical works that placed at the disposal of scholars worldwide materials that otherwise would have remained obscure. Her 1936 publication for the U.S. Government Printing Office, *A Selected List of Books by and about the Negro,* was the beginning of a facet of her career that changed forever the way people of African descent were to be studied. Her bibliographic production included *Catalogue of the African Collection at Howard University,* published by the Howard University Press in 1958; *The Negro in American Cities: A Selected and Annotated Bibliography,* which she prepared for the National Advisory Commission on Civil Disorders in 1967; *The Negro in the United States: A Selected Bibliography,* published by the Library of Congress in 1970; and *Afro-Braziliana: A Working Bibliography,* published by G. K. Hall in 1978. The latter is thought to be one of the richest mines of information on the subject.

Wesley's awards and honors include an honorary doctorate of letters in 1971 from Susquehanna University; an appointment as a 1988–89 visiting scholar at the W. E. B. DuBois Institute at Harvard University; an honorary doctorate of humane letters from Syracuse University in 1989; the Olaudah Equiano Award of Excellence for Pioneering Achievements in African American Culture from the University of Utah in 1989; and an honorary doctorate of humane letters from Radcliffe College at the 1990 inauguration ceremony of Linda Smith Wilson as president.

Dorothy Burnett married James Porter, an artist, in 1929. After his death in 1970, she married Charles H. Wesley, a historian, in September 1979. He died in 1987. Retired from Howard in 1973, Wesley remained an active researcher and consultant to the Moorland-Spingarn Research Center until her death on December 17, 1995. She died at the home of her daughter in Fort Lauderdale, Florida, where she had moved recently from Washington. Her 1971 book *Early Negro Writings, 1760–1837,* was republished in 1995 by Black Classic Press.

ARTHUR C. GUNN

White, Eartha Mary (1876–1974)

Eartha Mary Magdalene White was born on November 8, 1876, in Jacksonville, Florida, to two ex-slaves. Her father died when she was five years old, and her mother supported the child—the only surviving one of thirteen—by working on a cruise ship. After graduation from Stanton School in Jacksonville, White attended the Madam Hall Beauty School in New York and the National Conservatory of Music. She sang for a year with the touring Oriental American Opera Company, which was an African-American company. Subsequently, she attended the Divinity School of Cookman Institute (later **Bethune-Cookman College**) and graduated from the Florida Baptist Academy.

White was engaged to be married to James Lloyd Jordan of South Carolina, but he died a month before their scheduled wedding day. She decided then never to marry. She taught in a rural school near Bayard, Florida, and, dissatisfied with the decayed condition of the segregated school, led a successful crusade to get the county to build a new two-room school. The rest of her life was a continuous campaign to improve the condition of all people. Most of her work was strictly voluntary, supported by her own funds and those of other private donors.

Back in Jacksonville, she began to invest in real estate. She served as acting clerk when the Afro-American Life Insurance Company was founded by her church, and she was its first woman employee. When Booker T. Washington founded the National Business League in 1900, White became a charter member and later was historian for the organization. She assisted in activating the dormant Colored Citizens' Protective League and became a speaker for that group. When a catastrophic fire struck Jacksonville, many were left homeless, and the elderly without a support system. White provided aid through the Afro-American Life Insurance Company for aid. White rescued the ledgers from the fire.

About this time, White revived an organization that had been dormant for sixteen years, the Union Benevolent Association (UBA). The UBA owned land that had been purchased with the goal of building a home for the elderly. As president of the association, White raised funds for a building, and in 1902, the Old Folks Home opened.

In 1904, one of her projects resulted in the Boys' Improvement Club. Land was donated, and White used her own money to hire recreation workers. The club was in existence for twelve years before the city of Jacksonville recognized the need for it and took over its operation.

Over the years, she established, made successful, and then sold an African-American department store, a laundry, an employment agency, a taxi service, and a janitorial service. She helped organize the Jacksonville Business League. During this time, real estate was also an important part of her business ventures. She amassed an estate that was estimated at more than $1 million, when becoming a millionaire was an extremely rare achievement, and gave most of the money for community services.

As a memorial to her mother, who died in 1930, White created the Clara White Mission. During the Depression she housed, fed, and sought employment for the homeless and hopeless in her community. The police brought her teenagers who would otherwise have spent the night in jail. The Works Progress Administration used the mission as an office for employment and cultural operations. The mission was a maternity home, an orphanage, and a community center. When it burned in 1944, it was rebuilt and expanded, and by 1965 it was free of debt.

Recognizing the need for child care for working mothers, White started the Milnor Street Nursery, which was supported by government funds as well as her own. She founded a tuberculosis rest home for African Americans, who were denied access to other such institutions, and agitated for the renovation of the grossly inhumane Duval County Prison Farm. For more than fifty years she led Sunday services at the farm and served as sponsor for many prisoners who were released into her custody. She also pressured legislators to open a correctional home for girls in order to keep them out of adult prisons. During World War I and World War II, White was active in support of soldiers and their families, working closely with the American Red Cross.

White was not interested only in charity. In 1941, she joined A. Philip Randolph in organizing his March on Washington movement to protest job discrimination, which influenced President Franklin Roosevelt to issue Executive Order No. 8802 establishing fair employment in the federal government and the defense industries. White's last major project was the replacement of Mercy Hospital for the Aged, which she had founded. The result was the 122-bed Eartha M.M. White Nursing Home, which she saw dedicated when she was past 80 years of age.

Honored in her own city and in the nation, Eartha Mary Magdalene White was active in her community until her death on January 18, 1974.

AUDREYE JOHNSON

Willis, Gertrude (1878–1970)

"Miss Gert," as Gertrude Willis was called by many who knew her, was a New Orleans business leader and community activist. She pioneered in a profession that was not the usual choice of women born in the nineteenth century. She succeeded as an insurance executive and funeral director and became an inspiration to later African-American women who entered the same professions.

One of three daughters born to Oscar and Louise Pocte, Gertrude was born in St. Bernard Parish in Louisiana on March 9, 1878, near the small fishing community of Happy Jack in the general area of Port Sulphur. While she was still young, her family moved to New Orleans, where she received formal schooling that did not go beyond the elementary grades. The family affiliated with St. John the Baptist Catholic Church on Dryades Street (now Oretha Castle Haley Boulevard). After the establishment of Holy Ghost Catholic Church in 1915, Willis became a parishioner and retained membership there until her death on February 20, 1970.

Twice married and twice widowed, Gertrude first married Clem Geddes, son of George Geddes, who operated a funeral home on South Rampart Street. Clem died November 12, 1913. In 1919, Gertrude married dentist and businessman Dr. William A. Willis. He died April 17, 1947. No children were born of either union.

Each of the three sons of George Geddes chose to become funeral directors, but each established his business independently of the others. One became proprietor of Joseph Geddes Funeral Home; another formed a partnership and became coproprietor of Geddes and Richards Funeral Home. Clem established a firm in partnership with a local barber, Arnold Moss, in 1909. Gertrude was part of the venture and continued the partnership, operating as Geddes and Moss, for several years after Clem's death. Eventually she filed for reorganization and thereafter operated the business under the name Gertrude Geddes Willis Funeral Home and Life Insurance Company.

The companies formed by the other two Geddes brothers no longer survive, but family members have continued Willis' tradition of service in the funeral and insurance businesses and now operate five establishments—three in New Orleans and two in Houma, Louisiana. All trace back to the firm started by Willis and Clem in 1909 and, further, to the firm of Clem's father,

George. Gertrude Geddes Willis Funeral Home and Life Insurance Company proudly boasts of "over 135 years of service." The original site on Jackson Avenue in New Orleans is still in use after periodic renovations and continual expansion.

During her long career, numerous awards came to "Miss Gert." One was a silver cup presented to her by her employees in 1915. Other honors came from organizations, both social and professional, to which she and Dr. Willis belonged. Among the groups were the Original Illinois Club; local, state, and national associations of funeral directors; and the Zulu Social Aid and Pleasure Club. Willis also held membership in the Ladies Auxiliary of the Knights of Peter Claver (Ct. no. 52), the **National Association for the Advancement of Colored People**, the Young Men's Christian Association, the Urban League, Crescent City Funeral Directors and Embalming Association of New Orleans, National Insurance Association, and many other organizations.

A prominent New Orleans business leader and community activist, Gertrude Willis was owner and manager of a funeral parlor and life insurance company. (FLORENCE BORDERS)

Willis is buried in the family tomb in St. Louis Cemetery Number 3, New Orleans, along with both of her husbands.

FLORENCE BORDERS

Chronology

1619

Brought ashore in Jamestown, Virginia, the first African women come to North America as slaves.

1644

The area of New York City now known as Greenwich Village is owned by a group of eleven African Americans.

1660

Boston, Massachusetts passes a law forbidding people from hiring black artisans.

1712

The Connecticut Assembly passes a law forbidding free blacks from buying land or carrying on business in any town without the permission of white residents.

1736

With her own capital, Mary Bernoon opens an oyster and ale house with her husband in Providence, Rhode Island.

1790

A slave woman known only as "Sally" is born. As an adult she hires out her own time as a cleaning woman. She uses her savings to establish a laundry and cleaning business in Nashville's business district.

1812

Elleanor Eldridge, opens a weaving business with her sister in Warwick, Rhode Island.

1819

Amelia Galle inherits the bathhouse she had managed from her former owner.

1822

Entrepreneur **Elleanor Eldridge** starts her second business, painting and wallpapering. With her profits she buys land, building rental properties on it.

1825

Jane Minor, operator of her own home health care enterprise, is freed. She later uses profits from her business to free sixteen women and children from slavery.

1831

Sarah Mapps Douglass opens the first high school for black girls in the United States.

1840s

The Remond sisters (Cecilia, Maritcha, and Caroline) operate an exclusive hair salon in Salem, Massachusetts.

1848

Madame Cecee McCarty, a New Orleans merchant and owner of thirty-two slaves, is reported to have a fortune worth more than $155,000

1853

Mary Ann Shadd [Cary] creates her own newspaper, the *Provincial Freeman*.

In the New York City area, blacks own property worth more than $1 million and have invested more than $839,000 in local businesses.

1856

Blacks in Philadelphia own property valued at $800,000.

1860

In New Orleans, Louisiana, African Americans own $15 million worth of taxable property.

Blacks in America have accumulated personal wealth estimated at $50 million, own 9,000 homes, 15,000 thousand farms, and 2,000 businesses.

Fifteen percent of free black women are dressmakers or hairdressers. Five percent operate boardinghouses or small shops.

1860s

Mary Ellen Pleasant creates a business empire in San Francisco that includes restaurants, boardinghouses, laundries, and an informal employment agency for African Americans.

1864

Rebecca Lee becomes the first black woman physician when she graduates from the New England Female Medical College in Boston.

Elizabeth Keckley dress designer to Mary Todd Lincoln, designs Mrs. Lincoln's inaugural ball gown, which is now on display at the Smithsonian Institution in Washington D.C.

1872

Charlotte E. Ray graduates from Howard University Law School and is admitted to the bar in the District of Columbia, making her the first black woman lawyer.

1883

Mary Ann Shadd [Cary] becomes the second black woman to earn her law degree.

1885

Sara E. Goode is the first black woman to receive a U.S. patent, for her "Folding Cabinet Bed."

1887

A.E. Johnson founds the monthly literary journal, *The Joy*.

1889

Ida B. Wells-Barnett buys a one-third interest in the *Free Speech and Headlight*, of which she will later become editor.

1896

Fanny Criss, a prominent seamstress, dressmaker, and clothing designer in Richmond, Virginia, designs a Second-Day (wedding reception) dress that is now on display at the Valentine Museum.

1897

Eliza Grier, a former slave, graduates from medical school after attending every other year, working during the non-attending years in order to earn the money for tuition.

1899

Maggie Lena Walker is elected secretary of the female benevolent organization, the Independent Order of St. Luke. She heads that group's reorganization, expanding it to twenty-two states and converting it from a provider of funeral benefits into a full-fledged insurance company.

1900

The National Negro Business League is organized to promote business among African Americans.

Amanda Berry Smith publishes the *Helper*, a magazine that focuses on the issues of child care, temperance, and religion.

1902

Under the leadership of **Maggie Lena Walker**, the Independent Order of St. Luke begins publishing the *St. Luke Herald*. The newspaper later carried on a major anti-lynching campaign.

1903

The Independent Order of St. Luke opens the St. Luke Penny Savings Bank, and **Maggie Lena Walker** is named its first president. She is the first black woman and almost certainly the first woman to become a bank president in the United States (except by inheritance from a husband).

Pauline Hopkins is named literary editor of the *Colored American Magazine*.

1904?

Josephine Silone Yates serves as the associate editor of the *Negro Educational Review*.

1907

C. M. Hughes and Minnie Thomas (both black women) become the editors of the newly created *Colored Woman's Magazine*.

1910

17,266 black women are working as schoolteachers in the southern states, representing 1 percent of all black working women in the South.

1912

Charlotta Bass, thought to be the first black woman to own and publish a newspaper in the United States, purchases the *California Eagle*.

1913

Mamie Garvin, a South Carolina schoolteacher, opens a dressmaking shop with two friends.

1915

Delilah Beasley starts writing a regular column for the *Oakland Tribune*.

1919

Beauty mogul, **Madam C. J. Walker**, dies. She is the wealthiest black woman in America and the first woman in America to become a self-made millionaire.

Georgia Hill Robinson becomes the first African-American policewoman after passing the civil service exam in Los Angeles.

1920

Sally Wyatt Stewart founds *Hoosier Woman*, a magazine for black women.

Violette N. Anderson becomes the first black woman to practice law in Illinois. Later she becomes the first woman prosecutor in Chicago and the first black woman to argue a case before the United States Supreme Court.

1922

Louise Evans becomes the first black woman admitted to the prestigious United Scenic Artists Association for costume, scenic, and lighting designers.

Bessie Coleman, the first licensed African-American aviator, gives her first exhibition on Long Island.

1925

L. Marion Fleming Poe is admitted to the Virginia bar, making her probably the first black woman to practice law in a Southern state.

1926

Marvel Jackson Cooke becomes an editorial assistant to W. E. B. DuBois at the *Crisis*.

1927

Sadie Tanner Mossell Alexander is the first black woman admitted to the bar in Pennsylvania.

1935

Marvel Jackson Cooke becomes the assistant managing editor of the *People's Voice*, founded by U.S. Congressman Adam Clayton Powell.

1939

Jane Bolin is appointed Justice of the Domestic Relations Court in New York City, becoming the first black woman judge.

Mary T. Washington is the first African-American woman to become a certified public accountant after graduating from Chicago's Northwestern University.

1940

Sixty percent of all black women in the labor force are still employed in domestic service, and 10.5 percent are in other service work; only 1.5 percent are in clerical and sales positions and 4.3 percent are in professional positions.

1942

The August cover of *Ladies' Home Journal* features one of designer **Mildred Blount**'s hats.

1946

Hazel Garland is hired as a full-time reporter for the black newspaper the *Pittsburgh Courier*.

1948

While working for the Associated Negro Press (ANP), journalist **Alice A. Dunnigan** travels with Harry Truman, covering his presidential election campaign.

1949

Dorothea Towles, the first African-American woman to earn her living entirely as a professional model, begins her career in Europe in Christian Dior's showroom.

1950

Marvel Jackson Cooke becomes the first black woman to be a full-time reporter for a mainstream newspaper when she joins the staff of the *Daily Compass*.

Forty-two percent of all African-American women in the labor force are employed in domestic service and 19.1 percent are in other service work; only 5.4 percent are in clerical and sales positions and 5.7 are in professional positions.

1951

Ethel L. Payne, later known as the "First Lady of the Black Press," begins work as a reporter for the *Chicago Defender.*

Arie Taylor becomes the first African American to be a Woman's Air Force classroom instructor.

1953

Vivian Carter Bracken is one of three founders of Vee Jay Records, which will represent such black stars as the Staple Singers and will introduce the Beatles to the U. S.

Fashion designer Ann Lowe designs the bridal gown, bridesmaid's dresses and mother-of-the-bride's dress for the marriage of Jacqueline Bouvier and John F. Kennedy.

Ernesta G. Procope founds the E.G. Bowman Insurance Company.

1954

Norma Merrick Sklarek becomes the first black woman to be licensed as an architect in the U.S.

1955

Jean Blackwell Hutson becomes curator of what is now the New York Public Library's Schomburg Center for Research in Black Culture and guides its development until her retirement in 1984.

Rose Morgan opens the Rose Morgan House of Beauty in Harlem, with a crowd of 10,000 in attendance and the Mayor's wife cutting the ribbon.

1957

Charlemae Rollins is the first black woman to be elected president of the Children's Services Division of the American Library Association.

Ebony Fashion Fair stages its first tour. In the following decades, under the supervision of **Eunice Walker Johnson,** it becomes the world's largest traveling fashion show.

1959

Ruth Bowen opens a talent agency for black artists called Queen Talent. It becomes the largest black-owned entertainment agency in the world.

Juanita Kidd Stout becomes the first black woman to be elected as a judge.

1960

Of all black women in the labor force 32.5 percent are employed in domestic service, 21.4 percent are in other service positions, 10.8 percent are in clerical and sales, and 6 percent are in professional positions.

1964

Alma Jacobs is the first African American to become a member of the executive board of the American Library Association.

Appearing on the cover of *Harper's Bazaar,* Donyale Luna becomes the first African American model to appear on the cover of a mainstream U.S. fashion magazine.

1965

Joan Murray is the first black woman newscaster on a major television station, WCBS in New York.

The National Association of Media Women is organized by Rhea Callaway.

1967

Nannie Mitchell Turner receives the Distinguished Editor Award from the National Newspaper Publishers Association.

1968

Clothhilde Dent Brown becomes the first African American woman to be promoted to the rank of colonel in the U.S. Army.

The **National Domestic Workers Union** is founded in Atlanta under the leadership of **Dorothy Lee Bolden.**

Naomi Sims is the first black woman on the cover of *Ladies Home Journal;* the next year she is the first black woman on the cover of *Life.*

1969

Employed by WAGA-TV in Atlanta, Georgia, **Xernona Clayton** becomes the first black woman to host a television show in the South.

1970

Essence, a magazine for black women, begins publication.

Of all black women in the labor force 17.5 percent are employed in domestic service, 25.7 percent are in other service positions, 23.4 percent are in sales and clerical positions, and 10.8 percent are in professional positions.

The **National Coalition of 100 Black Women** is founded in New York.

1971

Fannie Granton serves as parliamentarian of the Washington Press Club, the first African American to hold office in that organization.

1972

Elizabeth Courtney becomes the first black woman to be nominated for an Academy Award in Costume Design, for *Lady Sings the Blues.*

1976

Clara Stanton Jones is the first African American to be president of the American Library Association.

1978

Charlayne Hunter-Gault joins the Public Broadcasting System's *MacNeil/Lehrer NewsHour* as national correspondent.

1980

Of all black women in the labor force 6.5 percent are employed in domestic service, 24.3 percent are in other service work, 32.4 percent are in clerical and sales positions, and 14.8 percent are in professional positions.

1981

Pamela Johnson is named publisher of the *Ithaca Journal.* She is the first black woman publisher since **Julia Ringwood Coston.**

Kitchen Table: Women of Color Press begins publishing.

Attorney Arnetta R. Hubbard is the first woman to become president of the National Bar Association.

1984

Ida Van Smith becomes the first African-American woman inducted into the International Forest of Friendship, in recognition of her contributions to aviation.

1986

The U.S. Supreme Court rules unanimously that sexual harassment constitutes illegal job discrimination.

The Oprah Winfrey Show goes national, making **Oprah Winfrey** the first African-

American woman to host a nationally syndicated weekday talk show.

Charlayne Hunter-Gault receives the George Foster Peabody Award for Excellence in Broadcast Journalism for her report on South Africa, *Apartheid's People*.

1987

Mae Jemison joins NASA—the first black woman to be accepted as an astronaut.

1988

Carole Simpson becomes anchor of ABC's *World News Saturday*.

Juanita Kidd Stout is the first black woman to serve on a state supreme court, when she is appointed to the Pennsylvania Supreme Court.

1989

Oprah Winfrey forms Harpo Productions, becoming the first black woman and only the third woman to own a television and movie production studio.

Jennifer Lawson becomes the executive vice president of national programming for the Public Broadcasting System.

1990

Marcelite J. Harris is the first African-American woman to hold the rank of brigadier general in the U.S. Air Force.

1991

Ethel L. Payne, the first black woman to work as a commentator for a national broadcast network, dies.

Ernesta Procope forms a partnership with her second husband John Procope and financier Alan Bond to found the investment company Bond, Procope Capital Management. In just two years, they manage to attract assets of three hundred and fifteen million dollars.

1992

Pearl Stewart becomes editor of the *Oakland Tribune*. She is the first black woman to edit a daily newspaper in a major U. S. city.

1993

Rosalyn McPherson Andrews is promoted to vice president of marketing for Time Life's Educational Division.

Ann M. Fudge becomes president of Maxwell House Coffee.

1995

The Ebony Fashion Fairs, under the supervision of **Eunice Walker Johnson**, have raised more than $45 million for churches, hospitals, schools, and other organizations.

Bibliography

GENERAL BOOKS USEFUL TO THE STUDY OF BLACK WOMEN IN AMERICA

Reference Books

African-Americans: Voices of Triumph. Three volume set: *Perseverance, Leadership,* and *Creative Fire.* By the editors of Time-Life Books, Alexandria, Virginia, 1993.

Estell, Kenneth, ed., *The African-American Almanac.* Detroit, Mich., 1994.

Harley, Sharon. *The Timetables of African-American History: A Chronology of the Most Important People and Events in African-American History.* New York, 1995.

Hine, Darlene Clark. *Hine Sight: Black Women and The Re-Construction of American History.* Brooklyn, New York, 1994.

Hine, Darlene Clark, ed., Elsa Barkley Brown and Rosalyn Terborg-Penn, associate editors. *Black Women in America: An Historical Encyclopedia.* Brooklyn, New York, 1993.

Hornsby, Alton, Jr. *Chronology of African-American History: Significant Events and People from 1619 to the Present.* Detroit, Michigan, 1991.

Kranz, Rachel. *Biographical Dictionary of Black Americans.* New York, 1992.

Lanker, Brian. *I Dream a World: Portraits of Black Women Who Changed America.* New York, 1989.

Logan, Rayford W., and Michael R. Winston, eds. *Dictionary of American Negro Biography,* New York, 1982.

Low, W. Augustus, and Virgil A. Clift, eds. *Encyclopedia of Black America.* New York, 1981.

Salem, Dorothy C., ed. *African American Women: A Biographical Dictionary.* New York, 1993.

Salzman, Jack, David Lionel Smith, and Cornel West. *Encyclopedia of African-American Culture and History.* Five Volumes. New York, 1996.

Smith, Jessie Carney, ed., *Notable Black American Women.* Two Volumes. Detroit, Michigan, Book I, 1993; Book II, 1996.

General Books about Black Women

Giddings, Paula. *When and Where I Enter: The Impact of Black Women on Race and Sex in America,* New York, 1984.

Guy-Sheftall, Beverly. *Words of Fire: An Anthology of African-American Feminist Thought.* New York, 1995.

Hine, Darlene Clark, Wilma King, and Linda Reed, eds. *"We Specialize in the Wholly Impossible": A Reader in Black Women's History.* Brooklyn, New York, 1995.

Jones, Jacqueline. *Labor of Love, Labor of Sorrow: Black Women, Work, and the Family from Slavery to the Present.* New York, 1985.

Lerner, Gerda, ed. *Black Women in White America: A Documentary History.* New York, 1972.

OTHER BOOKS

The one general book that deals with black women in a profession (other than the fields of science, medicine, and nursing, which are covered in the **Science and Medicine** volume of this encyclopedia) is:

Streitmatter, Rodger. *Raising Her Voice: African-American Women Journalists Who Changed History.* Lexington, Kentucky, 1994.

Contents of the Set

(ORGANIZED BY VOLUME)

Education

Religion and Community

Bowman, Laura
Burke, Georgia
Burrill, Mary P.
Burrows, Vinie
Bush, Anita
Canty, Marietta
Carroll, Diahann
Carroll, Vinette
Carter, Nell
Cash, Rosalind
Childress, Alice
Clough, Inez
Cole, Olivia
Dandridge, Dorothy
Dandridge, Ruby
Dash, Julie
Dearing, Judy
Dee, Ruby
Dickerson, Glenda
Douglas, Marion
DuBois, Shirley Graham
Ellis, Evelyn
Evans, Louise
Falana, Lola
Foster, Frances
Foster, Gloria
Franklin, J. E.
Gaines-Shelton, Ruth
Gentry, Minnie
Gibbs, Marla
Gilbert, Mercedes
Goldberg, Whoopi
Grant, Micki
Grier, Pamela
Grimké, Angelina Weld
Hall, Juanita
Hansberry, Lorraine Vivian
Harvey, Georgette
Haynes, Hilda
Holiday, Jennifer
Holland, Endesha Ida Mae
Kein, Sybil
Kennedy, Adrienne
Lafayette Players
LeNoire, Rosetta
Livingston, Myrtle Athleen
   Smith
Mabley, Jackie "Moms"
Martin, Helen

McClendon, Rose
McDaniel, Hattie
McIntosh, Hattie
McKee, Lonette
McKinney, Nina Mae
McNeil, Claudia
McQueen, Butterfly
Miller, May (Sullivan)
Mills, Florence
Mitchell, Abbie
Monk, Isabell
Moore, Melba
Negro Ensemble Company
Nelson, Novella
Nicholas, Denise
Nichols, Nichelle
Norman, Maidie
Parks, Suzan-Lori
Perkins, Kathy A.
Perry, Shauneille
Preer, Evelyn
Prendergast, Shirley
Rahn, Muriel
Randolph, Amanda
Randolph, Lillian
Rashad, Phylicia
Richards, Beah
Rolle, Esther
Sands, Diana
Sanford, Isabel
Scott, Seret
Shange, Ntozake
Simms, Hilda
Sinclair, Madge
Smith, Anna Deavere
Spence, Eulalie
Stewart, Ellen
Sul-Te-Wan, Madame
Taylor, Clarice
Taylor, Jackie
Taylor, Regina
Teer, Barbara Ann
Thomas, Edna Lewis
Tyson, Cicely
Uggams, Leslie
Walker, Aida Overton
Ward, Valerie
Warfield, Marsha
Washington, Fredi

Waters, Ethel
West, Cheryl
White, Jane
Winfrey, Oprah
Winston, Hattie
Woodard, Alfre

Social Activism

Allensworth, Josephine
Alpha Suffrage Club
Associations for the Protection
   of Negro Women
Avery, Byllye
Ayer, Gertrude
Baker, Ella
Barrow, Willie
Bates, Daisy
Black Panther Party
Blackwell, Unita
Bolden, Dorothy
Boynton, Amelia
Brooks, Elizabeth Carter
Brown, Elaine
Brown, Linda Carol
Burks, Mary Fair
Clark, Septima
Cleaver, Kathleen
Combahee River Collective
Cosby, Camille O.
Cotton, Dorothy
Davis, Angela
Davis, Henrietta Vinton
Devine, Annie
Edelin, Ramona H.
Edelman, Marian Wright
Evers-Williams, Myrlie
Foster, Autherine Lucy
Garvey, Amy Ashwood
Garvey, Amy Jacques
Hamer, Fannie Lou
Harris, Louise
Hernandez, Aileen
Higgins, Bertha G.
Highlander Folk School
Housewives' League of
   Detroit
Huggins, Ericka
Hurley, Ruby

Science, Health, and Medicine

Contents of the Set

(LISTED ALPHABETICALLY BY ENTRY)

Index

Page numbers in **boldface** indicate main entries. *Italic* page numbers indicate illustrations.